The History Of Times Square Records

A tiny New York City record store
located in the subway that
would become a legend
along with the man
Irving "Slim" Rose!!

Nadine DuBois

The History Of Times Square Records

ISBN 978-0-6151-4009-4
Second Edition

Contact Nadine DuBois by email. The email address is
timessquarerecords@yahoo.com

Dedication

This book is dedicated to my friend, JW.......who was always there to give advice....lend a hand.....anytime.... day or night......

This truly has been an exciting journey ......one which led to a road........ to a "magical" place back in time..........you traveled this journey with me.....when I wondered off ......you showed me the way back......when I came to a fork in the road....... you showed me the correct path to take......

THANK YOU for helping to make my dream come true......

All the best to you my friend............Bunny

Acknowledgments

Where do I begin.....the list is too long to name everyone.....my heartfelt thanks to each and everyone for your memories....you all know who you are.......

A special thank you to Wayne Stierle who never tired of my endless emails.....believe me when I say many I MEAN MANY....for sharing your knowledge, photos, articles and music......

A special thank you to the great song stylist, Billy Vera, for sharing his memories and wit.

A special thank you to David Hinckley for supplying his memories and observations about the era of Times Records.

A special thank you to Val Shively who encouraged me to write this book......for sending me all his memorabilia.....photos.....

A special thank you to Al Trommers and Donn Fileti for taking the time to answer my many questions and for sharing their memorabilia with me......

A special thank you to Robert Rose for sharing his memories, photos & documents of his dad, Irving "Slim" Rose...

A special thank you to Jerry Greene for his memories and photos....

A special thank you to Eddie Gries for sharing your memories photos and documents...

Thank you Lou Rallo and Ralph Corwin for your photos.....

Thank you Jess Porter who helped to get this project started and off the ground....

A special thank you to "Genni" Miscavage for her memories, and for setting the record straight about "Slim" and the car.

A special thank you to Arlene Rose for sharing her memories of "Slim" with me.

Thank you Irving "Slim" Rose for creating something so "magical".......Times Square Records will live on forever between the pages of this book......

Nadine DuBois
2007

Foreword

This book is strictly about Irving "Slim" Rose, the store Times Records and Times Square Records along with his Times Square Records label. The time line of this book tells what happened within the realm of "Slim's" world from the years 1953-1954 up and including through the year 1965. These are approximate years; however I do have documentation to show that "Slim's" days at Times Square Records ended in 1965. For those who continued on in the music business after this time line your contributions are duly noted by this author. Having made this clarification I continue on......

A question was asked through an email list "whatever happened to "Slim" Rose after his days at "Times Square Records". At first I was not going to respond to the email....I was just going to let it go by the wayside. After doing a little research on the internet, my instinct told me there was a story to be told.....Irving "Slim" Rose needed to be remembered....There were teens working behind the scenes......each one had their own story and memories. Record collectors had memories of having a place where they could go to buy/trade records or just hang out...It was a "magical" time for all....these written pages will preserve that "magical" time forever.....

I responded to the email. At first my intentions were to find out where and when Irving Rose passed away or find corporate records that listed the officers in the company. Little did I know my search would take me on a journey that would change my life forever. Each road I traveled had crossroads that took me to a new research destination. I knew I was headed on the path of discovering something important that made an impact on so many....as each day passed I found myself being drawn in...for me it was like going back in time....it was as though I were there reliving the memories.....I began to feel the excitement....the more I discovered...the more I needed to know......each story no matter how big or small made me want to go farther on my journey....It was only a matter of time when I knew I had to complete my journey by writing this book.

Within the covers of this book are different chapters...... you will read memories shared with me by those working behind the scenes. There are memories of those who visited the little shop in the subway arcade. The words written are not my words. They are the words of those who were there....those who experienced this "magical" place in time. I am simply the communicator or storyteller of these words. I have tried to provide as much documentation to substantiate what has been written.

You may ask yourself....Why after all these years do a book now? The answer is simple.....preserving memories......setting the record straight.......putting an end to rumors that have existed for almost fifty years.

Although Irving "Slim" Rose was slightly gruff or "rough around the edges" he made a contribution to the world of music that should be recognized and remembered.....this is my way of giving "Slim" his recognition. I never had the opportunity to visit Times Square Records or to know the "man behind the counter", however after all the research, interviews etc.... I feel as though I know "Slim" and I really like that "man behind the counter".....

Times Records and Times Square Records made a difference.....
....friendships were formed which have stood the test of time and continue to this day. Many became successful in the business....

This is a story that needs to be told...... must be told......and will be told.....After reading the words within the covers I hope you will agree too....

Nadine DuBois
2007

Table of Contents

There Was A Sink In The Store Window

Al Trommers

AND SO THE STORY BEGINS

The year is 1953-1954......a kid in the Bronx by the name of Al Trommers is listening to R&B and harmony groups on "black" radio stations. The sound he hears is phenomenal.....it is unique. It's the type of music that decades later would be known as "doo wop".

He begins to send letters to the record companies asking for promo photos of these vocal groups. The record companies would fill his requests sending press kits of the groups and every so often free records too. A list of the names, addresses and phone numbers along with a list of inventory are meticulously kept. Some of the record companies written to were Vee Jay, Gotham, Grand, Specialty, and Chess. In his letters he asked questions about carrying back stock and pressing reissues. This information would be documented and used later years.

At the same time he begins to increase his knowledge of the music business while at the same time building a stock piled inventory of these rare records. At one point he toyed with the idea of starting his own record label as everyone else was doing it. He becomes a walking encyclopedia on the subject and during this time the only visibly known person in the area to possess this knowledge.

With a box of records off he would go to the record shops in or around 42nd Street. The buyer of the shop would go through the box of records selecting what he wanted.......he was now selling records to these shops. While there he would observe conversations between the proprietor and customer at the same time listening to the names of vocal groups being requested such as the Solitaires and Fi-Tones. Once he knew the names of the vocal groups people were looking for, he began to stock pile these records.

On Saturdays he would meet teens at different record shops in the area always bringing his box of records with him. Meetings would take place around noon. Since there was no phonograph to play the records Al Trommers always gave a 100% refund guarantee to each customer. He would say

"If you don't like it the next time I see you and I will give you back your $2.00 or $3.00". Names and telephone numbers were always exchanged.

Brief recap of time line.....Between 1953 through 1957 Al Trommers went from a kid in the Bronx listening to R&B on "black" radio, writing record companies asking for promotional items, receiving press kits and occasionally free records....to a kid who had become a walking encyclopedia on the music business, who now possessed a small "phonolog" of his own and sold records to local record shops in the area. He knew which record companies would sell back stock to him, along with a list of companies who would press reissues. He is buying quantities of records. He has six years experience behind him. He has become a freelance record salesman selling to record shops as well as customers on the street. In fact, many say he was one of the first visible record collectors in the New York City area. He has become known to the collectors as "Broadway Al".

Briefly in 1956 Al Trommers worked for Cousins Records which was a "mom and pop" store in his neighborhood. The neighborhood was a blend of Italian, Jewish and Irish people. To buy this music playing on "black" radio stations you had to travel to Harlem where they stocked theses records. The owner, Mr. Cicchetti, was buying music played on "pop" radio stations. He had no idea that these vocal groups existed. Although Cousins Records had been in business since the 1940's, Mr. Cicchetti knew nothing about this music. Al Trommers began to do the ordering of records from the distributors for the store....buying five of one record...ten of another record. He continued to listen to the radio stations at night to see what new records were being played. It was not long before Cousins Records had an array of vocal groups in stock.

His first meeting with Irving "Slim" Rose..... The year is now 1957-1958.....Al Trommers is now working at J. Press Clothing Store in an office located at the corner of Madison and Vanderbilt Avenues right next to Grand Central Station. The exact address is 47 East 44th Street. It is at this office Al Trommers conducts all his music related business. It was a great setup at the time as he had his own office, access to telephones were he was able to receive incoming calls and also make outgoing calls. He used this address for business purposes only.

Quite often on his lunch hour at work he would visit this shop on 43rd Street that sold magazines, still photos, jewelry and records. Standing behind the counter was a tall slender built man who was cantankerous and a little rough around the edges. It was evident that he was a heavy smoker. His voice was so unique you could be in a room with a hundred people and know right away it was "Slim" without turning and looking. The man behind the counter was Irving "Slim" Rose.

"Slim" was selling a few of the current pop records, however the store had rows and rows of cutouts & used jukebox records that "Slim" had never heard of.....these were marked with a "circle" which represented a dime. Selling for a dime were such artists as Spaniels or Moonglows...as well as many others .... "Slim" was always happy to see him enter the store as he would purchase fifty or sixty records at a time continuing to stockpile his inventory.

Customers would come and go at this shop looking for vocal group records. Al Trommers would strike up a conversation with the customer.....learn which vocal group they wanted and sometimes he would turn around and sell the same record he had just purchased from "Slim" for a dime to this customer for as much as $2.00, $3.00 or even as high as $5.00. "Slim" was amazed by the fact that you could actually sell a record for more than a dollar. "Slim" thought this couldn't be done. He had seen Al Trommers do this many times at his shop.

The actual date of the closing of this store on 43rd Street is unknown to the author. Al Trommers went to the store one day and found a closed sign in the window. The store was empty...."Slim" and all the merchandise were gone....there was no forwarding address notifying customers where the store had moved too. The reason why "Slim" closed the store on 43rd Street is not known at this time. It may never be known. According to Arlene Rose, "Slim" had incorporated using the name I. Rose, Inc. **Author's note – I was not able to find any documentation with the New York State Corporate Division that said corporation ever existed. ** However, "Slim" did rent the store.

The display window was on the right hand side facing the store; done in "Slim" fashion so to speak. There was a sink complete with water running from the faucet displayed on velvet with lightning. A woman by the name of Frieda helped "Slim" when he was busy. She was around the same age as "Slim". "Slim" always referred to her as "Frieda" never revealing a last name. "Slim" sold novelty items, jewelry and records. The store was a "novelty shop" with no name. The interior was long and narrow leaving little room for customers to shop.

Al Trommers never saw Arlene Rose at the store.........I was told by Arlene Rose in an interview, she worked at the store for approximately two weeks in the beginning.... "Slim" did not want her to work at all and he did not want her at the store. "Slim" was always alone behind the counter when he visited the store. Al Trommers is certain that "Slim" was at that location a little over a year to eighteen months.

Moving forward along the time line.... It is 1959.....Irving Rose moves to the new location in a subway arcade. The address is 1475 Broadway. The exact date of the move and the opening of the store are unknown. This time the store is filled with costume jewelry. The size of the shop is small and the condition is decrepit.

It was by chance or fate that Al Trommers would find "Slim" again. There was a new store opening in a subway arcade that was selling jewelry. The year is still 1959. Al Trommers observed what was going at this new store and saw that it was Irving "Slim" Rose. He walked into the store...."Slim" recognized who he was from the previous store. This is the beginning of something that would become a legend....Times Square Records.....

Al Trommers gave "Slim" his initial start in 1959. "Slim" knew next to nothing about the record business. He gave "Slim" his "master list" of names, addresses and telephone numbers of the record companies he knew carried back stock....who were willing to press records....he told "Slim" what labels to look for, etc. Also, once a record was given air time on the radio "Slim" needed to have a stock piled inventory for that record. One copy of a record wasn't enough...you had to have quantities of each record at the store...."Slim" had to be ready for the people who would come to the store to purchase what they heard on the radio. "Slim" came up with the idea of the "want lists"....Al Trommers advised him of which records to put on the list....He told "Slim" to hang the list on the wall along with the price offered in credit....with the hope that a craze would be started amongst the collectors where they would bring in rare records for credit.

He helped "Slim" get the quantities needed to meet the demand of his customers. "Slim" was giving fifty cents credit for everything including vocal groups...Al Trommers tells him he can't be doing this...he is taking in too many records that he won't be able to sell...He tells "Slim" he needs to be much more selective...he needs to listen to what he is taking in...play it first on a phonograph to see if it is R&B, group harmony, pop, etc. then give the credit. He taught "Slim" how to negotiate with the record companies when it came to purchasing or having a record reissued. Remember Al Trommers already had the knowledge and six years experience before he would be reunited with "Slim" at the 1475 Broadway location.

Once "Slim" learned how to go about doing things Times Square Records was off the ground. On Saturdays, Al Trommers would sell to collectors outside the store. The store was very small... collectors waited in lines to get inside. The collectors did not mind the wait nor did they mind the store's dé-cor...what they cared about was that "Slim" sold great records. During this time he would bring several boxes of records which held twenty-five records each, sometimes he would also bring a box that held one hundred records. He was selling all original records to the collectors. One of his customers at that time was Jared Weinstein. "Slim" looked on and knew what Al Trommers was doing...however "Slim" never gave Al Trommers a hard time simply because he knew deep down inside that he didn't have any of these original records that he could sell. "Slim" knew to leave Al Trommers alone because he was supplying "Slim" with all the information needed to start a successful business.

By this time Al Trommers has a car and is traveling out of state to purchase records for both "Slim" and himself. His record excursions take him to New Jersey going to cities like Camden, Trenton, Newark, and to Philadelphia. A subway is taken for local record excursions which include going to Queens and Harlem. These excursions were known as a "two fold" deal. Quantities were sold to "Slim" and all prices were negotiated. "Slim" received his inventory and Al Trommers received enough in payment to cover his expenses, plus make a few dollars.

Once "Slim" began to buy time on the Alan Frederick's show Night Train; Times Square Records really took off. Al Trommers met Alan Fredericks at the store on several occasions. "I was like an agent on behalf of the store"...He would loan Alan Fredericks records that no one else had or heard of to play on the show and it would be announced where you could purchase these records and of course it was Times Square Records.

The business arrangement between Al Trommers and Irving Rose began to taper off several years after the 1959 opening of the store. Al Trommers is not sure of the year...he does know that he went to the second location only a few times before business between himself and "Slim" stopped. The store began to get stale...sales were dropping off..."Slim" began to be very selective and bought fewer and fewer records from him.

One day on his lunch hour Al Trommers stopped by the store to see "Slim". While there a COD shipment from Dot Records arrived (Al Trommers had helped "Slim" to get records reissued from Dot). The name of the record was "Darling Dear" by the Counts. "Slim" had no money on him to pay for the COD. He asked Al Trommers to borrow the money so he could pay for the delivery as the shipment would be returned, redelivered the following day and if not paid on the third day the records would go back to Dot. Al Trommers did this on many occasions to help "Slim".

It was not long after this that "Slim" stopped having records pressed. The business was slipping. At some point "Slim" was not able to buy radio time. The business arrangement between Al Trommers and Irving Rose came to an end.

****Author's Note – Personal information pertaining to the description of the store, the store front window, and confirmation that Arlene Rose did not work at either store came directly from Arlene Rose in an interview with the author.

****Information provided in this chapter came from several interviews with Al Trommers in March – August 2006.

My Memories Of Times Square Records

Jerry Greene

My memories of Times Square Records go forty-eight years, to when I was fifteen years old. In those days, I listened to Alan Freed on the radio during the week and heard many great songs by different vocal groups. That began my infatuation with vocal groups and R&B records. When I heard a song I liked, I had to have the record.

On Saturdays, my friend Marty Dorfman and I would go up to Manhattan looking for any recordings by artist that we did not have in our collection. We bought used records for five and ten cents a piece, paying up to twenty-five cents for those hard to find records. At those prices, I was able to build a massive collection.

The best store Marty and I came across was a little store off the corner of 43rd Street and 6th Avenue. The owner of the store sold both costume jewelry and records. The price of the records at that time was twenty for a dollar. I guess I must have visited that store six or seven times and got most of the records in my collection there. The store's name escapes me now, but I do remember that a couple by the name of "Slim" and Arlene owned it. As winter approached in late 1958, our trips to the store had to stop due to the weather and our responsibilities as high school students.

In April or May of 1959, we went back to the store and found it was no longer there. On our way back from the record stores on 42nd & 8th Avenue, we entered the subway at the foot of the Times Building at 42nd Street & 7th Avenue. As we walked down the first flight of stairs to the landing, I glanced into the store near the entrance and saw the person who had owned the store on 43rd Street, "Slim".

I remember walking into the store and meeting "Slim" at the doorway. I noticed he did not carry records any more; his new place was strictly a costume jewelry store. I asked him what had happened to the records from the other store. He told me he had them all stored in boxes at the back of this new store. He said he did not think he wanted to sell the records here, since this new store was small, and selling costume jewelry was much more profitable. I asked him if it would be all right for me to go through the boxes of records in the back room; maybe I would find some records I could buy from him. Out of five or six thousand records that I looked through, I picked out maybe three to four hundred that interested me. I only had about two or three dollars with me at the time, so I asked "Slim" if he would hold the records I could not pay for; I would come back the following Saturday to pick them up, and he agreed. I asked if he thought about putting the records out in the store again and if he would be getting any more new records in. He said he really did not know.

I asked "Slim" if he would be interested in letting me work in the store after school every Friday, and on Saturdays and Sundays so I could pay for the records I had picked out. He said he really was not doing enough business to be able to afford any help; it was just him and his wife. Besides, he did not feel there was any need for another worker in the store. I suggested that maybe if he brought the records out from the back, I could run the "Record Department" for him. "Slim" laughed and told me that with the amount of money he had been taking in on the records in the other store he could not even afford to buy lunch.

Then I suggested to "Slim" that he would not even have to pay me in cash, he could pay me in records. I thought it could become a very profitable business. The records he had were very desirable and he probably could do a lot better than a nickel a record. He did not really understand what I was getting at, and I showed him that if we took the sleeve of the record and wrote on it the artist, title, the release date, and put $2.50 or $1.00 or whatever on the sleeve, we could take in more money than just the fifty cents. Because of the larger profit, it would make a lot of sense for him to hire me. He really was not getting what I was saying; he could not comprehend that someone might actually want to pay more than a nickel a piece for these records. I said, "Let's try it for a week and see what happens. You don't have to pay me unless you take in more than the nickel a record you were getting before."

I wrote up the info on the sleeves of maybe fifty or seventy-five records, took pushpins, and put them along the back wall of the store, the wall facing the customers as they walked in. With a magic marker, I wrote the word "Records" on a piece of paper and stuck it in the window. The following Friday after school I came back and asked "Slim" if he had sold any records for more than the nickel he used to charge. He said he figured he had taken in about $23.00, and maybe $21.00 of that was more profit than he had made at his old selling price. Since my idea seemed to be successful, he agreed to let me work in the store and I got paid seventy-five cents an hour, with the equivalent in records being fifteen 45-rpm records per hour. He only let me work five hours, until we could generate more business. Needless to say, the completely back wall was written up and I tried to do as much business as I could, so I could make this a regular part-time job on the weekends. The following week, the Record Department took in around forty dollars, and from that point on, I HAD A JOB!

I had been working part time at "Slim's" store for maybe three months. In that time, the business never really did more than a hundred dollars per weekend with the oldies, but "Slim" was very happy with that, and so was I. Nevertheless, I also felt there was tremendous potential in what we were doing, if we could make people aware of it. After all, we were in a sort of remote location, with not much traffic walking by the store.

On Saturday nights, I used to listen to an oldies show on WHOM called "Night Train with Alan Fredericks". I felt that if we took out a couple of spots on the Night Train Show, we could bring in a lot more business. One Saturday right before closing, at about 11:30, I went over to the radio station where Alan Fredericks was broadcasting and waited for him to get off the air. I remember bringing about five or six records with me I felt would fit right in, and that I had not ever heard on the Night Train Show. Being that the show was only an hour every week, I got to know the music and remember the records he played, because they all happened to be records I liked.

I introduced myself to Alan Fredericks as he came out of the radio station. I said I was a listener of his and I worked at a record store that sold exclusively the kind of music he played. I told him the store had many records that fit in with the show, and I was wondering if he could play some of them and perhaps in turn promote the store. Alan said that he did not feel he could do something like that, because the mentions would be commercials, and since radio stations make their money on commercials, they would not go along with his promoting something without being paid. I believe he said spots at that time in the evening were ten to fifteen dollars each and I should check with my boss and see if he was interested in taking out maybe two or three spots on the show promoting the store, and he would be glad to do the commercials. I told Alan Fredericks I'd have to talk to "Slim" the next day (Sunday) and get back to him, stopping by the station the following Saturday. When I told him about Alan's suggestion, "Slim" looked at me like I was crazy and said there was no way he would spend fifteen dollars on a spot to promote the store. He said there were so many record stores it did not make sense to do anything like that.

The following Saturday, I went back and explained the situation to Alan, giving him more records to play. I then suggested to Alan that perhaps while he was playing some of these records, he could once or twice mention that they were "lent to him by Jerry who works at Times Square Records at 42nd and Broadway." In doing that, maybe we would get a response and I could eventually convince "Slim" to advertise on a regular basis, if it proved to be successful.

I remember some of the records I had given him that week were "Tormented" by The Heartbeats, "Dream Of A Lifetime" by The Flamingos, and one of my favorites, "Without A Friend", by The Strangers. Also included was a record by the Five Crowns, either "A Star" or "You're My Inspiration" (I am not sure which side he played). Alan was familiar with the Flamingos and the Heartbeats, but he did not know these songs. He had never heard of either the Strangers or the Five Crowns. At the time, Alan was playing what you would call more "mainstream" records, by groups that were more familiar, like the Heartbeats, the Valentines, and the Cleftones, groups that were known by many collectors. What I tried to do was give Alan alternative music, things that were not heard all the time, which would give the show more interest. Alan said he was getting many phone calls asking for different records, and he would mention my name along with the name of the store during the show in exchange for lending him the records. That week, Alan mentioned the store twice during Saturday night's show.

The Sunday hours at "Slim's" store were 12:00 to 9:00. The Sunday after our first mention on the Night Train show, I got off the subway at about 11:30. As I headed towards the store, I could not help noticing a crowd of people. I walked through the concourse and got out on the other side of 7th Avenue, because there were not any people on that side. I crossed the street and tried to make my way through this huge crowd to the subway entrance where the record store was located. I asked some of the people, mainly kids, what was going on. They said they were waiting for the record store to open. I pushed my way through the crowd of kids and after about five or ten minutes, I got close to the steps where the store was and waited for "Slim" to show up.

By 12:00, "Slim" still had not arrived. My usual routine on a Sunday after opening was to go across the street to Grant's, buy "Slim" two hot dogs, and a soda, so I thought I should check to see it he was at Grant's. Sure enough, "Slim" was sitting at the counter. After I told "Slim", the reason for the crowd outside, we ventured back across the street and opened the store, and we were busy until closing. It was so exciting to see that many people interested in the kind of music I liked; I felt we were on the right track with the advertising.

Many of the customers who came in those early days objected to the prices. They did not like the idea that we were selling some of the records for more than a dollar. I told them that if they had a copy of say, "Secret Love" by the Moonglows, which we were selling for three dollars, I would be glad to give them in credit towards anything they wanted. At that point, I began to offer anybody half in credit for anything that they brought in that we had on the wall at a higher price. The records we offered at a higher price were those I felt were harder to get, and did not see that often. I had been to ten or fifteen different shops as a collector, and I could tell hard to find records from the more common ones by their availability.

The customer realizing they could make money inspired collectors to get rid of the records they did not care for and exchange them for a record of interest. I would go through customer's collections and pull out records they wanted to trade in and give them half the amount in credit using the wall of record prices as my guideline. For example if a record normally sold for one dollar, I would give fifty cents credit toward any other purchase. If there were records, I did not know by major groups, I would also give fifty cents credit. I also gave fifty cents credit for records that I thought would not sell well at the store.

We made out very well with that trade in system, because in many cases we would pay a nickel for a record and end up selling it for a dollar, making twenty times the initial investment. The records that we were paying half a dollar for, I would listen to at night. If I thought they were good, I would sell them for two, three or five dollars each. By the end of the summer of 1959, I had to return to school. By that time, the store had already set a record by selling on 45-rpm for ten dollars. I remember "Slim" was thrilled to make that much of a profit. Since our inventory was growing so quickly, "Slim" and I came in early on one Sunday and built counters along the left and right walls. We expanded the counters, making the store one hundred percent records. Both "Slim" and I packed the costume jewelry in boxes that were stored in the back room of the store. Because of the trade in system, our inventory over the course of time grew significantly. We sold the records at the back counter and along on the radiator opposite the counter for three for a dollar (we could not watch those that much, so if we lost them it would not be that big a deal). We put the seventy eights all the way in the back of the store. We did very little in seventy eights, but because they were group records and the kind of music we were selling, and occasionally we did get some people asking for seventy eights, we took them in on trade. The most we paid on a seventy-eight, I think was twenty-five cents and if it were a group record, we would pay fifty cents. Customers would leave the records at the store even though we were not interested in them.

In September of 1959, I had to go back to school. Up until then, it had just been the three of us at the store, "Slim", his wife Arlene and I. I then suggested to "Slim" and he agreed that someone else would have to be there during the day, so I hired one of the customers I liked and used to go to lunch with, Harold Ginsburg. Until that time, I had been the only one giving credit for records, since "Slim" was not that knowledgeable about oldies then. Therefore, I taught Harold what to do; I showed him to be fair with the customers using the trade/credit system.

I attended The School of Visual Arts located at 27th Street in Manhattan from September 1960 to November 1961. School let out at about 2:00, and I would get to the store around 2:30. Every Friday, as soon as I got to the store, "Slim" and I would go straight to Portem Distributors located on 10th Avenue to purchase forty fives. We paid, I believe, about twenty cents per record. We always took a big checker cab back from Portem, giving the driver an extra five dollars so we could bring back forty or fifty cartons of records.

Also on Fridays, I would pick out about fifteen records for Alan Fredericks to feature on the weekly Night Train Show. I would write notes about each of the records. For example the name of the lead singer on the recording, the name of the record label along with other pertinent information. I would leave the store at around 9:00 on Fridays and go over to 53rd Street and 1st Avenue, where Alan lived at Sutton Terrace. I left the records with the door attendant. We did this for about a year; Alan would get the records, play them that Saturday night, and when I brought new records on Friday night, I would pick up the old ones.

Occasionally, I would call Alan to ask what he thought of the records, what were the most requested records, and if there was anything special, he wanted. Alan was a very easy person to deal with. I'd call different record companies and ask them to reissue certain titles and when we got them in, Alan would say that "Times Square Records" now has available for the first time on the Atlas label "I Belong To You" by the Fi-Tones, and "Yvonne" by the Parakeets. If there was anything we had just gotten in that week, Alan would announce that as part of our spot. If records received a lot of requests, or people were looking for hard to find records, he would sometimes play them and offer five, ten, fifteen or twenty dollars or whatever it might be for the record in credit towards other records.

I recall that once on a trip to Philadelphia I picked up a record by the Hide-aways called "Can't Help Loving That Girl of Mine". I had never heard it before and thought it was a great record. I remember programming the record on the show and offering five dollars in credit. Maybe two weeks later I offered ten dollars. I think the record went up to one hundred dollars in credit towards another purchase, but we were not able to get another copy.

Many records got their values from that show, because of their availability or their rarity. Many records were introduced on the show by using the trade/credit system. If the demand became great, we would try to contact the companies and have them reissue them. The first record that we reissued was "Sweetest One" by the Crests on the Joyce label, for which we received hundreds of calls. I contacted the record company and we ordered three thousand copies of the record. In the first two weeks, we sold close to one thousand copies.

Night Train had a very loyal audience. As time went on, the show's popularity grew and our sales in the store increased steadily and things were going along very well. Occasionally, though, we had a few problems. Many times collectors would come in or congregate outside the store and deal and trade records among themselves. Then they began to approach customers who were on their way into the store, asking to see what records they were bringing in to sell or trade for credit. At times, I would have to ban some collectors from coming into the store because of their soliciting other collectors outside. This did not make me too popular at the time, but I felt a responsibility to "Slim" and I took it upon myself to do these things, since I felt part of the business and a lot of their success was due to my efforts.

Probably the most interesting part of my job at Times Square Records was tracking down different manufacturers and getting them to reissue different product on their labels. I enjoyed dealing with the various people at these companies. I remember going to Hull Records and meeting Bea Kaslin and persuading her to reissue some of the Hull titles for which we received requests. I bought her overstock on all the old records by the Heartbeats, the Avons, the Beltones, the Legends and the Desires. There was a new record out at the time by the Desires, and it was always interesting to get new titles.

I met and dealt with George Goldner of Rama and Gee Records, Hy Weiss of Old Town Records, Ben Smith of X-tra Records, Bobby Robinson of Red Robin Records, Paul Winley of Winley Records, Syd Nathan of King Records, and Herman Lubinsky of Savoy Records. There were also people from a lot of the smaller labels, like Gil Snapper at Worthy Records (the Interiors), and Bob Schwaid at Music Makers Records (the Imaginations), Hiram Johnson at Johnson Records (the Dubs, the Shells) and Jack Brown at Fortune Records.

In retrospect, maybe contacting Jack Brown was not such a good idea. I had made a deal with him to get "The Wind" along with eight to ten other Diablos records reissued plus ten or fifteen records on the Fortune Label. This led to an unfortunate situation. In my discussions with Jack, he mentioned that he had a warehouse in Detroit with about fifty thousand records. “Slim's” wife Arlene’s mother lived in Detroit. Arlene offered to take a trip to Fortune Records. She could go through the records and let me know what was there, and pay her mother a visit as well. I bought Arlene a round trip ticket at the Greyhound bus terminal.

Soon after arriving in Detroit, Arlene called me to say she was not coming back and she wanted me to tell “Slim”! I told her I did not think it was my place to tell my boss that his wife was leaving him. Therefore, Arlene told “Slim” herself, and she did not come back. Arlene and “Slim” had a little boy Bobby, who “Slim” raised on his own. Over the a period of several months "Slim" became more and more depressed causing him to withdraw from the business. He would come in late and did not seem to care very much, about what went on at the store.

When “Slim” came around, about two or three months later, he went completely the other way. He tried to control what the people heard, forcing his musical preferences on the customers. He concentrated on playing more up-tempo songs, like "Silly Dilly" by the Pentagons.

Some of these records did well, like the other side of "Ankle Bracelet", "Hot Dog Dooly Wah" by the Pyramids, which was one of "Slim's" favorite records and became fairly popular. All the Charts records and things like that were very popular. Nevertheless, there were certain records that were a little bizarre, that many people did not like. One of the people that did not like this new direction was Alan Fredericks. In the summer of 1960, Alan objected to playing many of these records, and it caused a lot of friction between Times Square Records and the Night Train Show. "Slim", in trying to be more active, took over the programming of the show and began alienating Alan. I believe they stopped speaking to each other altogether.

I left the store in November of 1961, when I moved to Philadelphia to open a record store that was the same kind as Times Square Records. I felt that I could not open a store in New York and go into competition against "Slim", because in spite of everything, I still felt very close to him.

There are a few reasons for my leaving Times Square Records. When I was starting my second year of college, in September of 1961, I had asked "Slim" if there was a chance of my getting a raise. I had been making the same seventy-five cents an hour since I started more than two years earlier. I was now receiving an hourly wage instead of the records. The cost of art supplies was quite high, and I really needed the cash. "Slim" told me that it if I quit art school, he would give me one dollar an hour. He would not compromise; if I did not quit school, I would not get the raise. After all, I had done for the store and my loyalty to "Slim", his giving me such an ultimatum really hurt.

The deciding factor in my leaving Times Square Records came about on the day "Slim" came in to the store, handed me a $2.995.00 bill for a 1960 or 1961 Plymouth Fury, and asked me to make out a check. (It was part of my job to pay all the bills and balance the checkbook each month.) Opening the checkbook, I said, "I thought you didn't have a driver's license." He said he was going to learn to drive; Genni was going to teach him. Genni was a girl "Slim" had hired to work in the store on a part time basis. "Slim" was infatuated with Genni; however, the feeling was not mutual. "Slim" got to the point where he would do anything to win her over. He bought her a car. I felt much slighted; "Slim" had refused to give me a raise without any reason, but he was spending $3000.00 to buy a car for Genni. Looking back now, the picture seems very clear, but back then I had trouble dealing with it; this was probably the main reason for my leaving Times Square Records. "Slim" never knew just how upset I was about buying the car for Genni and saying no to my raise.

When I left, there were five people working at the store. They were "Slim", Genni, Harold Ginsburg, Johnny Esposito (another friend I made at the store and ended up hiring), and another gentlemen "Slim" had worked with years before in a different business that came back to work with him again. I had been attending The School of Visual Arts five days a week until 2:00 in the afternoon and the Fashion Institute three nights a week, but when I quit my job at the store, I quit school as well and moved to Philadelphia.

The Record Museum, my first store, opened in Philadelphia on the day after Thanksgiving in 1961.

***Author's Note – I interview Arlene Rose on May 5, 2006. She indicated the reason for her going to Detroit was to visit her biological mother. Arlene Rose was raised by Martha and Julius Garcia. Martha Garcia was in fact Arlene's aunt not mother. The marriage was over between her and "Slim". "Slim" knew where she was leaving him and he knew she would never return.

There was never any intention of her visiting Fortune Records in Detroit. "Slim" was so upset over her leaving him Arlene told me that he fabricated that story as he was too embarrassed to have anyone know the truth.

I questioned Arlene Rose about "Slim" having a driver's license and owning a car. He had a driver's license in both the state of New York and California. See the "Slim" archives for photo of license. In fact "Slim" taught Arlene how to drive.

The information provided in this chapter acquired from the liner notes from the "Memories Of The Times Square Record Shop" CD collection. Permission was given by Jerry Greene to use the liner notes. I also interviewed Mr. Greene on November 10, 2006. A few minor changes were made to the liner notes after the interview, with his approval after reviewing the changes.

Mr. Greene was grateful to hear the true story about why Arlene Rose went to Detroit. He indicated to me in the interview on November 10, 2006 he blamed himself all these years.

My Life: Hanging By A String From The "Times" Ceiling

Wayne Stierle

"What I mean is.............I KNEW at the time that it was crazy and wonderful......I never took it for granted...............It was nuts in a way that only "magic" can be, and so many things that would become famous or iconic were happening on a regular basis..........It was all moving forward at a rapid pace, and I thought everything would continue to get better and more exciting, but the sand was running through the hour glass faster than I could know........."

"I could go from Times, and Teddy the Raccoon running wild there, but thankfully in his cage most of the time, and "Slim" and Jenny, and Rosalie and Harold, and Mike, and others including Jared and Jerry, and minutes later be in The Brill Building at 1619 Broadway, riding the elevator with Jackie Wilson and Mike Wallace......to name just a few..............And, Jack Dempsey waving to you from the window of his restaurant............ ....it was THAT strange..............It really was.........Still, it was the reality of that point in time............"

"When I put the "Slim" 45 out (the EP), in the early 70's, I tracked "Slim" down to the store where he was working...........He didn't own the store.........But the owner had known him since the early fifties.............."

"I brought him 50 copies of the record and he almost cried.........He was so pleased that his son, Bobby, would be able to see a touch of what he had done...........To me it was bittersweet, because I had always been carrying between 50 and 400 copies of singles from here in Jersey over to Times by bus, and lugging them from The Port Authority to Times................(Stuff that Donn & I, or myself had re-issued......Such as "Rama Lama Ding Dong", "Baby Oh Baby", and others, all records that had been bombs in the late 50's.........BUT,...That were about to become national hits in the early 60's....).......”

"So here I was giving him these records a decade later, in what seemed like a different, sadder universe.................He was slightly confused and clearly beginning to lose his memory somewhat................(I never knew his age, and

I'm glad I didn't).......He would never say, but sometimes he would lie about it as a joke................"

"Arlene he referred to as "the big redhead", and sometimes when I'd answer the phone she would be calling and he would signal me to say he had just left........He seemed to be dodging something, but what it was I do not know............He gave me that impression.....................He said she was in Delaware, but I don't know..............."

"You know, the only early escapades that "Slim" chose to talk about was that crazy in time 1n 1953 when Marilyn Monroe & Playboy magazine both became famous....."Slim", like countless people around the world, was knocking off those photos and selling bogus "Marilyn" calendars.................He was proud of that............"

"By the way........................I assumed the "Slim" 45 would sell to the fans of Times Records..............Those people like to say they were there..........BUT.............they didn't support the record.....................It was a cold reception, in that I couldn't understand HOW anyone would NOT want it................But...........record collectors are not always lovers of music at all...........but rather collectors of what they can sell for a profit, in the same way that stamp collectors act.................Which I hate...This was music for the heart......."

"I was a kid when rock n' roll was born. It was time unlike any other time. Without Times Square Records, and the willingness of "Slim" to deal with anybody who came through the door, (and the early help of Donn Fileti), I never would have realized my childhood dream of actually putting out my own records. I might never have walked into a pressing plant and experienced the sheer mind-numbing smell of records being pressed. The little squares of plastic being melted and molded in 45 RPM dreams. Dreams and hope. What else is a record you like, if not an audio playback of your own emotions? To be on the inside of that elusive world was all I ever wanted in life".

"We moved Times with shopping carts. We actually moved the store in shopping carts. Here's a store that is a part of history, and it was carried out piece by piece and pushed and dragged over to the new location. As this was going on, I was watching everything and knowing that this was a true "point in time" that would be seen as fiction in the future. It was also a sad ritual, because the closing of the original store was a dramatic passage of an era that seemed to be closing itself. Sure, the new location might be bigger and better, but the nagging feeling that this was wrong haunted me. I can't stand endings......."

"The second store was big, and clean..........and had none of the charm of the original store, which was the craziest place in the world........The second store became like "home" after a while..........But it just lacked.......what I already said............."charm".................... (It would be GREAT today...........but at the time, it was second best)................That's how things are in their own time...Sad to say..........."

"When I brought my first released record into the store, it was a big event for me. (Candlelite #410). It was red plastic, and the only Candlelite single that never bore the candle I drew as the logo for the label. What a moment for me! "Slim" telling Harold to "write it up"! The title written on the white sleeve and having it pinned on the wall! Then, the biggest moment, when a copy was hung by string from the ceiling along with the other records hanging in that mystical place".

"I remember going up the subway stairs with Harold, and walking around The Times building. (Where the latest news rotated continually in lights). People would stare at us, and even the police did a double-take. You see, Harold had Teddy the raccoon on a leash! It seemed normal to us, in the context of a world that was tilted in a wonderful way. Down the stairs, beneath the street, Huberts Flea Circus was still in business, featuring sideshow freaks, and fleas that Hubert claimed did acrobatic tricks. In that environment, what would seem strange about walking a raccoon on a leash? After all, Teddy was the pet that "Slim" had, instead of a cat or a dog".

"If you look closely you'll see our coats piled up over the records...........We were just closing.............And Slim had his own way of closing.........He'd throw the customers out and lock the door, and there'd be the regular closing...............He came to believe that a customer might hide there, and then steal everything later on, by breaking OUT........................... He was right about that..........Crazy stuff happened there all the time................."

"My best memories of "Slim" are not directly attached to records, but rather to sitting behind the counter and having buttered toast with "Slim", or sharing a bunch of hot dogs from Grants. It was at these times that he talked about things in general. These were real conversations. I respected what he was doing, and what I thought it meant in musical history. I didn't want that world to end".

"Slim" would call on the phone to order records or ask questions..........he'd talk to my Mother for long periods of time, about "the old days". My Mother liked talking to him, and "Slim" would always inquire as to how she was doing."

"You see I loved the whole scene............42nd. Street when it was real........The X-Rated theatres were bad, but the pizza was the best............The hot dogs that Slim liked so much at Grants...........Grants...where the hot dogs were 15 cents, right out front, while in the back a bar was filled with drunks and people who seemed to have left society behind them................"And the music was there..............And even Slim and the buttered toast I'd get for him and me................Just sitting there eating toast with Slim as the store kept rolling along was magic to me.............Slim and his outlook on life, and his view of things, all colored by the fact that he was a world-weary adult who didn't really know the music, ...EXCEPT he LOVED the crazy record .... So he was the oldest fan of some of this music that there was.................. "

"He'd hear the craziest record and say "That's cute", and that was the stamp of approval, for if he could get 100 copies of it, you knew he was going to push it...........On the other hand, if he didn't like a record, he would resist selling it even if there was a demand for it............. ""It was nuts, but it was right.................The stars were in line.........All was right with the world................"

"Rosalie worked at the store. She was one of those girls with a bubbly personality that made everyone feel good. Rosalie ended up marrying Harold. Harold was short and slight, and about half the size of Rosalie. It may have not been a marriage made in heaven, but it made sense by Times Square standards. Harold was terrific working at the store, but Harold actually preferred working with cameras over working with records, which was very confusing to me. Rosalie always liked the records I put out, or at least she always said she did, and if "Slim" wasn't quite as thrilled, she'd berate him about how good it was".

"Mike worked at the store. Mike was probably 50 years old or older. He was weathered, and "Slim" said that Mike had spent most of his life at sea in the navy. Mike didn't know anything about records, and his job was to stop kids from stealing records. I don't know where he came from or how he got there. He was just there. He didn't say anything unless you spoke to him. I felt that he knew "Slim" from the early 50's, or late 40's, but I never knew".

"The records that were not behind the counter were in bins you could browse in, across from the counter. These records ranged in price from 5 cents to 50 cents, and varying prices, subject to "Slim's" Mood. String was run between them, so a whole row was attached together, and no one could steal one without lifting up the whole row. If you wanted to buy a record from that section, the string had to be cut, and the record brought out, and then the string had to be knotted up where it was cut Primitive? It was very primitive. It was great!!"

"Record collecting is almost exclusively a male pursuit, which is not to say that females aren't supporters of this music. The girls who worked at Times were not collectors, and were not very well versed in the music at all, with Shandy being the only exception. Shandy was the nicest girl there, and she really knew the music, far better than the customers who would try to impress her with their "knowledge". She had a self-taught musical philosophy that covered many areas of the pop culture, but she never flaunted that. Shandy was the youngest person to work at Times, and though she was seen as one of the cute girls from Times, hardly anyone knew she had started at age 12, and wasn't the older teenager that customers assumed her to be."

"Slim" hired several girls, and that didn't hurt with his male customers. Genni, Shari, Shandy, and Anita had their followers or "fans". Anita was only in the second store, and seemed to possibly be a Genni replacement, in some bizarre way. Anita knew nothing about records. Nothing. She was pre-occupied with her hair, makeup, and posing in rather outrageous outfits. I'd say the posing is how she got hired. Given her odd "fans", maybe she was replacing Teddy, and not Genni."

"For awhile the back room of the new store was large and clean, but soon was filled with records and cardboard squares and boxes. The back room of the original store was something else. That room was like a crawl-space from hell, and the ceiling would crash down at times when the subway would rumble overly loud. It had mice, and god knows what else. It took nerve to go back there".

"Slim" would cough in a way that only smokers cough. I thought that possibly he was ill, beyond the smoking, so I'd ask him why he didn't see a doctor, and maybe get a penicillin shot. He held up the cigarette and said, "....penicillin can't cure this......"

"One day at Times I had terrible stomach pains. I could hardly walk. "Slim" had Harold walk with me to the Port Authority Bus Terminal, and I was off to New Jersey, earlier than I should have been. When I got home, 'Slim" had already called my Mother twice, to see if I was ok."

"Times was like a strange "family", and I honestly think that fact, is a very large part of why people are so emotional when they speak about the store."

"Times Records, later known as Times Square Records found its way into your heart and soul".

***Author's Note – Information provided in this chapter came from actual emails to this author from January 2006 – April 2006.

The New York Attitude

Donn Fileti

It was the spring of 1959 when I first learned about Irving "Slim" Rose and the store known as Times Square Records. I was seventeen at the time and already an obsessive collector. I was at Tin Pan Alley Records located on 50th Street and Broadway copying down the numbers of vocal group records when I heard about this store located in a subway arcade. Someone came up to me and told me they sold records for a dollar and there was a store down on 42nd Street in the subway arcade that was selling the same record for $3.00 or $5.00.

It was September, 1959 when I heard my first Alan Frederick's radio show on WHOM which sponsored "Slim". Alan Fredericks would tell his listeners about this store where you could take rare records and in exchange you received credit. Naturally Donn was fascinated by hearing this on the radio.

Approximately a month later Donn called "Slim" and told him he could help him with getting records reissued or possibly get copies of some of them. Of course "Slim" not knowing it was Donn he was speaking to, was very interested. At the time Donn pretended to be a disc jockey simply because his prior trips to the store were not pleasant. There was "Slim" saying how he didn't like to deal with customers. Also, it was quite apparent that "Slim" was condescending and slightly rude. Behind the counter is a nasty sharp kid from Brooklyn known as Jerry Greene. Another employee was Harold Ginsburg who was nice enough, however he had the "Brooklyn attitude".

It was on this trip to the store Donn would learn just how nasty and rude everyone there actually was......Donn had found a record store in New Jersey that carried some very rare records at the time. He purchased them and took them to Times Records to do business with "Slim" or an employee. Behind the counter was Jerry Greene, who asked Donn where he got these rare records. Donn wouldn't tell him so Jerry Greene continued to badger him unmercifully.

After that, every time Donn went to the store to buy a record or trade in credit for another record, Jerry Greene would purposely give him the worse copy that was in stock. For example Donn asked for the Moonglows "Most Of

All".....Jerry Greene gave him a bad copy....when Donn asked him for a better copy Jerry Greene would say "what's the matter with this one"....and then he would say "fine" and get him a better copy. This was totally uncalled for on the part of Jerry Greene. "Slim" would stand there watching, making nasty remarks about the customers and other things.

It was Christmas, 1959 Donn brought in three records. "Slim" offered him $4.00 apiece. Donn made the deal thinking he could always purchase the records again. Two of the records were "Tony, My Darling" by the Charmers on Central which was purchased at Brooks Record Shop in Plainfield, New Jersey for 89 cents, and "That's My Desire" by the Flamingos on Chance, which was red plastic. Immediately "Slim" gave the records to Harold to put up on the wall for $20.00 apiece. It was like a slap in the face to Donn. It was totally contemptuous on "Slim's" part. Donn felt he could have at least waited until he left the store then put the records up on the wall. This was the way things were done at the store....Donn referred to it as their "New York attitude along with nastiness".

It was after that experience that Donn dealt with "Slim" by telephone only; pretending to be Donn Fileti, disc jockey who worked for West Orange Broadcasting Company in New Jersey.

Enter General Records Distributors......Wayne Stierle was Donn's best friend in high school. Donn had no money back then. Wayne had $400.00 to $500.00 in the bank which he saved from receiving birthday gifts. Donn knew that one of "Slim's" most wanted records was "My Heart's Desire" by the Wheels on Premium. He began making telephone calls along with reading Cashbox and Billboard to locate the owner of the master. It was not long before the owner was found. It was a man by the name of Saul Weinstein from Boston, who owned Rainbow Records. Sending Wayne's $350.00, Donn ordered one thousand copies of "My Heart's Desire". About a month later a huge transport truck shows up at his home in West Orange, New Jersey, unloading ten one hundred count boxes of records pressed exactly with the original label. Since Wayne and Donn were "sidekicks" at the time, Wayne brought the records into the store for "Slim". The records were purchased for 35 cents each and wholesaled to "Slim" at 50 cents each. "Slim" in return sold them retail for a dollar apiece.

"Slim's" biggest thing at the time was to control exclusive sales rights to a record. He didn't want it all over the city; meaning he wanted it all to himself to advertise on the radio and to sell at his store only. Donn told "Slim" that no one else would have this record ("My Heart's Desire" by the Wheels) etc. etc. etc. About a month or two later, "Slim" called Donn letting him know the record was playing all over the city. What happened was Donn had ordered the original 1000 copies, however Saul Weinstein in Boston wasn't satisfied with that....he pressed up more copies and sold them to a record distributor in New York which in return sold them to every record store in the city.

Donn told "Slim" this was all out of his control. Being a naïve boy from West Orange, New Jersey, he believed Saul Weinstein when he told him he wouldn't be pressing anymore copies of "My Heart's Desire" by the Wheels. This is exactly what the record companies did back then.

The next joint adventure Donn and Wayne embarked on involved three records that came out in 1957 on the Acme masters in New York. Looking up the address in BMI; off they go knocking on doors trying to locate an apartment on 44th Street hoping to locate the owner of the masters. Unable to find the owner, they both decide to press them, without contracts, since Donn had the original copies of the three records. They were sent to Beltone Studios in New York where acetate records were made of all three. Next came the making of 1000 labels at ten cents each for a total of $10.00 in Newark, New Jersey. Once the labels were finished the next step was to go to Silver Park Records in River Edge, New Jersey to press copies. Donn had approximately 300 pressed of each record for 11 cents each which was good at the time as one hundred copies were already sold to "Slim" for 50 cents each. "Slim" always balked at buying more than 100 copies of anything as he didn't want to tie up his money. As you can see very little profit was made on a record back then. A note worth mentioning.... One of Donn's friends who was seventeen at the time, the only one who had a car and could drive, along with his girlfriend took Donn, the records and labels to River Edge, New Jersey for pressing......

The name of the three records pressed were "On Your Radio" by Richard Lanham and the Tempo-Tones, "Get Yourself Another Fool" by the Tempo-Tones and "Walking the Streets Alone" by the Love Letters. Donn requested his records back from Beltone. Two of them arrived in the mail broken....both by the Tempo-Tones...."Walking The Streets Alone" was never returned..... According to Donn this record is worth approximately $1,000.00 on today's market. The original owner of "On Your Radio" was the brother-in-law of John Halonka, who was a well known record distributor. The brother-in-law passed away sometime in 1959. Soon after Donn's mother received a telephone call from John Halonka asking if she knew anything about "On Your Radio".

Moving along the timeline.....Donn along with Wayne traveled to the city along 1650 Broadway, 1690 Broadway, 1610 Broadway, and 1697 Broadway knocking on the office doors of tiny record companies asking if they still had any of the old records stored away and if so, were they willing to sell them for a very cheap price. They would pay maybe 25 cents or 30 cents or less a copy and then sell to "Slim" for 50 cents a copy.

It was decided by Donn that they (Wayne and himself) needed a name. At the time Donn's father was working at Prudential Insurance Company in Newark, where he had a mimeograph machine. Going to the office Donn made copies of a flyer which included the name General Records Distributors, Donn's name and address.......along with twenty-five or so records they had pressed or bought to sell wholesale. Before the flyer could be mailed to any record store in New York and New Jersey; the flyer had to be cleared with "Slim" as one of the records listed was "My Heart's Desire" by the Wheels. "Slim" had his "exclusive" now for two or three months. Donn still had almost 800 copies that needed to be sold. "Slim" finally gave his approval and the flyer was mailed sometime in March, 1961. Thus began General Records Distributors.

Again moving back along the time line to late 1959.....the next project to come along was the record "Baby Oh Baby" by the Shells on the Johnson Label. "Slim" really wanted this record. Donn located the owner of the master which turned out to be Hiram Johnson, Buddy Johnson's brother. (Buddy wrote "Since I Fell For You"). Hiram Johnson at the time was represented by Jim McCarthy whose office was located at 1619 Broadway in the Brill Building. It was late 1959 or early 1960 that Donn and Wayne became involved with the Shells and Jim McCarthy. This meeting would turn out to be a pivotal point in Wayne Stierle's life. The publishing on "Baby Oh Baby" was owned by Alan Freed who by now had been kicked out of New York City. He was now working at KDAY in Los Angeles.

"Baby Oh Baby" was reissued for "Slim". It is now two or three months later after "Slim" got the record in the store, when Alan Freed was able to get a copy and started playing it on his radio show. (Wayne remembers that Jim McCarthy sent copies to Jack Hooke, Alan Freed's manager, and Hooke who owned the publishing with Freed, sent it quickly to Freed). It soon began to take off in key cities, eventually hitting as high as #19 nationally by Christmas of 1960, and on into early 1961. Between 300,000 to 450,000 copies were sold nationally. "Baby Oh Baby" was one of the first actual hit records that "Slim" was responsible for......after that Donn and Wayne worked with the Shells...Wayne in particular worked with The Shells for many years producing the majority of their sessions. The follow-up to "Baby Oh Baby", "Explain It To Me", failed to "click" on the radio. The Shells continued to make new releases, including some success with "Happy Holiday", "Deep In My Heart", "Sweetest One", and "Baby, Walk On In", produced by Wayne, and best known in New York City, among other major cities. (Donn and Wayne chose to do "Sweetest One", when The Shells original lead balked at their first choice of "I See A Star". The lead then quit the group, and the re-grouped Shells recorded with Wayne, as Donn had gone to college in Virginia in September, 1960).

Next was another song that "Slim" really wanted. It was an up-tempo sound teenagers really liked. The record was "Lama Rama Ding Dong" by the Edsels which was released by a small record company located in Little Rock, Arkansas. Donn called the owner to ask if he had copies of the record. He was told by the owner of the company that he had just sold all his copies to a guy by the name of Sid Taback in California. Sid Taback bought records for a penny or two and then resold them for a dime or more. Contacting Sid Taback, Donn was able to purchase 100-200 records at fifteen cents each and sold them to "Slim" at fifty cents each.

"Lama Rama Ding Dong sold quickly and soon all copies were gone. Donn and Wayne tried to get Johnson Records or Jim McCarthy to take over the master. There was a gentleman in Ohio who owned one half of the publishing rights and who also originally cut the record; he would not give up his rights to the publishing therefore foregoing any deal on "Lama Rama Ding Dong". Donn believes what happened next......Jerry Greene went to Hy Weiss of Old Town Records and was able to persuade him to make a deal for the master. The deal was made, the record reissued. They quickly got air time on the radio stations in New York and soon it became a national hit. (Oddly enough, "Rama Lama Ding Dong" peaked nationally at almost the same point that "Baby Oh Baby" did, and yet "Rama Lama Dong Dong" is regarded today as much bigger hit than it was.) (Not long after this, the Arkansas record label gave the rights to Wayne, asking him to stop Hy Weiss, but it was too late). The name "Lama Rama Ding Dong" was changed to

"Rama Lama Ding Dong", by mistake, and the rest is history. This song is still a standard "doo wop" hit to this day, and has in fact become a part of the slang language of the pop culture, showing up periodically in the strangest ways.

Donn had gone away to college by this time. When the record started to break in New York, Wayne called Sid Taback in California and told him to send all the copies he had of "Rama Lama Ding Dong" which were about 500-600 copies. Wayne began to sell them as was his right to do same. Weiss began threatening Wayne to stop selling "Rama Lama Ding Dong", but Wayne defied him, and proof enough that Weiss was wrong lies in the fact that Weiss tried none of his usual rough tactics on Wayne, although he called Wayne, and getting his Mother on the phone, he threatened to kill Wayne. In 1998, Hy Weiss apologized to Wayne, and put the blame on his brother, George Weiss. Wayne was not amused. So ends the story of "Rama Lama Ding Dong".

Moving right along.....the next record that "Slim" was responsible for....."There's A Moon Out Tonight" by the Capris. Speaking with Donn about this...he has no recollection of the following as he was away at college.....However, Wayne Stierle says that it was Donn and himself who went and got copies of "There's A Moon Out Tonight" on the original label and sold them to "Slim". According to Wayne: Wayne, alone, then went back to the record label and set up a price to buy the master. Wayne then explained this to "Slim", with Jerry Greene listening, and Greene found a way to raise the money and get there with the cash before Wayne could proceed. That's entirely another story in itself.........

According to Donn Fileti most of the time Irving "Slim" Rose was a true visionary, however was a horrible businessman. He had a unique quirky personality. "Slim" never made the connection between Donn Fileti the kid who would come into the store and Donn Fileti the disc jockey.

Donn graduated from college in June, 1964. At the same time he started conducting business with Eddie Gries. Business was tapering off between Donn and "Slim" and it was time to move on.

****Author's Note – Information provided in this chapter came from an interview with Donn Fileti on March 26, 2006.

When He Spoke...You Knew Right Away It Was "Slim"

Our Memories Of "Slim"

Record collecting got its start at Times Square Records. Back then twenty-two dollars was a lot for a teen who was at the age of fifteen or so in 1960 or 1961. Those prices are long gone. As "Slim" would say "One dollar records, three records for two dollars and eight records for five dollars" promoting his store on his radio show called "Swingin' with Slim". "Slim" was pretty honest, giving eighteen or nineteen dollars in credit for a twenty-two dollar record, etc.

Some of those teenagers that went there in the early years around 1959 were the early R&B pioneers. We know who they are as they are telling us the story that is written in this book.

I went to Times Square in the summer of 1964, and although I was there for a short four hours, it was my only trip, however a trip I have never forgotten, and never will. My mother and I took the train from Philadelphia to New York. I was given a choice of going to the New York World's Fair or visiting Times Square Records. My answer was short and swift. I didn't need to think about it. Naturally I chose Times Square Records.

I hung out in West Philly with some of those pioneers such as Mike Adler, Jack Strong, and Val Shively. Val used to take the bus to Times Square on Saturday. The bus fare round trip was twenty-five dollars.
Jess Porter

I grew up in the Bronx [Locust Point] during the 50's/60's. My one foray to Times Square Record Shop had to be 1959-1960. I went to replace my copy of "Mary Lee" on Red Robin. I had come by this from my cousin in Brooklyn [Bushwick] who had given me quite a few records. The original was left in a window sill and looked like a roller coaster track after an afternoon's sun-shine.

Anyway...I remember walking into the shop and a nice guy of sixteen or seventeen came up to me and asked if he could help. I like to think it was

Jerry Greene or Donn Fileti but I don't know. He takes me to a bin and pulls out a copy of Mary Lee on Fire and earnestly tells me this is the original label. My thirteen year old self, who knew virtually nothing of Group Harmony and R&B outside of what I had in my small collection, loudly proclaimed "no it's not, it was issued on "Red Robin". The bottom line is I bought that copy for the princely sum of $3.00 and still have it today.

Rick Studer

I'm almost 59 now which made me a young kid then touring NYC and eventually landing at Times Square Records. I would guess somewhere in the neighborhood of 1959-1962 I found myself shopping at Times Square Records. My friend who lived in my building in the Bronx sang with the original Excellents (John Kuse - lead) and he turned me on to Times Square Records before their own hit, Coney Island Baby, 1962.

Slim" was a strange dude, at best. Kind of a nervous, constantly smoking type, not overly friendly but knew his stuff about the records. I remember he would do his best to obtain any record you wanted, if not in stock. I had never met anybody that knew more about the Doo Wop era than "Slim".

Soon after that, one day, without any warning, I saw a sign on his front door stating the store was permanently closed -- no forwarding address. I was heartbroken and never saw him again.

Steve Hiller

The most amusing part of the whole scenario is when I listened to Night Train on 1480 with host Alan Fredericks, Times Square Records was the sponsor of the show. Alan Fredericks referred to Rose as "Swingin" Slim". "Slim" was entirely different meeting him in person.

The record selection was unreal. He was the only game in town. We traveled from Brooklyn all the time just to go to Times Square Records. The shop itself was a hidden store located on the second landing down the subway stairs. If you blinked you missed it. It took me a couple trips just to find it because there were about six different staircases on six different street corners all going to the same stations. For a while I thought the place was a myth. I will never forget him in a million years!!

Bob Young

I went to Times Square Records mainly in 1962 - 1963. When you went into the store then, the records were on the opposite wall on the left side. The aisle was narrow. I do remember seeing the raccoon (Teddy) on one occasion. I also remember "Slim" being there, but don't remember him as particularly gruff or intimidating. He was just there. Of course when I went to Times Square Records I usually knew in advance what I wanted, as I'd make my "want list" from what I'd heard on his radio show. I probably never had more than $10.00 - $20.00 to spend at a time, and usually tried to stretch it by sticking to $1.00 records. And you could get some great stuff without ever leaving the $1.00 bins. It was a very COOL experience."

Times Square Records seemed to figure into the lives of so many of us who became collectors/doo-wop lovers during the early 1960's. One of the interesting things I noticed was on one of the record lists. It shows "Lama-Rama-Ding-Dong" by The Edsels. Now this is how it was listed when it was originally released in 1958, and how I first knew the song, since I discovered the record through Times Square, probably some time during 1961. Most of my high school friends were not into the whacked. A few months later the record was re-issued as "Rama Lama Ding Dong" and did pretty well in the New York City market. Now I was vindicated, as my friends didn't remember whether I'd called it "Lama-Rama" or "Rama-Lama", I didn't pursue the fine points of the minor title modification".

"Slim" was also good at disseminating misinformation. When he started pushing "My Reverie" by the Larks, he promoted it on the radio, as being from 1949, which probably increased the desirability of owning a copy of what at the time seemed like an "ancient" recording. It wasn't until many years later that I discovered that it really came out in 1951. Not that it really matters. It still ranks with my all time favorites.
Jim Dunn

As for my thoughts, I miss the old original Times Square Records store. It was cramped with musical charm. We lived the music; it was part of our essence. It was something we owned. What "Slim" Rose unintentionally accomplished was the uniting of young people in a bond of captivating musical harmonies and melodies, the likes of which had never before been heard in musical history.

An imperfect man, a man with flaws, Irving "Slim" Rose nevertheless achieved historical status by spreading the collecting of what we now call doo-wop music among an entire generation. He instinctively knew "the sound". "Slim" and his record store and radio program must be ranked even above legends such as Alan Freed and Dick Clark because he was at the "grass roots" level of the street music of the day, being passionately in love with the doo-wop group sounds, and he introduced all the various styles of doo-wop music to us over only a four-year period, 1960 through 1963, but what he started continues to mushroom decades later. New generations will discover how enjoyable and pure doo-wop music is, since these groups sing the harmonies and melodies straight from the heart, with no pretensions. All these groups sang, and the new waves of groups still sing, in group harmony for the love of the music and the euphoric feel it gives to both the singers and the listeners.

The fast songs are great fun and the love song ballads are emotionally-charged, sung with passion. "Slim" Rose expanded our affection for this musical genre we now refer to as "doo-wop", and therefore he is one of the most important personalities in musical history, and ensures that this unique form of Americana will live forever.

Pete Chaston

I visited Times Square a few times a year whenever I had a bunch of money from my grocery delivery tips. It was a small place and I was always nervous going there. "Slim" liked to yell and scream which was unsettling to me. I never came across a store owner like him".

I always listened to his radio show but his voice was terrible for a DJ. It was so unpolished, nothing like Alan Freed, Jocko or Alan Fredericks. For all my visits to the store I probably spent $200.00. I always looked for the bargains and not the expensive stuff on the wall. I was a listener and not a collector.

Stanley Starr

The area of wall behind the counter was pasted with new releases as well as $2.00 to $8.00 records. There always seemed to be a few (records) hanging from the strings as well. When we used to go there Val had a camera a lot of the time. I used to wear a derby just to keep them honest. The photos on the covers of the Collectibles "Memories Of Times Square" were either taken by Val or me. Maybe not all, but there is one with Val with "Slim" where Val is wearing my derby. We always busted on "Slim" & Harold.

I remember buying a new pair of shoes at Flagg Brothers which was located a few blocks away from Times Square Records. We put my old shoes in the Flagg bag and hung it on the wall in the far corner with a tag saying Jack's shoes $30.00. After awhile Val asked "Slim" if he could see the condition of the shoes. That was the kind of fun we used to have there. As far as purchasing I mostly stayed with the $1.00 stuff. Got a few originals before I stopped going, however the memories are golden.

Jack Strong

Growing up in the Bronx, I had a friend whose older sister would send us both to the Times Square Record Store to buy records for her. We traveled by train from the Bronx to Times Square. I remember the store would rattle as the trains would pass.

At the store, we learned of the Times Square Records Radio Show with "Slim" Rose as the DJ. He played many records not heard on other shows and so we would venture time and time again to his store. I remember seeing records on the wall, at prices well above what we were paying at local stores and knew that one day records would be a collectible item.

The first records I purchased from "Slim" was "Sunday Kind Of Love" by the Sentimentals and "There Goes My Love" by the Fantastics. By the way, I never did see the raccoon but did hear about him!

Chris Buccola

I passed Times Square Records a few of times without really realizing what it was. I used to listen to WADO and WWRL late Saturday nights and wondered at the nighttime quality of the music. There was something otherworldly about a play list that contained nothing that could be heard on the mainstream stations. They even gave Murray the K a run for the money.

Times Square itself, populated with characters out of a Grove Press novel, had that same weird quality that fascinated a Jersey girl. I spent Saturdays in New York with my mother. When we went into the subway, we would pass by a record store, which would fascinate me to no end.

When I was a high school junior or senior—I can't remember which—I went to visit some friends in Brooklyn. On the way there, I decided to seek out the record store and I found it. All I recall are an older guy and bins and bins of records, and records on the wall. No raccoon, though.

I'd gone to Relic before, so I wasn't totally confused, but I was enchanted that all these things—most of them completely foreign to me —were there. I had limited funds, so I bought one record. I believe it was "No, No, Don't Make Me Cry" by the Youngones. I still have it.

The effect still lingers—the strangest few blocks in what to me was the world, and a record store that was truly underground.

What more could you want in a memory?
Kate Karp

I was at this show with my friend Jay Helfrick. I remember our shock that the leader of the Kodaks was a GIRL, Pearl McKinnon. We thought how smart that was; a Frankie Lymon type voice with no worry about an adolescent voice change! I remember "Slim" & Genni on the radio show on WBNX.

I used to date Genni when she went by the name Jenny. Her last name was Miscavage. Genni was blonde and living in Great Neck, New York in the 1950s. She attended St. Mary's High School in Manhasset. I saw her after high school when I went to Times Square Records and found her working behind the counter. She told me she would dedicate a song to me and Jay on the radio show she did with "Slim" (WBNX). She did!

Great times in that store with the raccoon and those shows were great too!!
Harry Hepcat

My knowledge of Times Square Records was by way of Alan Fredericks and the oldies show, "Night Train", he hosted on Saturday nights from a little radio studio, WADO, in the meadows, (now called the Meadowlands), in New Jersey. I lived in Oradell, a few miles away from there and across the river from NYC. I was in high school and was really into the music of the day like early Elvis, Chuck Berry and especially what eventually came to be called doo-wop. I don't know how I discovered Night Train, but the way Alan Fredericks presented the music was more like a teacher rather than a huckster. He was the one who pointed out that groups like the Diamonds and the McGuire Sisters to say nothing of Pat Boone were not doing original stuff, but covers of black musicians and groups. I came to realize that even Elvis was doing some of that, but his was more honest, trying mainly to learn from and help popularize those people rather than stealing from them. I listened even more attentively to learn more about where this music had started. Turned out there was a whole world of music out there that I came to love.

My older sister loved the Mills Brothers. My parents listened to big band and Broadway music. My family was not only tolerant of my music. I shared it with them by way of my little 45's and American Bandstand. That Philadelphia sound was interesting, but I really got to like the likes of Frankie Lymon, the Harptones, and Little Anthony. I understand that Lee Andrews and the Hearts were from Philadelphia, but I only remember seeing people like Fabian and Frankie Avalon on Bandstand. But I digress. When I first heard the Flamingos, I was hooked.

Times Square Records sponsored the Night Train show. Alan talked about the little store in the subway station under the NY Times Building with such reverence and enthusiasm; I had to go there, if nothing else, just to see it. At some point before I could drive, a friend and I took a bus into the Port Authority one Saturday for the single purpose of finally seeing that little goldmine. My foggy impression after all these years is of walking down the subway stairs to the first landing where the stairs turned to the right with a window and door to the left which was the entrance to Times Square Records. I remember first seeing a wall, out of reach but prominent behind the counter, covered with rare 45's with little hand lettered signs saying things like "Oh, What a Night" the Dells $15.00", or "Golden Teardrops", the Flamingos on Chance, $50.00". I don't remember exact signs or prices, of course, but when the latest 45's could be had for 79¢, the prices were outrageous. But they had bins and bins of records to poke through running the length of the one aisle store. We spend probably close to an hour flipping through hundreds, maybe thousands of records, 90% of which I had never heard of. I bought "Just For A Kick" b/w "Would I Be Crying", by the Flamingos, my favorite group, on the Checker label. I have no idea how much I paid for it, but it couldn't have been more than a couple of dollars. I still have it.

I probably saw "Slim" Rose. I may even have handed him my money. I don't know. I have no recollection of the people behind the counter. But I do remember the sense of discovery, of the world of obscure (to me) music opening up. I have since come to realize that by exposing the rhythm and blues roots of what became rock and roll, Alan Fredericks and "Slim" Rose (and Alan Freed, of course), could almost be considered the Jackie Robinsons and Branch Rickeys of popular music. For a few short years, some of those black acts actually got popular and out sold their white imitators, no thanks to the northern music business establishment. They opened the door for Motown, Stax-Volt even Ray Charles to get airplay leading to the recognition and success they deserved.

Jeff Medler

I guess it was 1958 or 1959 and rock and roll had been sweeping the country by storm for several years now. My best friend Wayne Stierle had gotten involved at the very beginning. We didn't listen to Patti Page or Pat Boone or people like that because that wasn't real Rock and Roll to us. Wayne had made friends with "Slim" at Times Square Records and I used to go over to NYC with him. "Slim" had the music we wanted to hear, "The Fires Burn No More", "Mexico", "Cora Lee", "and Peppermint Stick" and all that other great 1950's music.

We would catch the bus at the corner of Mississippi Avenue and Harrison Avenue in West Orange, New Jersey and get off at the Port Authority Bus Terminal in New York. We would walk a while and then go down a stairway that led to the subway and at the first level off to the left was Times Square Records. I remember all the records on the walls. They were 45's. There was also a list of records expected in that week and I believe there was also a top forty list. Prices were posted on the various records and some were expensive even fifty years ago.

I remember Wayne and "Slim" always talking about locating a record called "Stormy Weather" by the Five Sharps. It was quite collectible fifty years ago and I wonder if anyone ever found it.

"Slim" also had a pet raccoon that he kept in the store. It was quite an attraction. Wayne and I spent a lot of Saturday afternoon's there over fifty years ago.

Robert Dickson

In the fall of 1959 I followed the advice of a friend and traveled into Manhattan in search of a new store that was selling old records for large sum of money apiece. What I found was a tiny store under the New York Times Building. Outside the front door, on your left as you were walking in, stood a showcase and inside the showcase were approximately seven or eight 45's, I remember seeing "The Closer You Are" and "I Really Love You" both by the Channels on the shiny Whirlin' Disc label. "Whew! I was home.

Times Square Records", well for me it was a hang out from 1959 to 1964. Now I'm the first to admit that I was never a major part of the crowd that made most of the noise over the years, or would be likely to be remembered, but I was there a great deal of the time, and I do remember.

At first it was a place where a fledgling group of young teens could meet and talk, buy and trade (not a very popular thing to do from "Slim's" way of thinking, it was absolutely not allowed in the store) records. We shared information on new discoveries, and in those early days we were uncovering lots of tunes that never got played on the radio, they were found in record shops in Harlem, Jamaica Queens and in mostly black neighborhoods in Brooklyn. When we found something special we would buy a number of copies and sell them to "Slim".

I said that I was there on a number of very special occasions in the history of the music, well in 1960 a box of records came into the store and someone played it, it was not bad, a white group for sure but those of us who were there liked it enough to buy a copy for a dollar, I never thought much of until it suddenly began to be played on the radio some months later, the song was "There's A Moon Out Tonight" by The Capris on the Planet Record label. A copy on Planet is worth a lot more than a dollar these days.

I met Clarence Johnson one day in the store. He was there to talk to "Slim" about this group he had as "Slim" was looking to start up his own label. "Slim" liked the song these guys had done, he thought it would be a great idea to drum up some hype for the tune by having a contest to name the group, well the rest is history and the Timetones were born. Clarence had been in the business for some time, he even had a few releases on his own Cee Jay label, I remember "A Beggar To A Queen" by DeRoy Green & the Cool Gents as a better than average tune. I was told that he was also involved with Danny Robinson and the Ladders on the Holiday label.

Another day that I was there some guy came into the shop with a couple boxes of records and asked Slim what he thought of them. One was by a group called the Teenos, the other by a group called the Edsels. The song was called Lama Rama Ding Dong on the Dub label. Needless to say "Slim" loved the novelty sound and bought them, yes I got one of those copies too. I also bought the Teenos tune though I never did like it very much.

I know that it was early fall of 1959, and as far as what I purchased? Well I know that it wasn't an earth shattering purchase. I believe this was the time I bought "Baby" by the Avons on Hull. The price was either $2.00 or $3.00. While there I also purchased a few more records for the same price, however it's so long ago I do not recall the names.

It is early 1960 not long after Christmas. I had a few extra dollars to spend. Off I go to Times Square Records. What made this day memorable was what I found at "Slim's" ten for a dollar box. This box was located along the right side of the store, where there were hundreds of 45s most without sleeves. I was casually going through one of the boxes and spotted a familiar yellow label with brown print; I took a deep breath and pulled out a copy of "I Don't Stand A Ghost Of A Chance" by my favorite group the Solitaires. I picked out a few other records and quietly passed them to "Slim". Now "Slim" wasn't the most knowledgeable member of the store as far as the music was concerned but he did know the name the Solitaires and asked about it, it caused a stir but I stuck to my guns that it was in the ten for a buck box and I wanted it, he gave it to me but I don't think he ever forgave me.

Jim Conroy

"Slim" was a tall, skinny cantankerous guy who smoked one camel after another. He had a distinctive voice....when he spoke you knew right away it was "Slim"....It is sad that "Slim" passed on without as much as an obituary notice. "I would have attended his funeral".

I saw Teddy the "infamous" raccoon many times. One time my friend Jimmy and I were at the shop when Teddy went over to Jimmy and started to crawl up inside Jimmy's pant leg. Jimmy is yelling get this "thing" off of me. You had to be there to appreciate what I'm saying. It was so funny....

Another time Jimmy and I had gone to see an Alan Fredericks show at the Audubon Ball Room. After the show we walked over to Times Square Records. "Genni" was behind the counter. Jimmy said to "Genni"..."Pardon me miss, do you have a restroom".... "Genni" said "whose it by"....we both laughed hysterically....but that was "Genni".....

The subway arcade was small in size....smaller than most living rooms....The ceilings were low that exposed steel girders...many times I hit my head on one of those girders. The atmosphere was one which is hard to describe...although dingy and in need of repair....it was the "in place" to be because there were records that you couldn't find anywhere else....It was located on the first level right hand side. There was something about this little shop......when you were there "you knew you were there"....

As a teen I saved all my money to buy records or to see the Alan Fredericks shows....I would travel on the train from Middletown, New York to Hoboken, New Jersey. I would either walk or take the subway to Times Square Records.

After all these years, at the age of 63; I'm still collecting and buying records. I have been able to obtain most of the records that were recorded on the Times Square Record label.

I spent my two honeymoons at that store. Oh yes....it was a "magical" time...an exciting time....wonderful memories ...."Slim" is responsible for where we are today.....Although it has been said that Jerry Greene is the one who help start "Slim" in the business.....in reality it was Al Trommers....he was at the original store located on 43rd Street......

I also have the entire Times Square Record collection"....I may be one of the few collectors who do.....

Ralph Corwin

During my teen years I lived with my aunt and my uncle in Levittown, Long Island. In my high school years I was given the opportunity to take a field trip to the United Nations Building in Manhattan. I wasn't too thrilled with seeing the United Nations Building, however I knew of a small record shop located on 42nd Street owned by a man named "Slim" called Times Square Records.

Taking the bus into Manhattan we soon entered the United Nations Building. A few of us quickly slipped out the door into the rain and rushed to West 42nd Street towards the Times Square Station. Walking down the cement steps you could hear music coming from the record shop.

Entering through the door I immediately noticed the records on the wall and those that were hanging from the ceiling. In fact there were records everywhere. The prices were a little high for me. I complimented "Slim" for atmosphere of the store and immediately went outside to wait for my friends.

Once outside I saw a few guys with boxes of records getting ready to sell them to "Slim". I interrupted them and asked "how much for the records". One quickly answered "ten cents each". I responded with "I'll give you a quarter for two". Eventually I was given the boxes of records to look over and take out what I wanted to purchase. I chose "Over A Cup Of Coffee" by the Castelles along with seven other records that day.

Soon it was time to get back to the United Nations Building as all of us didn't want to miss the roll call or the bus.

Florence Fox

Times Square Records brings back many fond memories for me. The very first time I visited the shop I was looking for a record store that sold oldies. I had ordered many records from other places but they always came back as unavailable, not in stock, back ordered, etc. Times Square Records proved to be a location that was very convenient and was in walking distance from my residence in New York. It became a regular stop for me, habit forming, to just go into "Slim's" place to both purchase and browse through his selections. Even after graduating high school I continued to go there and often spent at least one half of my pay check on records.

I remember going in and being surprised to see a raccoon on the counter. It was something that you did not expect to see in the city. He added to the atmosphere of the store! I was amazed to see 45 records in sleeves hanging from the walls. It was an awesome sight you just didn't see anywhere else. "Slim" also had a store policy where you could trade records you had for other records he had in the store. This worked out very well if you wanted a certain record (i.e.) "There's A Moon Out Tonight", on small label) to add to your collection. The very first record I bought from Times Square Records was in the 50 cents - $1.00 box and was "Think" by the Five Royales.

I know of one incident where it was not greatly appreciated that I had stopped at the record shop. I was taking my date out for a movie and dinner but we stopped at Times Square Records, I was just going to look. As it turned out, I spent most of the money I had on records and we ended up with pizza and just going home that night. Even though our date was cute short, I did manage to get some great records.

It was not unusual for me to spend $40.00 to $50.00 on records. "Slim" also had a radio station and he even had mystery records. You needed to know the name of the song and artist and had to send it in on a postcard which was to be postmarked no later than Sunday, midnight. I remember the record, "Ooh Wee Baby" and wasn't sure of the group so I called the record shop and asked the clerk who answered if they had "Ooh Wee Baby" by the Jets, she corrected me and said, "Oh no, that's by the Hearts". I had the answer I needed, so my postcard got mailed in with the correct song and group. I won! Still have the record, today.

"Slim" was a very wise business man. He hired a lot of young people to work in the store and always kept them in line. He appeared to be stern but he was always good hearted and had a heart of gold. His store was run neatly and efficiently and he was frequently out on the road looking for new records for his shop. When he came back, his radio station made the announcement that "Slim" was back with fantastic new records. You know how that would draw people into the store. You just couldn't wait to see what was new!

I continued to shop in Times Square Records until 1963-1964 when I got married. I had to cut back on my big purchase for records because my family was growing. Times Square records will always hold someplace special in my memories.

George Hauser

I first started going to Times Square Records in 1961.

The year is 1964....I am a junior in high school with limited funds. I had a girlfriend at the time.... (We would marry and are now married for over 40 years) I would bring my box of 45's to play when I went over to her house to visit. Her father would tell me to go over to Hyman's son's record store to buy my records. "He has a lot of records," he would say. I would tell him to forget it that I only bought my records at Times Square Records. My girlfriend's father would shrug me off and walk away. Once I started getting serious with this girl, I spent more and more time at her home.

Hyman Ginsburg was my future father-in-law's best friend. They had been friends since the age of nine. Hyman was a television repairperson who worked for a hotel in the city. My father-in-law was a dockworker, but repaired televisions and stereos on the side learning from Hyman.

Hyman lived right behind Buddy's Kiddie Land on Flatbush Avenue.
It was about fifteen minutes from Canarsie. Hyman liked baseball and would

come over to watch the game. One night he was at my girlfriend's house watching the game when he mentioned his car had broken down and his son would be picking him up. At the end of the game when his son came in, I could not believe my eyes. There was Harold from Times Square Records.

He immediately recognized me since I was a regular person who was always at the store. I knew Hyman's last name was Ginsburg, but I only knew him Harold from the store as Harold....Up until then I did not know his last name.

He once offered to sell me his complete Red Robin collection but saving for my wedding, I just could not do it. I married in 1967. Harold along with his father attended my wedding.

Harold's father passed away after a long battle with prostrate cancer. It does not surprise me that he has not contacted you. Although he was really, a good person he was very sensitive and somewhat private about many things.

He would love to tell me about record trips out of state and how on a trip to Ohio he discovered all the sides on Aladdin by the Five Keys (five copies of each!)

In 1966 I was in the military. I was stationed at Fort Hamilton in Brooklyn. I would call Harold at his tiny store on 6th Avenue and he would bring home the latest Acappella albums for me to pick up at his home or his father would bring them over. I would then pay Harold or his father for them.

I remember Harold told me about tons of vocal group tapes that "Slim" never got a chance to go through and they were then in storage. I asked Harold what he planned to do with them but he did not think it was worth paying the storage fee and going through the whole thing because the business was not the same anymore.

Harold's first love was always photography and last time I was in contact with him, he was working at a camera store. I always got the impression that when he started to talk about Times Square records other things going on at the same time in his life (which I heard between my father-in-law & his father, of course not knowing whom they were talking about at the time) would dampen his spirits. This may be the reason why he seems to want the past to remain the past. Of course this was just my impression, but I did know a little of his personal life. Maybe record collectors only saw Harold Ginsburg as a memory of Times Square Records.

Lou Mandracchia

I learned about "Slim" and Times Square Records in 1959. It was the spring of 1959 as I recall I had just gone to see on of Alan Freed's shows in New York City.

I used to go into New York City to buy records I could not find here in Connecticut. I would listen to the black radio stations in the New York and New Jersey area.

Doc who worked at the Tin Pan Alley Record Shop told me about a little shop under the Times Building located in a subway arcade. This shop was selling old 45s. It was Times Square Records. Record shops had old stock; however, they did not pull it out of their basements until Times Square Records came along.

Tin Pan Alley stocked the very latest in 45s. I would ask for an "older record" and the answer would be they did not have it in stock.

Tin Pan Alley was located on West 50th in midtown Manhattan.

I can recall groups coming in from the street and singing in the store for "Slim". "Slim" also broadcasted his radio show from the store.

I would take the train in from Connecticut and walk up 42nd Street to the store.

I would ask for records and "Slim" would tell me it did not exist. The next time I would visit the shop he would have the records.

"Slim" was a cool "beatnik" type person, who wore "coke bottle" glasses. He had a pet raccoon that would walk over the records. Although "Slim" was older, he knew the "stuff" we rock 'n rollers wanted.

I recall meeting Jerry Greene, Marcia Vance, Wayne Stierle, Harold Ginsburg, Lou Silvani and others who worked at the store.

Times Square Records was the roots of group harmony record collecting of old out of print vinyl 45s. I bought new records starting in 1952 as you heard then on the radio, however after I discovered Times Square Records in the spring of 1959, I started buying records I did not know existed. Although at the time it was not known, this is how "rare record" collecting began.

I visited Times Square Records many times to buy group harmony and blues. If you looked long enough you always found something. "Slim" had the first "back stock" shop that started a trend across the United States.

May we all never forget "Slim" Rose and Times Square Records.
Bill Nolan

My best friend back in the day was Bob Campbell. He is the one that took me to Times Square Records my very first time. I believe it was September, 1962. I remember walking into this small dingy shop seeing records hanging on a wall for $5.00 or $10.00 each….records that I had never heard of…..to me a record was only suppose to cost a dollar… At the time I thought people were nuts to be spending this kind of money for a 45….It would not be long that I realized how important owing a 45 on an original label would become…..I was hooked!!

Here I am 18 years old and to me Times Square Records was like being "a kid in a candy store". Music was always playing….you had to stand in line sometimes waiting to get into the place….teenage kids, younger kids, even adults would be there looking through bins of records…rows of records….it was amazing!! It was "magic"…."It was the place to be"…..

"Slim" was like a father figure to all of us….He was always "puffing" away on a cigarette….was grumpy allot…but had a big heart….I was always playing tricks on him….going behind the counter which was a "big NO " with "Slim"…..You knew it was "Slim" speaking without looking directly at him…He'd say to me "What do ya want kid" in that scratchy gruff voice that stems from "chain smoking" over the course of time…even though he was cantankerous and nasty at times you couldn't help but like him…..I can say this about him…."he was one of a kind"…..

One time I was at the store with my friend Jack Strong….Jack bought a new pair of shoes….he put his old ones back in the box…put the box in a bag…and then hung them up on the wall asking "Slim" how much did he think he could get for the shoes….I took a picture of Jack's shoes hanging on the wall and to this day still have the picture….

Another time while I was on my Saturday visit to New York I stopped by a place that made newspaper headlines...you could have anything printed....I had the headline printed "EXTRA Times Square Records Folds..."Slim" Selling Pretzels"...I took the newspaper into the store to ask "Slim" what was going on....he laughed...took the newspaper and hung it up on the wall where it hung for a long time. I had my camera with me that day and took a picture....

"Slim" was my inspiration that got me started in the music business. "If it weren't for "Slim" doing what he did with Times Square Records; I would never have gotten my start".

Val Shively

****Author's Note – All information in this chapter came from interviews and emails from those individuals who shared their memories. These memories are from January 2006 to February 2007.

I'd Stop & Browse At The Times Square Records

"Slim...Me & JFK

Billy Vera

I was Class of '62, Archbishop Stepinac High School in White Plains, NY, one hour north of Times Square. In sophomore year, along with two friends, a tone deaf guy whose father had bought him a guitar and amp and another guy who'd never played a drum in his life and I won 296 out of 298 votes in the sophomore talent show. This, because we played a rock'n'roll song, Eddie Quinteros's "Come Dance With Me," and because we went down to the Army & Navy store and bought shiny, metallic black shirts and string ties like Chuck Berry wore on the cover of his album, One Dozen Berrys.

From that point forward, I was the cool kid in class. As such, I sat at the head of a long table in the lunchroom.

Soon, a kid named Johnny Lea started coming around to my table, wanting to talk about music and records. He talked about a store down in the subway at Times Square. He mentioned records and groups I'd never heard on Alan Freed, much less American Bandstand. Titles like "Over A Cup Of Coffee" and "Hoping You'll Understand" sounded exotic, and nothing like the typical teen stuff I'd been listening to by Chuck Berry and Little Richard and Frankie Lymon, all great, but these things Lea talked about with such enthusiasm seemed, somehow, more hip.

By junior year, I was going down to the City after school to try and make a record myself. Sometimes, on the way back to Grand Central from my rounds at the Brill Building or 1650 Broadway, I'd stop at Times Square Records and browse.

I had no money to speak of and the music was more important to me than having the original label items. So I bought the reissues of the Strangers and the Four Buddies or albums, like "The Paragons Meet the Jesters" instead of the old 45s. The Flamingos Chance recording of "Golden Teardrops" on red plastic hung on the wall for five bucks. "Who'd ever pay five bucks," I asked myself, "when you could have the same thing on Vee-Jay for a dollar?" I'm too embarrassed to admit what I paid for that same red plastic Chance record last year, but I will confess that, back then, I needed the five dollars more than I need the price I paid today.

Once "Slim" and his crew got things rolling, he made deals with labels to reissue rare items. One of these, thrust upon me by one of the guys behind the counter, was "These Foolish Things" by the Dominoes, a great record by any measure. Lead singer Clyde McPhatter outdoes himself in a breathless, and breathtaking, performance.

Later, back in White Plains at the local Alexander's department store, I found both Dominoes albums, one of which contained a different take of "These Foolish Things". Not knowing that this was the version on the original single, I referred to it as "the album version" until I found out the real story. As it turned out, "Slim's" version was far superior.

Cut to November, 1963. Times had moved over to the Sixth Avenue subway and one day, I was alone in the store with only Harold for company. In my hand was a record from the dollar bin by Johnny Ace, the singer who had died ten years earlier in Texas by a gunshot to the head.

In walked Slim, his face ashen, drained of all color. He said to me and Harold, "Hey, did youse guys hear? Da President just got shot in the head down in Dallas?

What a place to be, on the day JFK was murdered...and me, holding a Johnny Ace record. I went up to the street, where bedlam ensued. In the windows of all those eternally Going Out Of Business discount shops were dozens of TVs, running the tape of the assassination. People were crying in the streets of Times Square and I went home with my Johnny Ace record.

*****Author's Note – This chapter was provided to me by Billy Vera via an email in the spring of 2006.

I Was Intimidated At First By "Slim"

Tony D'Ambrosio

The first broadcast of the radio show that I heard was in the spring/summer of 1961. I was flipping through the dial of my transistor radio, while laying in bed and heard what sounded to me like the most unprofessional radio DJ I ever heard...but the music was great. (I had actually started to accumulate vocal group recordings about a year earlier, but never considered it collecting as in stamp or coin collecting). I recall on the first occasion hearing only a few minutes at the end of the show.

It was not until September 1961 that I again heard the show. Again, it was by accident. On this second occasion, I heard that entire one hour. It was like magic. Sure, I liked vocal group recordings and they made up the vast majority of the 45's I owned, however I remember my reaction was "where did he get this stuff". The Pyramids "Ankle Bracelet", the Castelles, the Dreamers...I was hooked, though I admit that at first I was always hoping to hear some records that I already knew such as the Five Satins, Mello Kings and other groups that I had heard Alan Freed play in earlier years.

On the radio show, besides "Slim", he had a girl named "Genni" (pronounced Jenny) who also was a "DJ". She was extremely pretty and "Slim" would encourage guys to "write in for a picture of Genni". I had two or three of them. I don't recall ever seeing her in the store.

While "Slim" always referred to the store as "Times Square Records" as he would usually say after playing a record "$1.00 at Times Square Records" or just "Times". "Slim" would also encourage you to write in for a free fan club card. The benefit of this card was a ten percent discount on purchases at Times Records. I recall that the card was silver in color and had the words "sink or swim with "Swingin' Slim" at the top. It also mentioned the radio station WBNX (which was a small Bronx station that was sometimes difficult to get in clearly in Brooklyn) at 1380 AM. The show was on Saturday nights, I believe between 10:30 pm and midnight. The fan club card was one way that "Slim" promoted and encouraged purchases at the store. The other was his "two for one special" that was rarely offered on a weekly basis.

In late 1961, he offered two for one, maybe once a month and soon they became even less frequent. I recall that the first two for one special; I bought was "Get Yourself Another Fool" by the Tempotones on Acme. The second one was "It Took Time" by the Upfronts on Lummtone. There were others too that I do not recall.

Another way "Slim" promoted sales was with his top 100 sales list. In spite of its title, the list did not really represent the top hundred sellers of the month. Instead it was a list of records he had in stock, usually new arrivals in quantity. Some customers walking into the store would pick up a list, and of course, go right to number one, two or three not to ninety-eight, ninety-nine or one hundred. If it was the number one seller it had to be good.... right?

The store itself was small at the original location. The ceiling, or at least part of it, was so low that you had to bend your head to avoid banging into it. There was one window, not very large and a door to the right of it. Of course the window on the door was pasted with a variety of things that made looking into the store somewhat difficult. There would be the top 100 list, letters from all over the country from people looking for or looking to sell a record, news articles and even fan club letters asking for a picture of Genni.

From time to time a record would be taped to and hung in the window. I recall that for a long time the center from the destroyed 78 of Stormy Weather by the "Five Sharps" on Jubilee. It was taped to the window with a note below it saying "Do you have this record" along with a dollar amount offered for it. Another fixture in the store in 1961 - 1962 was the "infamous Teddy the Raccoon". I say "infamous" because it was Teddy who broke Billy Pensabene copy of the Five Sharps' "Stormy Weather", which set off a hunt for the record which still continues. After the record was broken, "Slim" on his radio show offered $5.00 in credit for a copy. This increased every week as no one brought in a copy.

"Teddy" usually sat on top or next to the bins of miscellaneous $1.00 records that you encountered when you entered the store. These were records that "Slim" had only a copy or two of and they were never listed on his top 100 list. "Teddy" was the size of a very large cat and was very playful. He was fairly tame, especially considering the number of people coming into the store were mostly strangers. They would pet him or do other things to prevent him from sleeping.

There were a couple of people who worked in the store. The one, who seemed to be there most, at least when I went which was usually Friday night, was Harold Ginsberg. He seemed to know a lot about the records he was selling and he also was the main person who handled their mail orders.

"Slim" was always in the original store, however not always at the second one. He sometimes took care of customers when the others were busy. I remember being a little intimidated at first by both "Slim" and other customers in the store. "Slim", because he was an old guy around my father's age selling and playing on his radio show my music. Remember at that time, there was big difference between what I would call my music and my parent's music.

The other customers were even more intimidating. While I was just looking for a copy of a particular record that was new, or not too beat up, these customers would be asking for records and asking about label color, print styles, etc. Other things that I later learned were so important to collectors. Another thing was that just about all the other customers I encountered in the store seemed to be older than I was. I was a sixteen year old high school kid, who sometimes barely had enough money to buy two or three records (which were always $1.00 records) and still take the subway home to Brooklyn. However, a number of other customers were in suits, apparently stopping after work and were spending $10.00 to $20.00 and more. They were buying the $2.00 and $3.00 records, not just the $1.00 ones that my "budget" limited me to.

The address at the original location was 1475 Broadway. It was one flight of stairs down, as you were going into the subway station at Broadway & 42nd Street. To get to the subway you actually had to make a short right turn, go down one more flight of stairs taking you to the level where the token booth was located. At times the store would shake from the subway.

The location was great for business as everyone coming up those subway stairs met the store head on before they reached the street. I have a very vague memory of a "Magic Shop" being in that location before Times Records was there, however I am not one hundred percent sure.

When you first entered the store you saw $1.00 records hanging on the wall at the right and to the left there were the "money" records. Also, there were several bins of ten cent records to the right of the door. Most were without sleeves, but in very good condition. I remember buying a DJ copy of "Bing Bong" by the Silhouettes, "Gone" by Jesse Belvin on Specialty and "Don't Be A Fool" by the Explorers on Coral for ten cents each. When the store moved to the 6th Avenue subway arcade location; the bin increased in price to twenty-five cents. There were still some good records in it.

It was after the move to the new location, that things at the store began to change. The once tiny store was now a big spacious one compared to the original store. The Saturday night radio show was gone. It was replaced by another show that "Slim" did that was not the same, or maybe it was that I was not the same.

Now that I had a job after school or in the summer I had even less money for records than before. Girlfriends were "expensive" and I was starting to focus on things like avoiding the draft and the war in Vietnam

As I mentioned, while I always recall seeing "Slim" in the old store, he was not always there when I visited the new one. I remember on at least two occasions when he was there, he would say to me something like "isn't she pretty"……referring to one of the girls who worked in the store. But it wasn't the beautiful Genni whose picture a lot of us were carrying. Instead it was a girl who to me at the time was very much overweight and sorry to say her dress looked more like a tent than a dress. I am sure that my perception may have been more than a little poor at the time, but then "thin was in" and the opposite wasn't at least with my friends and me.

I somehow recall, between the time "Slim" closed his store and Lou Silvani opened his, there was someone else in there. It was not for too long a time, if my memory is correct. Later Lou Silvani would move Times Square Records to the Bronx; the same location was no longer a record store, although in the same 6th Avenue Subway arcade. It was at this location Roy Adams and his partner opened up Downstairs Records in approximately 1970.

****Author's Note – Information provided in this chapter was sent to me by email from Tony D'Ambrosio on January 18, 2006.

"Slim" Becomes A Music Publisher
(The Story Of Clarose Music)
Wayne Stierle

The Promo DJ Copy Of "Here In My Heart"

The name Clarose was created from a combination of "Clarence" & "Rose", resulting in the name Clarose, for Clarose Music. (Clarence Johnson & Irving Rose were the two people). It ended up a few years later being totally owned by "Slim", and I now own a few of those songs.

Clarence Johnson was a part owner in Holiday Records, and produced records with The Bop Chords, and others. With Everlast Records he recorded The Charts, and co-wrote many vocal group songs, including the classic "Deserie". (Clarence was also known as "Jack Rags").

Clarence showed up at Times to see what was going on there, as "Slim" and Donn & I were trying to get him to re-press his early records. (Clarence ended up making a deal with "Slim" on the re-pressings). Clarence was a great "basic" producer, and he produced "In My Heart" by a group that "Slim" would call the Timetones, when he & "Slim" went partners on the session. Clarence also produced a few records that I own, including among others, "Go Back Where You Came From" by the Summits.

"Slim" was surprised and disgusted with the headaches caused by new recordings, because of tremendous problems with the distribution of "In My Heart", which had gotten action in several cities. (The record hadn't actually sold in quantities equal to its' inaccurate chart status, because charts were rigged at that time, with a major chart fixing story involving Gone Records about to be exposed only a half year after The Timetones release.) Given the problems and headaches, the follow-up, "Pretty Pretty Girl", found "Slim" glad to be able to sell it to Atco Records. Clarence died of a heart attack in about 1962, (just before we were going to do a session together on a very hard core group sound that I had arranged with a group from East Orange, New Jersey).

Clarence was very interesting to talk to, but he didn't see a lot of magic in the music. He had produced "Deserie", but he called the song "God awful" and "totally unfinished". I used to tell him that if that were true, then that was the real charm of it, but he just shook his head, saying that when The Charts had first sung it on amateur night at The Apollo, they were booed off the stage because the song didn't seem to end, or make sense. (Interestingly enough this was before Clarence worked with The Charts, so his own writing credits are suspect, but that didn't stop him from telling the story anyway, and it is possible he changed some of the original words later on before the recording session.). The Charts were not his favorite group, as they gave him a major headache on the recording session following the success of "Deserie". As Clarence told me, "....these guys came into the studio and acted like such stars that they wouldn't talk to each other....It wasn't a good situation at all. They had their mics far enough apart so they wouldn't accidentally touch each other. It was really bad. I hated it...."

Clarence and "Slim" got along well, but "In My Heart" was a pain for everyone involved in it. The song was originally titled "Here In My Heart", with the opening line and a quarter being, "Well, Here In My Heart There's A Story Untold, Of A Girl...", which is the exact opening line and a quarter of The Nutmegs classic, "Story Untold". (A big pop hit for The Crew-Cuts annoying cover version). "Slim" was threatened very strongly by the publisher of "Story Untold", who wanted a title change, but really expected a fast financial settlement, or part of the publishing rights. "Slim" opted to change the title, and destroy the remaining labels, and a few thousand copies of the record, with the pressing plant providing the requested proof of destruction documentation. There was no real legal reason to change the title, but the publisher was aggressive and nasty, and was ready to go to the radio stations and have his lawyer point out that the song was the subject of a copyright case. This would have been enough damage to bring the record to a grinding halt, as radio stations fold up like cheap cameras if they think they are in the middle of a legal situation. The fact is that the publisher of "Story Untold" could never have won a case against "Slim" over one line of lyrics, or over a title, but radio stations were still very nervous from the payola scandals, as well as Alan Freed being driven off two New York radio stations in the recent past, to name only two reasons of the many reasons that radio stations were so jumpy at that time.

The explosion over this record would have been less severe if the lines were from inside the song, but the 12 words copied, were indeed the opening lines of the original song. Hearing it for the first time, you would think it was a modern up-tempo recording of The Nutmegs ballad. To understand fully the impact of taking the opening 12 words of a famous song, and using it as your own, consider adding words to the opening of a song that you wrote, as follows: How about taking these eleven words for your song, "You ain't nothin' but a Hound Dog, cryin' all the time", or what about these nine words, "Heavenly shades of night are falling, it's Twilight Time"? Maybe you'd like to use these 8 words, "Little Darlin', Little Darlin', oh where are you.....", or these 8 words, "Earth Angel, Earth Angel, will you be mine ..." The lesson is that there is enough trouble out there, without looking for it.

Although "Slim" dabbled in a few more new releases, he did it in the context of the store, and pulled away from regular distributors, and other thieves. "In My Heart" was a tough but clear lesson.

***Author's Note – Wayne Stierle wrote this chapter and emailed it to me on August 6, 2006.

The Song: And Then..."Slim" Said

Wayne Stierle

In 1956 a recording, "The Flying Saucer", had a profound effect on anybody who was half awake. The record simply combined actual short clips from current hit records with dialogue, and became a staple item, that was still a viable concept as late as the mid-seventies. (While everything that followed was a "Flying Saucer" type recording, the term to describe this was mutated into a dumb phrase, "cut ins").

That first recording was amazingly literate in its almost biting satire of disc jockeys, rock n' roll, song titles, artist's names, and the mid-fifties pre-occupation with outer space beings. What made it so great was that in the midst of the satire, there was a love for rock n' roll that pervaded every second of the record. No record that followed this ever came close to the original, even though the hits in this genre went on for two decades.

I was so taken with this recording, that I attempted versions of the concept at least four times. One of these attempts never saw the light of day, and it was probably the most inventive of the batch that I created. It was a song, in a "Coasters" mode, called "And Then "Slim" Said..." The concept was based on lyrics about troubles that we all can relate to. For example: your car is constantly breaking down, and you can't figure out what to do, and you turn on the car radio and "Slim" says, "....bring it in to Times Records and get $2.00 credit for it..." The "Slim" statement would be an actual clip of "Slim" on the air, and put into the song. So it would go for about five verses. It was funny, and it was crazy as only rock n' roll can be.

"Slim" liked the idea, and even gave it the highest praise, which is to say that he called it "cute". "Slim" called whacky up-tempo records that he really liked, "cute". The next step was to simply record a group doing it. I knew exactly how to do it, and I couldn't wait to get going with it.

Ah, but it was latter 1964, and "Slim" was waiting for the lull that had fallen over the store to lift, before he would release a very odd record like this. I felt such a record not only celebrated Times Square Records, but "Slim" himself, who was in many ways a reluctant icon in this strange universe. But, "Slim" said it had to wait, and I couldn't do it myself at that point, because "Slim" had already agreed to put it on Times Square Records as a 45.

The cloud that hung over the store got darker, the sun never shone again, and the record never was made.

PS If a group would volunteer their time, I guess I would still do it, but then again, maybe I wouldn't.

****Author's Note – Wayne Steirle wrote this chapter. He emailed it to this author on January 30, 2006.

"Slim" And The Creation Of Accapella

Wayne Stierle

Everything has a starting point.....a genesis. Especially in the pop culture of the United States of America, this is the most vibrant pop culture in the world.

The word "Acappella" started in the early sixties. Until then, as your dictionary told you, "a 'cappella", means a vocal with no musical backing. It's a word that most people didn't relate to, and was only brought up when something in the "opera" type area was being described. It was a high brow word used by musical snobs, for the most part. Generally it wasn't used at all. People have always sung without music, and that includes the most prolific period of vocal group history, the fifties. In those days, if you sang on the corner, you were singing "group music". It was that simple. All groups singing that way were either copying records or aspiring to record with music for a record company.

At one point in history a new word, "Acappella", was created to describe vocal groups singing rock n' roll and R&B. This is the story of how that came about.

Donn Fileti and I had been re-releasing and causing to be released, more records than you might ever suspect. This was done primarily to sell these records to Times Records, and "Slim". In these pursuits we came upon a large cache of unreleased master recordings that we wanted to own, and were able to make a deal for. There was just one problem, and that was that we couldn't afford to do it. We knew that if we could make this happen for someone else, we might at least be some part of it, and we took it to an interesting older record biz person, Leo Rogers of Bruce Records, at the infamous 1650 Broadway building which housed everyone who wasn't in The Brill Building. Leo was a funny guy, who was very much like you might imagine Bela Lugosi playing a record label guy from New York, without the Dracula accent, and none of the menace. Record label adults in those days, (the early sixties), either wanted to work with you, or they wanted to toss you into the street. Leo was cool. One day he played a group of tapes for us and wanted to know if he should put a record out from his pile of stuff that was lying around gathering New York dust. Among these recordings was a sound that made us jump in shock, as it was an unreleased Harptones recording. We voted a very loud positive, and Leo pressed it up for us to re-sell to "Slim". The song was "Loving A Girl Like You", and it was a sixties release, although recorded in the mid-fifties. (You've seen it listed as the fifties, but that's a function of people assuming things and not checking).

The deal with Leo on the master recordings eventually fell through. Leo decided it wasn't worth it, as he was still managing to get attention with some new recordings he was making and leasing to larger labels than his own. Now it was in limbo, and may well have remained there forever, as few people really cared about this, or would invest in it. "Slim" had been so much against starting Times Square Records as a re-issue label, that despite my continued harping on it, he only started with new releases, prompted by the success of our re-issues as "new" records, and the circumstance of having Clarence Johnson supplying the two new recordings. ("In My Heart" and "Go Back Where You Came From"). However, as "Slim" pulled back from the hot stove of putting out new releases, he didn't really have any product to keep the label going. It was this fact that made this deal attractive to "Slim", and he saw in it, the same potential for a series of 45's that we had planned to do. So, just like that, the deal was done, and "Slim" ended up with the pile of masters, and set on a course to make Times Square Records a primarily re-issue label, as I had already started with Candlelite Records. (Unmarked tape boxes, scratchy demos, and reels of tape sometimes unwinding into a pile that looked like a nightmare in a plastic factory).

Slowly, for weeks, we went through the recordings during regular store hours. The demos were rough, scratchy acetate discs that 'Slim" would play, and watch the reaction, or lack thereof, from whatever customers happened to be standing around. He took mental note of the recordings that seemed to "grab" people. Often he would ask what made sense to me, and I'd explain why I especially liked, loved, or hated a particular recording. Much of it was very bad by the standards of the fifties. It was little wonder why this stuff had laid around for years, and yet the fact that it had been kept was odd, for most of this type of thing had been thrown out by so many small and medium sized labels or studios, before the sixties had even dawned.

We took the tapes over to Sanders recording studio and made acetates so they could be listened to in the store. It was really tiring, and not exciting, as I know it must sound. Sometimes weak recordings can drive you crazy. So here were old acetates and new acetates, and a confusing mix of junk and good stuff that was very hard to sort out. Some demos got smashed, and are lost for all time. Some were too defective to be saved, at least considering the technology of that time period. In among the lackluster recordings were standout performances by The Five Satins, and the edgy group that was among the absolute best ever, The Nutmegs. "Slim" was not a Nutmegs fan for a few simple reasons, being that "Slim" liked insane up-tempo records and really pretty ballads. The Nutmegs did not fall into either category, and he offered to give me most of The Nutmegs tracks, but I believed in Times Square Records, and was not about to simply take something that I knew mattered in the basic scheme of rock n' roll. (Over the years I've been beaten over the head for this attitude, but that's how I see it, and I was there when rock n' roll was born, and I have trouble understanding why anyone would see it any other way). I very strongly advised "Slim" of the pivotal role played by The Nutmegs "Story Untold" in the history of rock n' roll, and eventually he understood that The Nutmegs mattered, despite the way he may have felt about them. (That The Nutmegs were the nastiest, most dangerous group that ever recorded is a whole other story).

Some of these recordings were practice tapes of groups rehearsing without a band. They were singing with no musical instruments. Tapes like this were made for only two reasons in the fifties and early sixties. The tapes were showcases for the groups to send to record companies to present themselves or their songs, or both. The other reason is that a record company can use such a tape to create a musical arrangement for a band, so that everything is in place for a recording session. The object of all groups was to make a record, and records were made with musical backgrounds. It's that simple.

Then came the day that changed the language and even changed the way people view music made by vocal groups.

"Slim" decided that the recordings made without musical background needed to be put into a category. I disagreed because these were just rare recordings by vocal groups in a style that you'd expect, and nothing was exceptional, except the lack of a band. "Slim" felt that if you sold a record without a combo playing on it, then you might get returns, because the buyer may feel the record was "less" than expected, or some similar reaction. We didn't agree, and while the logic on both sides was ultimately flawed, the fact is that "Slim" was 100% correct, for the wrong reasons. What followed was weeks of talking and arguing about what to call this type of record. I came up with a few names that I felt summed it up, such as "Subway Sounds", "Street Corner

Style", "City Sounds", and other gems. Finally with "Slim" wanting to put the records out, and not totally sold on the various ideas, he turned to, of all things, a dictionary. There, naturally was a cappella. In a move that took seconds, "Slim" created a word that had never previously existed:"Acappella". The word was put onto the record labels, and pushed on his radio shows, and it stuck in the "pop culture", even though initial releases when sent to regular New York City stores, were filed under the Italian or foreign language sections at first. Nobody, outside of a Times Square Records customer, knew what it was!

So, this new word came to stand for rock n' roll and rhythm and blues vocal groups singing in the style of the 1950's, without musical backing. Sometimes it is even used to describe any fifties music, which is a gross misusage. (Whereas a'capella still applies to everything else sans a band, including the snobby music it always was used for). This word is now used to describe a time in which the word didn't exist, and even known groups can be found quoted as saying things like, "....we sang acappella back then..." Like hell you called it that.

This style became a part of the vocal group scene from that time forward, with groups beginning to deliberately be recorded without music for an actual record release. Records released in this genre are thought of as "normal" today. Music fans who weren't there actually believe that this way of recording groups was a typical "fifties" thing. (I ended up producing over 80% of the acappella done in the sixties, as well as the first acappella album ever done by a true 50's group).

I wish it had been a different word, but once the genie is out of the bottle, it takes on a life of its own, and God knows that "acappella" is now a world-wide word. It was created in the early sixties by "Slim", and sometimes wrongly seen as a fifties word. "Slim" had made yet another milestone contribution to the way people talk about, and view, the music of vocal groups.

***Author's Note – Wayne Stierle wrote this chapter and emailed it to me on August 6, 2006.

The Start Of The Times Square Label

Wayne Stierle

I couldn't believe it, but "Slim" didn't really care to have a record label.

I pushed him to start a label for almost a year. The main argument was simple. With all the re-issues we were causing to happen, why not lease some of the available recordings and have a record label. Why shouldn't the premier oldies store have a label? Why not record some of the groups that constantly came through the store? But "Slim" was caught up in the day-to-day store, and wasn't thrilled with the idea of adding more possible grief to whatever troubles came along with this type of success and blossoming fame. This was understandable, but a record label fit the image of what Times Records was all about, much more than a raccoon did. (Crazy as that may sound).

As 1960 began turning into 1961, "Slim" finally relented, do in no small way to the actual hit records that some of us had started, from the initial inspiration of "Slim" and Times itself. "Slim" finally saw that he should be a part of the releases that he was selling and advertising in spots of time bought on the radio. The appearance of Clarence Johnson, vet record arranger/producer, whom we were buying re-pressings from, provided the chance to make an actual new record, as opposed to a re-issue of a previously pressed and available group record. Clarence showed up because he couldn't believe his older records were actually finding such interest, and since Clarence had produced most of his own records, the decision to jump right in, was made easy for "Slim". A group, given the name "The Timetones" would record "Here In My Heart" aka "In My Heart" as the first record released on the new label, with the new name "Times Square Records". The store was "Times Records". (See "The Clarose Story" regarding the song title changes).

One day "Slim" was casually filling out a simple one page form, which turned out to be the initial order for the actual labels. The paper labels that when pressed right along with melting plastic, actually become the "record label", in a process that I saw as nothing short of magic. What a process to be a part of. I had died and gone to heaven. To my surprise, "Slim" was not paying particular attention to the style of type or label color. I was truly shocked, and launched into one of several lectures and/or speeches, (depending on how you look at it), about why the label had to look substantial and carry that "fifties mystery" with it. At first it was an uphill campaign, since "Slim" had not been a rock n' roll fan when the music was born, and didn't know the sheer mind-bending power of seeing an early authentic record label on a brand new rock n' roll 45. You had to have been a kid at the time, and already into records, to see why these new singles had a strange aura about them, that you'd never find on an RCA or Columbia label. The majesty of the black Gone Records label with its beautiful silver letters could put you into a trance for days. "Slim" finally handed it over to me, and I selected as bold and gothic a type as I could, and the great colors of Gone Records simple yet stunning black and silver. (The idea was to conjure up that "feeling", without looking like Gone). The first Times Square Records label was designed to look as an impressive label with a "history" should look.

I won the first label battle, and I lost the second one. Following The Timetones single, and The Summits single, the label would gain speed with releases not intended as new releases. (See the "Slim" & The Creation Of Acappella" chapter). At this point, only six months into existing as a label, "Slim" decided to make the label itself fancier, and he totally and I mean totally, copied what he regarded as the best "rare" label, Chance Records. To say I lobbied against this, would be putting it mildly. Chance was great for what it was, no doubt, but I knew in my heart, as I do today, that Times Square Records did not need to have an image that was just a reflection of an already legendary labels' design. This was Times Square Records, and not some copy label, was exactly how I put it to "Slim". "Slim" was so taken with the Chance Records design that he refused to alter it at all. I pointed out that while the one word "Chance" looked good in that thick script, the two words, "Times Sq." looked clumsy and hard to understand. It difficult to read, as who expects to see the famous word "square" depicted as "sq." in large print at the top of a record label? It's not that it was horrible, but more that it wasn't necessary, and frankly beneath the giant image that the store, Times Records, had become. At least, I kept saying, drop the thick script and use the gothic type, but no deal. I tried to sell him on the concept of a city skyline with his own profile drawn as one of the buildings, and keeping the black and silver colors. I tried to convince him to use an art rendering of himself at the top of the label, and other variations on this theme. He was not to be moved by any of these pleas, and the label became, for me, a label that I really didn't like the "look" of. I still don't like it, because I know that it could have reflected the overwhelming image of the store and its' creator, as it well should have.

****Author's Note – This chapter was written by Wayne Stierle. He emailed it to me on November 30, 2006.

The Story Of The "Times Square Stomp"

Wayne Stierle

The second release for Times Square Records was "Go Back Where You Came From" by the Summits. The record was produced by Clarence Johnson, and featured one of the three styles that "Slim" liked the most, this one being a "crazy" bass voice. This record pushed the limits of that style, in that the bass sang the entire lead of a very serious/comic song that featured extremely in-your-face lyrics.

Upon listening to a demo from the session, "Slim" heard the band track from "Go Back Where You Came From", and decided that it was a good instrumental for him to use as a theme song for his radio shows. (The ones that he hosted, as opposed to those on which he might buy advertising spots). He dubbed this basic track "Times Square Stomp", and put it on the flip side of "Go Back Where You Came From". (In this way, both sides have the same instrumental track!)

"Times Square Stomp" is just a backing track, but like most early band tracks, it has a repetitive hypnotic beat and sound that is very nice to hear in short bits, as used in theme songs or under a voice over. These early tracks provided the foundation over which so many great vocals would be recorded. (This was still the early years of stereo, when record companies no longer had to do the session totally "live" at one time, as was the case with early rock n' roll, 1954-1958).

"Go Back Where You Came From" was never the success that "Slim" thought it would be, but it is a unique recording that reflects his taste in vocal group recordings. Today I own this master, and I must say that it still has that same basic, urgent, nervous excitement about it, that it had the first day we heard it on a demo, at 1475 Broadway, with the subway rumbling agreement through the walls.

****Author's Note – Wayne Stierle wrote this chapter. He emailed it to me on August 6, 2006.

It Was Another World...A Better Place To Be

What It Was Like To Go To Times

Wayne Stierle

Before I was a distributor to Times Records, before I produced some of "Slim's" radio shows, before I hosted a few of his shows, before I helped " Slim" start his label, before I worked behind the counter at Times, and before so many other things, before all that...I was briefly........a customer......a customer at Times Records...

Among the positive events that shape your lifetime, there are special happenings that change you forever, and alter and widen your view of the world. Things that are, for whatever reason, like electric power to your soul. Times Records was one of those things that changed your life when you just walked through the door. It was stamped so vividly in your mind that you would take it with you, wherever you would wander. Oh, you'd find bigger places, and fancier places, but you knew you'd never find anything like this again. This wasn't just another "store", for this was the original design, or template, on which all locations dealing with this wonderful music would be copying, right into the next century.

It was a cold, clear day. It was too early and too bright. Streets were quiet. It was Sunday. We waited in the brisk chill for the bus. It was a De Camp bus, which meant it would be sending up a dense, gray cloud of poison into the New Jersey air, long before we would even begin to think of it as air pollution. This was Jersey, so we could take it. Finally the 66 bus pulled up, and we were on our way to Oz. Donn (Fileti) was checking and re-checking his trusty notebook, and I was going through the 45's we had pooled together as legal tender in this venture. We were going to Times Records, where records were the coin of the realm, second only to hard cash. "Slim" would give you "credit" and then you'd spend that "credit" getting records. But, "Slim" was tough, and the $2.00 record you expected to get $1.00 in credit for, might only bring fifty cents. So, Donn and I were re-working the possibilities, to try to determine the value of what we had. We arrived at a price that was our lowest price, and even though we agreed on that price, we knew that if "Slim" undercut that number, we would accept his terms. That's how it was when you went to Times Records in the heart of Times Square, in the greatest city on earth.

We had a list of records we wanted. We had lists for other people too. There was Donn's sister Barbara, and my friends Dixie (Bob Dickson), and Lou. (Lou Rallo). Lou would say how much he wanted to spend, and ask me to get him whatever I thought he'd like. "You know", he'd say, and in fact, I did know. There was very little money to spend, which made the credit records so important, and oddly enough, that's the same reason, in reverse, that they were actually important to "Slim". (In the very early days, one of the main sources of records was the 45's brought in by customers for "credit" or small cash payments). It was a kind of give and take trade that you'll see portrayed in old movies about the wild west of over a hundred years ago. It was a lesson in basic bartering and haggling. It was fair and unfair at the same time. It was exciting. It was a journey and an adventure, and look at the final results, great records! Sounds of magic that would leap off of grooved pieces of plastic that were the 45 rpm wonders that we sought more urgently than if it were gold or diamonds. Truth be told, these records were better than gold or diamonds. (Even though a "want list" is a list of records you don't have, it's also a history of who you are, and how you see yourself, and what you aspire to be).

At Times Records, you'd wait until "Slim" would look over the records you'd brought in for "credit". Finally "Slim" would grab a handful of records and shuffle them like a deck of cards, and put them down, and bark out a price. You could argue, and maybe you'd improve your luck by a buck or two, but it was hard dealing with Slim, because he gave you the feeling that he didn't need your records. Sometimes you could pull out a few records that you'd rather not trade in, and try to do the deal all over again. Usually you ended up making some kind of deal. How could you not? After all, you were carrying records you clearly intended to hand in for "credit", so it was obvious you didn't have a great bargaining chip. "Slim" could be patient, sometimes, but you would be nervous and off-balance as you gazed at the wall, covered with absolute treasures that were so close, and yet so far away. It was nerve racking bliss. Hey, if you didn't move fast, somebody else was going to get the last copy of that record you couldn't live without. What choice did you have? You had to act fast. If you had looked over your shoulder, you might have seen the devil laughing, but you couldn't afford to take your eyes off the wall. Behind you, the customers were pushing and shoving! You might lose your place up front by the counter, and "Slim" might decide he didn't want your records! Then what? You didn't have any extra money with you. You'd go back home without any records from Times. You're jolted out of your nightmare haze by "Slim" saying, ".....well..." What?

You better answer. This sounds close to doom. "Slim says, here...." and he hands back your records and tells you, ".......go outside and think about it, there's a line here..." Oh no! You might never get back in. Who knows? You hand the records back to "Slim" and blurt out, "I'll take the credit...", and your heart is beating like a drum, because now you suspect he won't take your records. An eternity goes by in three seconds. You're looking at the end. It's over. But, "Slim" says "ok", and makes a note of your "credit", and you step out of the firing line and breathe a sign of relief. Somehow you were saved, at least this time. From behind the counter you hear "Counting the Stars" by The Ladders playing and trouble comes back into your life, for "Counting the Stars" is on your "want" list! Now you got to hope there are multiple copies available, or that someone will decide not to buy it, if there's only one copy. To make matters worse, the playing of a good record would sometimes cause a surge of customers wanting what they just heard. The drama starts again, as you edge nearer to the counter, clutching at the hope that you'll get a few of the records you came in search of.

The whole "credit" situation was usually transparent. It happened right in front of you. It was not unlike those scenes you see of Wall Street trading. For example, you might bring in a copy of "Two Hearts Are Better Than One" by The Paragons, although I'd have advised you to keep it, that's your choice. You hand it to "Slim" and he calls out to the air, ".......Paragons...."Two Hearts"....". Harold leaps into action from his already frenetic constant motion mode and digs through records under the counter. Harold calls out to "Slim", ".......11 copies......" Now "Slim" knows he doesn't really need your copy, and you get fifty cents in credit, because the record is selling at that point for one dollar. Now, if Harold would have found there were no copies, you might have gotten a dollar in credit. That's basically how it went, record by record.

The bus is coming out of The Lincoln Tunnel, leaving Jersey behind, and climbing the cement hill into The Port Authority. We get out of the bus, stepping into the cold carbon monoxide fumes that envelope the bus area. The game is afoot, and we head to 42nd Street from the Eighth Avenue exit of the Port Authority. Chestnuts are roasting on an open fire, and the cold weather aroma they add into the strange mix that is New York City, helps to clear my head from the sickening bus fumes, and the lingering headache they always inflict. Forty Second Street, between Seventh and Eighth Avenues is about as sleazy as it gets, with the exception of a Puerto Rican pizza place that makes truly great pizza. The guy in the window is tossing the pizza dough up into the air, and the edges of the window are foggy with the light icing that happens when the cold air outside hits an overly warm window. We're getting closer to Times Records. It's colder than I thought it would be, and the wind whips between the concrete canyons with no mercy at all. But we are prospecting for gold, and not about to let a sandstorm on this desert stop us. We forge on because we have a noble quest. This is as much about a true belief as it is about records.

We arrive at the stairs that go down into the ground, eventually leading to the subway. There's no crowd, in fact Times Square itself seems rather deserted. It's earlier than we planned on, and Times won't be open for another hour or two. This means we will walk up Broadway to Colony Records, to see what we can get from their back stock of records they never sold, but never returned. But first, a fast look at Times, and we start down the stairs. An odd character, a very "New York" looking guy, is halfway down the stairs. He's just waiting there, and seeing us, he somehow senses that we are a part of what he's waiting for. He looks up at us and his eyes light up with a crazed purpose, and he says those words that have haunted me now for over four decades, "............FETHAHS ...I got FETHAHS......." He pulls a small cardboard box from inside his coat and carefully opens it, staring into it as you might look into a crystal ball. He looks up at us again, and pulls the box back as though we might try to get it away from him. He mutters," ....FETHAHS...", and we start walking down the stairs from our momentarily frozen position, but he blocks the stairs and opens the box again, now seeming to trust us. We have no choice but to look, and there in the box is what seems to 15 or 20 records by The FEATHERS! I see this and I say, ".....Feathers....", and he says ".......yeah, Fethahs..." in his heavy New York accent. (The Feathers are high on the list of almost mystical vocal groups, and yet a distant second to the enchanting Castelles). "......Here, look ...you want "Nona"...I got "Nona".......", and he displays a copy of "Nona". It's very tempting, but because of this approach, I am suspecting some sort of cosmic trap to be waiting. Suppose these records were stolen from Times, and I end being seen with them? I could be banned from the store, or worse. (Although' I don't know anything worse). Donn examines the labels, and I walk down the stairs a little further, and there, closed and dark is Times Records! I look to see if it has been broken into, because maybe that's what this "Feathers" sale is all about, but Times is secure. (This is a time before bootlegs of rare records were being made, and so the 45's were all original, and the only detective work to be done, was to conclude if they were a first or second pressing, and determine if there should or shouldn't be any color plastic available.). We decline to buy anything, and he informs us he'll be around, and he walks down the stairs toward the subway platform. We stand in front of Times; just drinking in the wonders of the window, and try to see the wall inside, but it's so dark and forlorn that we just can't be sure of much. But, we'll come back in an hour, when Times Records will probably open. We back away from the window and turn to head up the stairs, and there, looking down on us is the guy with The Feathers, and his hopeful leer says that he expects we might now be customers. We aren't buying, mainly because we don't want to be engaged in the trade of records, right outside of Times, plus the simple fact that we only have a few bucks. We hit street level and make a hasty trek to Colony, Tin Pan Alley, and The Automat, all in about an hour and a half. But, we got to hurry.

After all, Times Records will be open very soon.

****Author's Note – Wayne Stierle wrote this chapter. It was emailed to me in the August 16, 2006.

The Store Rumbled When The Subway Went By

Lou Rallo

The bus from New Jersey pulled into the Port Authority Bus Terminal and I'd get off, go down a flight of concrete steps to one of the levels, then down the escalator and out into the always honking, bustling street. It seemed like there were thousands of yellow cabs right there. I'd do a half walk, half run to 42nd Street, trying not to bump other pedestrians, and head east one long block. I could feel my heart beating in anxious anticipation. Maybe the book store windows and movie theaters added a little to the heart rate, too. I could smell the hot dogs, pizza, French fries, and $1.99 steaks as I quickened down the wide sidewalk. There was often a small group of people listening, semi-circled, around someone speaking loudly about one political or religious cause or another. I ignored the guys trying to sell me watches and marijuana; finally reaching the last crosswalk to the Times Building. The light was always red. On green, I zigged and zagged through hordes of oncoming people walking in the other direction, flew down the one flight of steps turning left into the store...... BAM I was there. I knew I could look at the stuff "Slim" had posted in the window AFTER I was done.

Harold and "Slim" knew I was Wayne's friend; always treating me well when I visited the store. There was truly a magical atmosphere in that little place and I breathed it in while looking at the "money" records on the two walls. To use the word "wander" in such a small place may seem odd, but that's what I did. The wooden floor sounded comforting "all the way" back twenty feet or so to the low wood ceiling beam with the little paper sign that said "duck or leave your brains"; leaving another fifteen feet to the very end. The whole place rumbled occasionally as a subway went by below. I remember the awe of seeing a 78 of "Golden Teardrops" on the wall priced at $20. 00. Then, back again to the front to browse the bins, pick up a printed copy of the top sellers, and ask for the ones I came in for. Even with records stuffed everywhere on shelves and in piles behind the counter, they knew where to find every thing.

Another thing I liked about Times was the "credit system" for records you brought in toward purchases of other records. For most records I brought, I received fifty cents in credit for each one. It was a form of record swapping.

Sometimes I could buy records right on 42nd Street for thirty five cents and go to Times Square Records and get fifty cents in credit for the same record. To me, this was great! Once or twice I saw seedy looking adults bring in records and "Slim" would discreetly pay cash.

I also sometimes convinced other kids in my neighborhood to give or trade with me their old group records or those of their older brothers and sisters. I remember the first time I brought in a significant amount of "credit" records, "Slim" took about ten or twelve, held them by the bottom corner of the sleeves, and shook them out in a pile to check their condition.

The other thing I remembered was all the records hanging from the ceiling by strings. I remember that they were all color plastic, which was very novel at the time......especially to the kids. They certainly existed for many years. One of the things Wayne Stierle pointed out to me was..."the next time you go there, look at those records...you'll see it's strange because under the label, the plastic is black but in the outside, where the grooves were, the plastic would be like, yellow, for instance." I thought to myself "that's impossible"....however when I went there, there were such records.

I had no idea how they could be made that way. Of course I realized later on that if each one was done individually, that could be done. If you put a black center in and then yellow plastic around the outside, and press up a few of them that way but those records hanging from the ceiling in yellow...red...... blue and green. I remember "Did It" by the Laddins on Times Square Records label in green plastic hanging from a string and I bought it because of the color and to this day the record remains in my collection.

I went to the second store......to me it was the second store but it was really the third store, I guess...... I went there once...and I hated it...it was clean and had no atmosphere whatsoever. The store had the feeling of plastic....stainless steel. It was cold.....there was no warmth there and it was even difficult to look through the record bins. You had to lean way over because they were long. I don't know of anyone who went to the second store and liked it. I went to that location once....maybe twice....I didn't buy anything if my memory serves me well.

I was in the candy store in West Orange and Wayne (Stierle) walked in.....he knew I was going to be there, I guess, and Wayne gave me...well, he actually sold me.... (for thirty five cents, the cost) a copy of the first Candlelite record....The Five Satins.........in red plastic Candlelite Number 410.....with 410 Main Street.

I remember talking to Wayne in, maybe, tenth grade and him telling me he was going to have a record label and I suggested a name and he said, "No that's not going to be it" and he showed me a drawing of a candle and told me "I'm going to call it Candlelite".

It was the year 1968 or thereabouts..... I was in Times Square when I walked into an adult book store and there he was...."Slim" at the desk......after all those years he was still working in Times Square. The store was on the south side of 42nd Street. If I had thought he would remember me I would have said something to him.

"Slim" was a character. I recall Wayne (Stierle) saying that "we knew it was something special; but had no idea how special or lasting it would be". No idea...."it just was at it was...in the present at the time you know (we knew even then)...this is cool...it's great...actually...but who knew, as they say, that it would be like it is today.

My friend, Florence Fox used to buy records for her collection, from junkies, on the steps leading down to Times. She'd pay them a nickel more for the records than "Slim" would give them. Of course there were others that had a good selection and would give you a deal too....who was to say whether it was right or wrong.....it was an opportunity....it was about the records. It's was always about the music.....only the music.....

I met Wayne Stierle when we were in third grade! By fourth grade we were talking about Nat "King" Cole and the Mills Brothers. We were talking about "the music" how much we both liked it. I was in seventh grade sitting in English class at the time. Across the street from the junior high school was a place where they gave guitar lessons and sold instruments. It was located right next to where Wayne lived. He said to me "this store have just received a box of records that were from a jukebox. The price for the records was two for a quarter. You ought to go over there, Lou". After school, (I still had my allowance money that I didn't spend on popcorn or bubblegum or whatever I usually spent my money on) I went over to the store, purchased my first two records that Wayne suggested to me. That very same day I became a record collector. The two records I purchased that day were "Wisdom Of A Fool" by the 5 Keys on Capitol and "Please Send Me Someone To Love" by the

Moonglows on Chess. I purchased the Moonglows record without hearing it first because it "was the Moonglows.

The teens that went to Times Square Records saved their allowance....if they cut lawns or whatever odd jobs, saved their money just so they could go to Times...... so they could buy records.

Harold was about 5'4" at most....maybe weighed 120 pounds. He wasn't very gregarious. He was friendly in a quiet way. He handled my requests very well..... for example I would ask him..."Ding-A-Ling-A-Ling Ding Dong" by Dickey Dell and the Bing Bongs or "Since You're Gone" by the Diablos or "Shombolar" by Sheriff and the Ravels or "I'll Never Tell" by the Harptones?, he'd "Yeah, we got that" and he'd find it. He was a nice enough guy but I don't think I can add anything else significant about him or his personality.

I never saw "Teddy the raccoon"; however I did see Genni (pronounced Jenny). She ignored me. Needless to say, there will never be another place like Times Square Records or another person like "Slim" Rose.

Time Records and Times Square Records are etched in our memories as well as things from the past.

****Author's Note – Information in this chapter came from an interview with Lou Rallo on March 13, 2006.

"Slim" Versus The Music Business
"Pretty Pretty Girl" (The New Beat)
The First Times Square 45 Sold To Another Company
Wayne Stierle

In this book, the story of "In My Heart" aka "Here In My Heart" is told. This is the story of the follow-up recording that might have spelled a new beginning for Times Square Records, but instead was an ending.

"Slim" was not about to release the second record that Clarence Johnson had recorded with The Timetones, and get back into that upside-down world of distribution and payola. For that reason, "Slim" was very pleased to sell the recording to Atlantic Records, and be paid a solid fee for doing so. Atlantic released the records on their Atco Records label, but "Slim" would usually say it was on Atlantic.

The song "Pretty, Pretty Girl" was one of those odd records that stood the outside chance of hitting the middle American market, because it was so catchy that the "sound" over-shadowed the fact that it was a basic vocal group recording. In other words, it was a record you could enjoy even if you didn't care for the genre it came from. "Slim", always on the watch for an "angle", felt that the recording had a "new beat" and tried to promote that aspect by adding "The New Beat" to the record as a sub-title. "Slim" was so deeply immersed in mid-fifties music, that he really thought the record had a "new" sound, when in reality; it was playing off of the hypnotic qualities of many other saxophone driven recordings, most notably the Ron Holden record of "Love You So", from a year earlier. But, his idea of trying to set it apart from other releases was a good inventive try, even if it made no common sense.

"Pretty, Pretty Girl" offered "Slim" a freedom he hadn't had previously. It represented the luxury of producing records that could be placed with a major label, and thereby cutting out the dangerous pitfalls of going it on your own, as had happened with the aforementioned "In My Heart". If "Pretty, Pretty Girl" had been a hit record, then material from Times Square Records would be welcomed by Atlantic Records, and eventually other labels. "Slim" was poised on the brink, and someone like myself, was more than ready to write material, or produce things for this growing enterprise (As I begin to do with The Shells). Yes, it was exciting, the possibilities seemed almost endless. Things were going great.

"Pretty, Pretty Girl" failed to hit. Clarence Johnson suffered a life altering health crisis. Atlantic did not want any more recordings.

Such as it may be...so much for the possibilities.....

****Author's Note – This chapter was written by Wayne Stierle. It was emailed to me on August 16, 2006.

"Slim" & The Night Of One Thousand Calls

One More Shot At The Charts!!

Wayne Stierle

There were four records on the Times Square Records label that stood the chance of making it, in one way or another. The fourth, and last of this quartette, was "It's Going To Be Alright" by The Decoys. However, This was following the severe problems of the first three: The over-pressing and under-selling "In My Heart" aka "Here In My Heart" by The Timetones; the failure to take off of "Go Back Where You Came From" by The Summits; and the lack of response from the master sale of "Pretty Pretty Girl" by The Timetones. The Decoys record therefore was handled as an in-store record that would be shopped around as a lease if it took off in any way at all. This tinny sounding recording should have been re-recorded, but "Slim" was through with spending money on "new" records, so it was pressed and sold as just another release for the most part. "Slim" liked this record, but wasn't going to bother spending money to get a form of perfection, that he felt, no one appreciated anyway.

Once upon a time, WINS radio in New York City was a legitimate station for music, and in the early sixties Murray the K, a former jazz dee-jay, turned rock n' roll dee-jay, would have a record contest each night. The winning record for each night would compete after five days to find a winner for the week. The votes were taken by phone calls to "live" operators. (There were no #800 numbers and no automated voting).

Well, this was hard to resist for any independent record company, as it was a chance to get at least one air-play, where you may have gotten none, and beyond that, who knows? These were the kind of odds a gambling chain-smoker would be naturally drawn to, so "Slim" was looking forward to it. The goal was to somehow get around dealing with record distributors by going straight to the radio station for a chance at grabbing the brass ring again.

I don't know if the voting was fixed. Following the Alan Freed/payola problems, it may not have been, however with cash deals possible, you never know for sure. At any rate, I had already been through this with The Shells, as we (Johnson Records crew & myself at night in The Brill Building), had phoned in like crazy to vote for a Shells record I produced. We won one night, but not the week. "Slim" found the possibilities in such voting for a record to present a very interesting set of odds, to say the least. "Slim" liked the idea of stacking the deck, and why not?

What followed is obvious. "Slim" sent the record to WINS, and we dropped off some copies in person as well. Sure enough, along came a slow enough week for new releases that "It's Going To Be Alright" got into the contest. "Slim" had an extra phone line put in temporarily, and put signs up asking customers to call in and vote for The Decoys record. On the night of the contest, we were there ready to call. "Slim" was handing out rolls of nickels to part-time employees and some trusted customers to go into the subway and use the pay phones. Once it was time to call, we started non-stop, right there in the store. The trick is to listen to the voice answering the contest line, so if it's a different operator than you spoke to 30 seconds ago, you could use your regular voice, but if it's the same operator, then you'd change your "sound" enough to sound like someone else. (Remember, there was no such thing as "caller I.D.") Sometimes you'd vote for "It's Going To Be Alright", and other times you'd vote for "The Decoys record". Variety is the spice of phone voting. You also paid for your calls. (This wasn't a free call, such as with "talk radio" or "reality TV" talent shows, etc.). These were the days before TV networks and radio stations became so desperate that they started paying for the calls. These were the days when you paid for your own phone calls.

To our surprise, The Decoys record won the night! Did we do it, or did the general public actually do it? We'll never know, but it seems that we probably did it. Now, you might think this is no way to win, but actually it is, because record companies, including major labels using promo people, were doing the same thing! Not only that, what chance would anyone stand in New York City against a new Four Seasons record? (I use The Four Seasons as an example of playing against the hometown team). These were all dial phones, also called rotary phones. None of that easy-to-use push button speed dialing junk that would be invented over a decade later.

Harold was a riot. With his very "New York" nasal sound, he really couldn't disguise his voice, but he tried, and maybe he conjured up an image of a hundred guys from Brooklyn calling in. I was able to do several voices, but even "Slim" was calling in, and he didn't sound like a kid voting, to put it mildly. I suggested to "Slim'" that he not call in, for obvious reasons, but he said, "....why not, it's a free country...", and in between puffs on his cigarette, he was placing raspy votes for The Decoys record. Did they count all our votes? We'll never know. Did they discount the votes from "Slim"? I'll never know.

Now the game was afoot. (I've always wanted to say that). Anyway, the voting for the winner of the week would be tougher and harder fought. Times Square Records was turning out signs and fliers designed to get even more help from the customers. It was a mini-political campaign of sorts, crammed into about four days. This had turned into yet another "cause" generated from the store. (In fact, although we didn't know it at the time, this would be the last real shot of natural, crazy, energy.).

The night of the contest to determine the winner of the week was a re-play of the first night, with the phones, pay phones, customers, and a general delirious feeling of insanity that so well summed up what it was like at Times Square Records. The unreality was so thick in the air that you could cut it with a knife. Somewhere in the night there was an audience listening and voting, who had no idea that a record store/record company, located underground was in the running.

The Decoys record won! It was an amazing thing, and it felt like maybe this record could take off as an East Coast out-of-left-field triumph, as stranger things have not only happened, but had a way of happening at Times Square Records. "Slim" was upbeat, but not nearly as happy as I expected he'd be, and his world-weary way of being "positive" seemed to say he didn't think much would happen. Perhaps he had regrets about not re-cutting this song, but he didn't say that, still, what sounds like a demo had won the contest.

The new week dawned and WINS wasn't playing the record heavily, but rather giving it a few spins as a "contest winner". Worse yet, the station called and wanted a better copy of the record, as they assumed their copy must have been a rough rushed release. (Now that "demo" aspect was coming into play). There were no better copies. Despite an increase in sales, and a handful of stores wanting a small stock of the single, there was no great public demand that you could measure. Air-play at other radio stations did not happen as a result of this win. "Slim" sent the record over to Atlantic Records, who had purchased "Pretty Pretty Girl" less than two years earlier, but they passed on it. In a matter of days, WINS dropped the record, and that was basically the end of that ride on the merry-go-round. (No brass ring). The Decoys record was generally liked by the Times Square customers, and even many years later, it remains well respected. (I obtained the master from "Slim" a year or so later, and I'm glad to have it.). I also have my memories of what was, and what could have been, all blended together with what should have been.

The times at Times were among the best of times.

****Author's Note – This chapter was written by Wayne Stierle. He emailed it to me the first part of September 2006.

"Slim" Versus Shoplifters, Con Artists And Smokers

A Typical Day At A Non-Typical Store

Another Day At "Times"

Wayne Stierle

Among the throngs of regular customers that flocked to Times Square Records, from all over the greater New York City Area, were some true "New York Characters". Some of these characters were shoplifters and/or con artists. This particular breed provided both charm and alarm at Times Square Records.

The store was a powerful magnet for all types of collectors, including the dime novel variety, who sometimes conjured up a cross between Alice In Wonderland and the villains in Batman.

What did they look like? Imagine a movie where a New York character wearing a heavy, worn down winter coat, opens the coat as you walk by, displaying 20 or 30 watches all pinned inside the coat, and offers you a great deal. He talks in gruff terms and seems tougher than he is.......Imagine a sleazy New York cab driver with a Brooklyn accent, who needs a shower and shave, but talks in colorful terms about the city, and then charges you $20.00 for a $4.00 ride, and when you point out it's really $4.00, he accepts the $4.00 but never admits he tried to get $20.00...........Imagine a guy rummaging through a trash can for God knows what, and wearing knitted hat pulled down over as much of his head as possible, and grumbling to himself..........Imagine a guy who grabs a donut from a diner counter on the way out, and has the nerve to start eating it as he is only halfway out the door, with crumbs flying around in the winter winds......Imagine that this guy, despite the above descriptions, won't hurt you, but he'll steal from you. He might buy you a cup of coffee today, and tomorrow if you have dinner with him, he'll duck out and leave you to pay the bill, even though' he invited you to dinner.

If you can picture all of the above, then you kind of know some of these "outcast" collectors who came into Times, and who hung outside, in heat and cold.

Outside of the original Times Records was another world. It was the world of collectors trying to make money from "Slim's" real customers, before and after they went into Times. In that shadowy world beneath the street, some of the odder collectors dwelled. Some would carry a "50" box with them most of the time. The box had whatever they claimed was "rare", and considering the time frame, the records were good, if not rare, as they were all records by vocal groups. They would make all kinds of claims, while trying to sell you anything and everything, and trying to buy whatever you were carrying for a small cost, so they could then re-sell your stuff to the next customer who came by.

"Slim" had created a multi-headed monster, for he was taking in records from people in return for store credit. So, these characters knew that customers heading for the store would be carrying records, and some of these might be far more valuable than the kids knew. (Kids were raiding their attics, grabbing records from their older siblings discarded 45's, and buying used records from anywhere they could, sometimes for as low as one penny). Here were the vultures of the day waiting to swoop down on you as you headed for Times. Waiting to get that rare record before "Slim" would even see it, and hoping to get you to spend your money with them, instead of at Times! There was an "air" of espionage and intrigue about this whole manic scene, and it wasn't really about money, as much as it was about 45 rpm records.

"Slim" was livid, especially annoyed by those who could not be chased away. Some people called them cockroaches, because they never could be gotten rid of, and seemed to come and go from the dark of the subway halls. They would get chased away from outside the door, but still they would actually stand in front of the door and proposition customers trying to get in. "Slim" or Mike would chase them away, and they'd go halfway up the stairs, and work from there. When "Slim" could get a local cop to chase them, they would then stand on the sidewalk looking at everyone heading towards the subway to determine if they were heading to Times. Countless people were approached and mis-identified because they were carrying a small package of some sort. It was something that started hours before the store opened and lingered after it closed, depending on the tempo of the area at any given time. After all, this was Times Square, the center of the world.

These collector/sellers would go into Times until they were ejected, just to learn the current price of the stuff they were carrying, so they could approach you and undersell "Slim" with the same record. It was like Times Records was Saturn, and these characters had become the rings of Saturn.

People would actually come into Times and try to get a cheaper price on records that they'd been offered on the street. "Slim" would tell them to go and buy them on the street, which shocked the customers, but that was "Slim", and he was fed up with the bickering caused by this situation.

(As anyone who has been to New York City knows, this type of thing has escalated into the tables set up along Broadway, selling books, posters, and everything else, while legitimate stores file complaints that don't seem to mean much, because the tables and the dealers return in a flash.)

The fights with these "gypsy" collectors never ended. They would sometimes be allowed in the store, and then they would do something wrong, and be kicked out again. It just went on and on.

My best memory of this, I think, sums up what it was like to deal with them, and I'll tell you about it with a story from just one small part of an average day at Times.

I'm at the register in the original store. People are milling around as usual. Everything is distracting. There are questions about the wall and records to be played. Questions about everything possible and people digging through stuff, and it all had to be monitored every second. It was crazy and it was New York. People would come in and want to know about the subway, and drunks would wander in, etc. "Slim" is behind the counter, but down the way, near to the back room. Harold is running back and forth from the back room to the counter and back again doing whatever he was doing. I don't remember where Teddy was, or if he was there at that point. Mike was standing guard on the floor. The door opens and in comes one of these "characters", wearing a very heavy coat that may well have been a few coats actually. He was hunched over as if you wouldn't see him that way. He went straight to an area of records all connected by string running through them and seemed to be casually looking at them. Clearly he didn't think he was noticed. But, Times was small, and this thief had a reputation well known to everyone there. I looked over at "Slim" to warn him, which is what I was instructed to do, but "Slim" was signaling Mike to get on it. So, I watched, like watching a movie in slow motion, and for some reason, I can see it playing right now in my head............

Several people came through the door and the cold air rushed in, hitting me first as I was across from the door. This diversion was what the thief was looking for, because he suddenly bolted for the door, bent over and moving fast. Mike grabbed him by the coat and turned him around, and while this weasel was protesting as only a guilty person can, at least 50 records, and maybe as many as 75 records came sliding out of his coat and onto the floor.

He stood there, caught. "Slim" seemed to ignore him and went to check the counter, and the strings had been cut AND re-tied, to look like nothing was taken! Mike got him to empty his pockets, and he had a switchblade. "Slim" never addressed it other than to say what he'd said other times.........."....You're not allowed in here anymore..."

He was escorted out.

But, he didn't stay away very long.

They never stopped hanging outside, and trying to come back in...

Once things got back to normal, "Slim" leaned over his chair and lit another cigarette. The door opened and in came some regular customers, and the first one through the door was smoking. "Slim" stopped him with these harsh words........ "Can't you read the sign, there's no smoking in here......take it outside"! Having said that, "Slim" took a long drag on his cigarette, and blew the smoke out into the store. There wasn't a "no smoking" sign at this point, but "Slim" would refer to things that weren't there in such a strong manner, that you didn't even consider that it wasn't accurate. Harold put on "When I Woke Up This Morning" by The Bop-Chords, and everything was cool. This mini-drama had been only a small portion of yet another fascinating day in the saga of Times Square Records, and its founder and personality, Irving "Slim" Rose.

****Author's Note – This chapter was written by Wayne Stierle. He emailed it to me mid summer 2006.

"Baby Oh Baby"
The First National Hit To Come Out Of Times
Wayne Stierle

"Baby Oh Baby" was the first of three national hits to happen directly because of Times Square Records (Then known as "Times Records"). "Baby Oh Baby" was the least likely of the three to make it, as you will see as you read this.

The thing about "Slim" was that he wanted a variety of previously "rare" records to sell, and in particular, those records that were already sought after. It was the eventual downfall of Times, because the records he showcased became popular enough to be distributed to other stores, which in the final analysis meant that Times was not going to remain as "the only game in town". There was no way around this puzzle, (although "Slim" tried to control the scene by creating a short-lived, ill-fated "one-stop", that would supply "oldies" to retail stores, but that never worked). Success breeds imitation in this world. (If "Slim" was Elvis, then the stores that would spring up copying him were Conway Twitty and Ral Donner).

In the late summer/early fall of 1959, Donn and I, who I met through Donn's sister Barbara, began a quest to track down as many "lost" recordings as possible, and try to get them re-released. It was quite a process, and judging from what I've learned over the years, there simply was no one using the oddly refined techniques we created, almost out of thin air.

But, without a place to sell these records, we really would have had nothing to drive us, save the great feeling of adding to a record collection. (And that is, make no mistake about it, a great quest). If not for Times Records, none of this would have happened. There were a few of us that were among the first actual "record collectors" as we know the term today, but "Slim" provided what fast became the Mother Church of vocal group records. (Much as The Grand Old Opry is known as "The Mother Church" of Country Music) This was about great "group" records, and not about harmony or unison, but the whole package, including strange out of tune combos, but more often than not, depending on great lead singers. The first golden era of rock n' roll had not yet ended, though its final days were upon us.

Among the records that "Slim" was partial to, was a record called "Come On Baby" by the Cordovans on Johnson Records. (The Cordovans, like most Frankie Lymon imitations, were labeled as "cute" by "Slim"). There were other records on the Johnson label, and all were wanted in what "Slim" called "quantity". ("Quantity" meant anything over twenty five records and usually at least 100 copies). One of these records was a single that had bombed on its' initial release, "Baby Oh Baby" by The Shells. The reason it was a true "bomb" was that the publishing was owned by Alan Freed, and because of this, Freed had played it for a few weeks in 1957, and it failed to catch on. It simply didn't have "it", in New York City, in 1957, on the #1 radio show in the world. "Baby Oh Baby" was over and done. It was a flop which was gone with the winds of chance; never; to be heard from again. Unlike most vocal group ballads, "Baby Oh Baby" featured a highly aggressive lead vocal that was close to being out of control, and oddly similar to a version of what would later be referred to as soul music. (There were those strange records that were played in New York City, and would then drive you crazy, as they would suddenly disappear. Records like "In Self Defense" by the Flairs, "Guided Missiles" by the Cufflinks, and yes, "Baby Oh Baby" by the Shells). Make no mistake about it, "Baby Oh Baby", complete with a bridge on which very few people can even understand the words, is an enchanting, urgent recording that transports you back to the sound of the late fifties, in New York City.

We contacted Johnson Records, through our means of locating people and companies, finding it by tracking down the publisher. The trail led us to a publicity office, not a record company, in the Brill Building. (This is not an example of our abilities, as Johnson Records was easier than others to locate). There was no actual record company at all, and its' founder, Hiram Johnson, (no relation to Clarence Johnson), did not work out of the office. The office was just a convenient address for Hiram, and sometimes for his brother, the legendary band leader/song writer, Buddy Johnson. It was an office run by Jim McCarthy, who spent all day on the phone with his bookies, betting on the horses. McCarthy hung out there, and picked up occasional "publicity" work just by virtue of being there on Broadway, in such a famous/infamous building. Because of his connection to the oft times drunk Hiram Johnson, McCarthy had inherited by proximity only, the use of the Johnson label and a quasi management arrangement with two groups that Hiram had originally recorded, The Dubs and The Shells. Nothing was happening there at all, except the bets being placed on the ponies.

McCarthy was happy to press up any records we wanted, but when we placed an order, in early 1960, but there was a lag time. (Unknown to us, McCarthy was getting something in writing with Hiram Johnson, and wouldn't proceed until an agreement gave him a free control over the situation of re-pressing whatever Johnson singles we wanted). When he was finally ready, we then found that he wouldn't press "Baby Oh Baby", and wanted us to do it! He owed money to the Long Wear Stamper Corporation, and was beating the bill, so we had to order the stampers to make the record, under the name of Hiram Johnson. We had to pick up the stampers in person, so Long Wear would get paid cash, and even then they almost balked at giving us the stampers. Finally, in the spring of 1960, we got the stampers for Johnson #104. ("Baby Oh Baby"). We pressed 300 copies and gave 25 to Johnson Records, with the rest going to "Slim", who went through them pretty fast. We re-ordered some more, and McCarthy, sensing that this was very unusual, began sending copies to New York radio stations, trying to build on the attention that "Slim" was giving the record. We took the record in person to the stations, and got a luke warm reception. In the summer of 1960, "Baby Oh Baby" was a steady seller at Times. And you know, having a solid seller at Times, meant something, even if it never got attention anywhere else.

But, where were The Shells? They existed, and they didn't exist. After the failure of "Baby Oh Baby" in 1957, the group disbanded, which is record-biz language for falling apart under the weight of trying to deal with the ego-driven alcoholic lead singer, Nathaniel Bouknight, and the lack of continuity that was the true hallmark of Hiram Johnson. (Nathaniel was also known as "Little Nat" and "Little Nate". He was about 5 feet tall, but his attitude was well over 6 feet). The Shells records after "Baby Oh Baby" had featured Nate along with anybody who was around, which accounts for the weak recordings that use The Cordovans and The Arcades as faux Shells behind Nate. Hiram ran into a young group hanging around at The Apollo, and asked them if they wanted to be part of a real group, and they agreed. The four new guys recorded with Nate on "Sippin' Soda", and when Nate quit to pursue a solo career, they recorded "She Wasn't Meant For Me" with a new lead they found, who had none of Nate's rough appeal. There was no plan for Nate to ever sing with a "Shells" group again, and the new "Shells" that Hiram now had, were agreeable in a way that Nate would never be, and why try to duplicate the raw, edgy sound of Nate, since "Baby Oh Baby" hadn't been a hit? But...the re-issue of "Baby Oh Baby" changed everything, because Nate was, after all, the total "sound" of "Baby Oh Baby", and by logical extension, the "sound" of The Shells. Nate was free to come up with his own group, but he couldn't care less, and so the new group, from "Sippin' Soda", was suddenly re-united with Nate, and facing what looked like what might be a breaking hit record. A record this group had never performed, or recorded. They didn't like Nate, and Nate didn't like them, and that's putting it mildly.

Unknown to most music fans, Alan Freed, who had been tossed out of two New York stations, was thriving in Los Angeles by mid-1960. Jack Hooke, who was Freed's manager, also ran their publishing company, Figure Music, which published the song "Baby Oh Baby". Hooke, when supplied with copies of the record, sent them to Freed, and Freed eventually gave it air-play in Los Angeles by the late summer of 1960'. In California, they thought "Baby Oh Baby" was a brand new record! Even odder, given its' early failure, they liked it. "Baby Oh Baby" was breaking on The West Coast as a new record, and picking up steam on The East Coast as well. Billboard magazine called "Baby Oh Baby", "the California Sound"! The California Sound! What Madness! Can you imagine a great New York group record having been recorded in California? (Who knew that surf music would soon steal that title of "California Sound" from the hard core New York group, The Shells, and hand it over to The Beach Boys.) It was crazy, and I do mean crazy.

At this point things kept getting stranger. "Slim" wanted to keep his exclusive on selling the record, but this was impossible, for Johnson Records now had major distributors willing to distribute the record. Then the stampers broke, and the original mold broke as well, meaning that new stampers could not be made. New masters had to be cut from the tapes, but Jim McCarthy was not about to try to get the tapes. The reason would surface later. For now he wanted a master, and he told me it was "no problem", to just get a tape of the record! What? But he was serious, and I took the record, my copy, to Tru-Tone Recording in Orange, New Jersey, and made a copy onto to a 15 1/2 ips tape, which was sent to a master cutter to be made ready for the mastering process. This was beyond the pale. Major quantities of "Baby Oh Baby" were going to be pressed from my copy, and as it worked out, no one would ever even suspect this had been done! (Your copy of this record may well be a copy of my record). At this point, Jack Hooke moved into the Johnson Records office, to watch the money personally. (Donn had gone out of state, and wasn't around for this day to day insanity that was building rapidly).

McCarthy couldn't get the master tapes because they were held by George Goldner, who had paid for the session. Goldner owned the publishing on the flip side, "What's In An Angels Eyes", and McCarthy just took the publishing credits so he wouldn't have to pay Goldner for the publishing based on sales of the record. He even changed the title to "Angel Eyes", and it worked, for George Goldner had forgotten about it, and never noticed. George Goldner had paid for the session because he had acquired Hiram's other group, The Dubs, and gave Hiram twenty minutes at the end of their "Could This Be Magic" session, and that free 20 minutes enabled Hiram to record "Baby Oh Baby" and the flip side. This information comes from Hiram Johnson, Richard Blandon, Cleveland Still, and Nathaniel Bouknight. Listen carefully to the release of the bridge on "Angel Eyes", and you'll hear that "Could This Be Magic" band sound very clearly. When The Shells first appeared "live" with Cousin Brucie at Palisades Park, I noticed Nate, who didn't like to talk to the group, huddled in the corner with Bobby Nurse, the great falsetto tenor from the new group. When they went on, Bobby sang the falsetto opening to "Baby Oh Baby", and Nate came in as lead on the song itself, which surprised me. Nate would repeat this at each "live" appearance, for the short time he remained on as lead of The Shells. I never did understand this, and neither did anyone else, but Nate would just say that the notes in the false opening were a little too high on some days. In the early 1970's, when I was producing and recording The Dubs, Cleveland Still, in remembering the "Could This Be Magic" session, claimed that he had sung the falsetto opening on "Baby Oh Baby", because Nate couldn't get it right. This is strange, since Nate wrote the song, writing credits notwithstanding. Frankly, it is possible, but it's only about fifty percent possible, because the chance that Cleveland just tutored Nate on the note is there too. Then again, with the studio clock ticking, who knows? It sounds like Nate, and yet, well... (I can make the argument both ways from the record itself in very convincing terms.). Nate never talked about it, and aside from pushing me to release his earlier recording, "My Cherie", Nate didn't talk at all. (Nate claimed that "My Cherie" was far better than "Baby Oh Baby", but in reality it didn't compare.). As for Cleve, he laughed when I asked him to sing the falsetto, but he never would actually do it.

"Baby Oh Baby" hit the national charts with a bullet, and began a solid climb each week, usually with the coveted red bullet! It was breath taking stuff. It actually hit the top twenty nationally! It got up to number nineteen on the national charts, and sold somewhere in the area of 400,000 copies, and made a lot of publishing money for Alan Freed. In many cities the record was top ten, and got to the top in Los Angeles, and number three in New York City. But, the real Shells background group never showed up! The vocal group that actually sang background on "Baby Oh Baby" was never to appear!

Never! Johnson Records didn't have to pay anybody but Nate, but they sweated it out every day, waiting for the original group to show up. Nate had written the song, but shared writing credits with others, though they didn't write a word of it. (The song was crafted by Nate, in his oddly illiterate fashion, which added to the charm of the overall hypnotic, pounding production.). Jack Hooke, (personal manager of Alan Freed), paid Nate a few dollars for the writing, but from what I could tell, he really cheated Nate badly. Hiram Johnson came around for awhile, but he wasn't making sense at all. What Hiram got paid, I don't know, but in his delicate condition, I doubt he was paid fairly. Among the odd things that happened was that Charles Brown covered the record, and actually sold 70,000 copies in the mid-west, with those figures being according to Jack Hooke. (Can you imagine the surprise to some kid who asks his father to buy "Baby Oh Baby", and the father comes back with the Charles Brown record?).

One cold evening at Christmas in 1960, I was in my 1952 Pontiac, at Main Street and Mount Pleasant Avenue, when Donn, (home for Christmas), pulled up next to me. I motioned to him to turn his radio on, and as we sat there at the light, "Baby Oh Baby" was playing on WMCA. Donn waved to me to change the station, and we opened our windows as "Baby Oh Baby" blasted out from WABC, and then on to WINS where it was playing as well. All the major New York stations were playing the record at the same time! What a strange feeling that was.

The off-beat sound that Nate presented vocally was copied six months later on a west coast recording, "Those Oldies But Goodies"(Remind Me Of You). (I wanted to "cover" that record with The Shells, and do it in a much harder, tougher version, and I created the arrangement and a spoken part, but since the publishing was not owned by Johnson or Freed, I was voted down at that crucial point. The idea was solid, because the Shells had some air-play automatically coming off of the momentum of "Baby Oh Baby". I have no doubt at all that The Shells would have scored another major hit single, had we done that song, in a hard-core version.

As a result of Jack Hooke moving into the Johnson Records office, I ended up doing the A&R for the album by Rosie and the Originals. (It ended up being just Rosie solo). Alan Freed owned the publishing on "Angel Baby", and Hooke signed Rosie to Brunswick Records, and they flew her into New York for a session. (Hooke promised to use one or two of my songs, but it didn't happen. He blamed the arranger, but Hooke was a big league liar and con artist supreme, and what would you expect from someone who was able to manage Alan Freed?). I tried to tell Hooke that they should do a basic session in a tiny studio, to get the "Angel Baby" sound, but he wasn't interested in anything like that. (The result was a "big session" with no results, except for a dull album, and the weak single, "Lonely Blue Nights").

I was never paid a cent on "Baby Oh Baby", not one copper penny, but I did get to produce the Shells recordings. In having a hot roast beef sandwich with Hooke, downstairs in the Brill Building, he introduced me to people like Big Al Sears, and Panama Francis. One day Hooke was on the phone, and after talking for awhile, he handed me the telephone, and I heard, ".....Wayne, this is Alan Freed, I just want to thank you for all your help to us...." At the time, I considered this payment in full, along with the hot roast beef sandwich at Jack Dempseys. Now I know better. At least, I ought to. But, in truth, I don't.

I produced a majority of the Shells following records. When the singles ended up being stocked at Times Square Records, it seemed strange to me, although it shouldn't have seemed that way. "Slim" would say things like, "....here's your Shells record.....how's it doin'?", or "...it's a good record, but it's not selling very well....." This was "Slim" being "positive". (My best productions were "Sweetest One", "Baby, Walk On In", "Happy Holiday", and "Deep In My Heart". For "Baby, Walk On In" and "Sweetest One", we got Cliff Driver and his combo, to get that "sound", as Driver had played piano on "Could This Be Magic" and "Baby Oh Baby", but he showed up in a bit of a daze, and his combo was stone drunk). If you listen to the intro of "Deep In My Heart", you'll hear the "Baby Oh Baby" opening being mimicked behind the word "...melody..." I was proud of that "touch", but no one seemed to notice. On "Sweetest One" I attempted to create one of the most hard-edged vocal group openings possible, and on the fade, I tried for the "perfect fade", or frankly, I was trying for the best fade ever made.) When Nate quit The Shells, he stole their song, "Stop Pretending", and took it to the Clovers, who recorded it with Nate in the background, rather than on lead. After that, Nate went solo, as he always wanted to do. ("Stop Pretending" by the Clovers was produced by Paul Winley, who had come close to obtaining both the Shells and the Dubs from Hiram Johnson, in 1957. The Shells might have been sort of good on Winley Records, but "Baby Oh Baby" would never have been recorded in the way it was. The Dubs without George Goldner would never have made their famous recordings).

Somehow that almost eerie introduction in the record "Baby Oh Baby" came to stand for the vocal group sound of the early sixties, an era in which it hadn't even been recorded. Let me tell you, it was a strange time for a kid like me, (still in high school), and it whirled by like a merry-go-round out of control. Some days I still feel dizzy from the ride, but most days I feel very depressed that it's all over and gone.

****Author's Note – This chapter was written by Wayne Stierle. He emailed it to me the November 14, 2006.

No Other Store Had "Slim" Rose

Remembering A Man.... A Store.... & The Music

David Hinckley

Since I first visited Times Square Records in 1963, I arrived a little after its relatively brief peak.

I never saw the 1475 Broadway store. "Slim" had already moved to 1104 Sixth Avenue which would later be changed to 55 West 42nd Street by the time I arrived.

I never saw Teddy the Raccoon.

But what I didn't see didn't matter, or even occur to me, until years later.

It also never occurred to me in 1965 or 1966 that someone could have acquired a world-class 78 collection at quite modest prices had they only known then what they could know now. Seventy-eights were almost a throwaway at Times; for an original pressing of a modestly rare 45, you could get a half dozen 78s that were each rarer than the 45.

Such is life, I suppose – a kiss, a rose and regrets over a lost copy of "Church on A Hill."

What I did see, in any case, was plenty at the time.

I was a kid from Connecticut whose experience with record stores was a rack of top - 40 hits, some rows of albums and maybe the occasional tray of "oldies" that might have a copy of "Mack the Knife."

Then Mark Ransom, who introduced me to "New York oldies," brought me to Times – a store comprised entirely of wonderful exotic records with a constant stream of fellow customers who felt the same way about them.

The collectors you met at Times were as striking as the music. Some were straight out of Damon Runyon, some out of "Blackboard Jungle," some more like Rod Steiger in "On the Waterfront."

There were hoods in black leather jackets, geeks in glasses and a lot of guys with a New York swagger. They didn't all like each other, but their common ground was that you could get them all to shut up and listen by slapping a Five Keys record onto one of "Slim's" low-fi turntables.

While Times was instrumental in spawning a mail network that expanded the collectors' umbrella to Boston, Pittsburgh, Philly and the West Coast, the patrons on any given Saturday were mostly from the city, where R&B vocal groups were the music with which many of them had grown up.

Almost none of these collectors were anything like anyone I knew or even saw growing up in a Connecticut suburb. As Ransom notes, it was such a different world that even though it was a legitimate enterprise, it felt almost forbidden.

By 1963 a handful of other stores also featured rhythm and blues vocal group records, like the Relic Rack in Hackensack or John Belmonte's and Skippy White's in Boston. But no other store felt like it was the center of that universe.

And no other store had "Slim" Rose.

The first time I saw "Slim", he scared me. His legend preceded him, and he was exactly what I expected. He looked like the kind of perpetually annoyed grownup who was always telling you to get off his lawn.

One of Mark Ransom's memories of "Slim" is pretty much just that, except in this case it was "Get out of my arcade."

One of the things about going to Times is that you always brought a box of records. Sometimes you'd be looking to trade them in for store credit. A $10 record, for instance, theoretically got you $5 credit – or "cridit," as Harold Ginsberg said.

Just as often, though, you'd run into other collectors with their own boxes and work trades.

It never occurred to me, as a dumb kid from Connecticut, that "Slim" might see this as cutting out the middleman, that is, "Slim".

It occurred to "Slim", though.

Times didn't open until noon, and those of us who arrived early would often end up chatting in the Sixth Avenue subway arcade, chat that sometimes continued after "Slim" had opened for business.

One Saturday afternoon when Mark and I were talking with a couple of other guys outside the store, "Slim" called a couple of policemen – one of whom was physically huge -- to chase us off.

It worked, too, except that "Slim" belatedly realized we were also paying customers. Once that occurred to him, he was apologetic and almost pleasant, a demeanor he adopted about as often as he spun Six Fat Dutchmen polka 78s.

We tried to be marginally more discreet after that, following the lead of long-timers who, if they were doing serious deals, would often repair across the street to Bryant Park and work it out on a bench.

Jerry Greene was also gone by the time I arrived, so the go-to guy behind the counter for me was Harold. Like "Slim", he seemed irritated much of the time, but he knew the music where "Slim" really didn't, and when he relaxed he could be cordial and funny.

Besides, the lettering on the hundreds of record sleeves on the wall – title, group, year and price – was in Harold's writing, which made him sort of the Picasso of the place.

I don't remember much of Jenny, but I do remember Shan and Shar, two teenage girls who weren't a bad draw for the almost entirely male collecting population and also had a reasonably good knowledge of the music. Shari Halpern commuted in from Port Washington.

There were several bins of 78s on the left as you walked in. For a dime or a quarter, you could get common records like "Deserie" by the Charts or "Sixteen Candles" by the Crests that clearly "Slim" had bought for nothing out of some warehouse.

Like most "sophisticated" collectors, I passed on these. I already had the 45, so why did I need the 78? I remember Walter DeVenne, a big collector from

Boston, sending me $20.00 to buy him copies of the common 78s, saying some day when they were no longer a dime apiece they'd have real value. He was right. What did I know?

Being on a teenage budget, I would occasionally buy a $2.00 or $3.00 record from the wall, but mostly stuck to the regular records, which were $1.00 apiece, three for $2.00 eight for $5.00. This kept my cash flow fully engaged; since I got a late start, I still had to buy all the standards that other collectors had bought years earlier.

Meanwhile, you didn't have to hang around Times for long to learn who most of the serious collectors were, or where we all stood in the collecting hierarchy.

At the top were the "big" collectors who had the one- or two-of-a-kind records we minnows could only dream about, records like "Estelle" by the Belltones. They often formed their own cluster in a corner of the store or the arcade, discussing the nuances of deep early R&B like "Dearest" by the Swallows while the rest of us were still picking up finger-popping teen tunes like "Peppermint Stick" by the El Chords.

Another group hung on the fringes of the big-collector circle, soaking up every word, every story of how someone acquired "They Say" by the Rainbows, glad to be allowed to listen to the stories and sometimes even the records. They dreamt of the day they too would find a copy of "Just A Lonely Christmas" on red plastic, a record that would give them respect.

There were other subgroups, too, including some pure music fans who weren't at all mesmerized by the "collector" aura, but just liked the sound. They didn't need original 45s. They were happy with reissues, LPs or even reel-to-reel tapes.

The serious collectors could be cordial to these fans. But what really got the action going was the arrival of a known or occasionally unknown wild-card person who happened to be packing a few good records, which of course the big boys immediately began trying to pry loose.

Sometimes this involved just buying the record, preferably before the other big boys even knew it had come in.

But sometimes the guy wouldn't sell, or wanted to test the market a little more, and that's the point at which, by the lore of Times, more intense means of persuasion might be employed. While this could be just a long persistent campaign that would wear the fellow down, there are darker stories – some, not all, of which is doubtless urban legend – about techniques that ranged from simple fraud (misrepresenting a record offered in trade) to intimations of violence.

When the opportunity could be arranged, flat-out theft was also employed.

I remember agreeing to sell a record one afternoon to a chap who promised to send me the money that very evening. If you ever see "Johnny Russo" and you can get him to stop laughing, tell him I'm still waiting.

In any case, these deals – legitimate and otherwise -- didn't really involve Times. But they would have happened a lot less if Times hadn't been there as a place to which people with records gravitated.

Sometimes, when a deal was being worked out, a collector who lived in the city would invite an out-of-towner to his place to finish it up. Mark, I and our friends took a number of trips around the city to the homes of various collectors, and the experiences were fascinating.

Not to mention, very often, intimidating. You might look down at your own 45 box with two or three $10.00 records, and then glance up at a wall with hundreds of carefully filed records worth three times that. It almost felt like a civic duty to take whatever deal was offered – and besides, crumbs to a big collector could look like pretty shiny stuff to the likes of me.

Sometimes visiting the home turf of a big collector could be a multidimensional adventure. When we were visiting a major collector's place one late summer afternoon in 1966, some of his rather squirrelly looking friends came into the room and tried to slip a couple of our records into the refrigerator. When we asked to get them back and the door was reluctantly opened, we noticed that this refrigerator held no food, just our handful of records and several shelves of containers and devices commonly associated with heroin use.

Decades before the Internet, those of us who lived up in Connecticut could send letters saying we'll be at Times on such and such a Saturday, take the train to the city, meet a dozen collector friends and be home by mid-evening.

Alas, being the hub of this small, devoted universe apparently didn't turn out to be all that lucrative for "Slim". In a 1964 edition of the "Keep the Big Beat Alive" newsletter – KBBA was a club formed by some of the eager young kids who met at Times, though the big collectors didn't get very involved –"Slim" put in a classified ad saying he was planning to retire and he'd sell the store, stock and all, debt-free, for $35,000.

A few months later he put in a similar ad saying the price was now $12,000 – with no mention of "debt-free." The ad said the new owner could take possession on Jan. 1, 1965.

So my personal history with "Slim" was a fairly short one. But it lives on, vividly, in the tapes of his radio show, for which he would buy time on low-power AM stations to play and plug his records.

By the time I tuned in, he had long since parted ways with Alan Fredericks – a serious mistake, most collectors now agree – and was doing his own show late Saturday afternoon. It aired live, so a few minutes before show time one of the staffers would rope off the right back corner of the store and "Slim" would set up with a stack of records next to his bad record player.

His radio show, as anyone who heard more than five minutes can attest, was one of the funniest productions in radio history.

First of all, his voice always sounded like he was talking at the wrong speed – 33 instead of 45. Second, he sounded as if he barely knew the titles of the records he was playing, which was probably accurate.

Everyone has a favorite "Slim" radio moment. He'd introduce a record as costing $50, drop the needle on it, and there'd be this crackling screech before it started skipping. "Slim" would try to fix it, doing everything but drag the needle across it, before he'd give up and repeat that this would cost you $50.

One of Mark's favorite "Slim" moments was when Genni was telling a joke about a yacht and she pronounced it "yatch-it."

At some point "Slim" actually closed the store when the radio show went on, which was an act of mercy.

Still, for all "Slim's" quirks, Times was the first place I'd ever seen where records were the center of the universe, the sun around which all else revolved.

I figure this is how jazz buffs felt when they went into Commodore, or show fanatics felt at Colony, or gospel lovers at Rainbow.

In the rest of my life, collecting records was at best an incidental pastime. You could mention popular music to your friends, but you discussed it, almost always, in passing or a brief burst. It had little importance.

At Times, it did, and here were hundreds of people who validated your own affection for it.

"Big" collectors, like the big men in any crowd, had and have their good and bad sides.

They find and preserve music that might otherwise be lost. They help document its history.

They can also be liars and cheaters whose primary interest is less in the music than in their personal ownership of it.

Many of the big collectors of R&B vocal group music, a lovely but little-known and consistently underappreciated style, do nothing to spread it, nothing to help the artists who made it. Their goal is personal possession, to be the only one with a particular item. They glorify themselves.

It's sad, but its human nature, and the way it relates to Times is that Times was so entwined with this small corner of record-collecting culture that the store often picked up the characteristics and style of its patrons.

Times never felt like a place where everyone was in it together, in spite of the strong bond from a common love of the music. It felt like a rabbit warren of intrigue, something close to 1943 Casablanca.

Yet conversely, it was also a full-immersion crash course in the music, which after just a few weeks became a second language in which anyone who paid attention could become fluent.

And this is just from a Connecticut kid who got there a couple of times a year. I can only imagine the impact on New York kids who went there every Saturday.

I remember going to the 1964 World's Fair with Mark and my family. We told Mom and Dad that Mark and I would like to explore a little on our own, if it was okay with them, and the minute they disappeared in the direction of the Pieta, we were on a 7 train to Times Square.

I'm not sure how we explained rejoining Mom and Dad later in the day with two boxes of records

For "Slim", I guess, Times Square Records was one more short-lived attempt to grab a brass ring, to become more than another subway arcade hustler whose concept of success was making the rent with enough left over to show a hot girl a good time on Saturday night.

The fact he happened to create a place that became a catalyst for collecting and preserving a great style of American music was doubtless to him entirely accidental.

You hope that gave him some satisfaction and that he didn't think of Times only as a place where most of the money never got to his cash register.

You hope that once in a while he laughed, which he never seemed to do at Times.

You hope that even as he helped popularize what's called street-corner harmony, he wasn't what he looked like – the kind of guy who, if he heard kids singing on the corner one summer night, would lean out the window and tell them to shut up.

****Author's Note – This chapter was written by David Hinckley. He emailed it to me on July 16, 2006.

Driving Along In My Automobile

A Gal.... A Guy & A Car.....

Genevieve Miscavage

I first learned of Times Square Records from a bunch of guys who lived in Great Neck, Long Island. Diane and I would take the Long Island Railroad into Times Square. In those days it was "cool" to wear a black skirt with a matching scarf which often we did. We were referred to as "commuting hoods".

I was not quite 16 years old when I first met "Slim". The year was 1960. The store was located at 1475 Broadway. I had gone to the record shop with my boyfriend at the time, Billy Marinan looking for "My Heart's Desire" by the Wheels. "Slim" had the record for $3.00. He let me purchase it for $1.00.

It was not long after that first visit I began to work at the store. "Slim" traveled out to Great Neck meeting with my mother. At first my mother was hesitant as she did not like the idea of my traveling back and forth into the city at night. "Slim" gave his word that he would look out for me; allowing no harm to come to me. After much discussion and badgering on my part; my mother finally gave her consent for me to work at Times Square Records. I was not yet 16, it was the spring or early summer of 1960 as my 16th birthday would be in August that same year. I needed to have my mother sign so I could get my "working papers" along with a social security number. "Slim" helped my mother with both. Soon I had my first job...working at Times Square Records.

I was working at the store when Teddy was a baby. He was too little to stay alone at the store at night. I would take him home with me. Teddy was so small he fit inside my purse which was the size of a feedbag. Back and forth we traveled on the Long Island Railroad together. Once Teddy was old enough to be on his own he stayed at the store during the night.

I would open a small spot in my purse and Teddy would stick his head out looking all around while we would ride the train. The conductor knew I had Teddy with me and often he would bring grapes for him.

Although Teddy was a cute little critter he became nasty. He would attack people's feet when they came into the store. There were many times that I remember jumping up on the radiator to avoid Teddy's claws. The little raccoon was good at ripping my stockings. Eventually, "Slim" placed Teddy on a farm in upstate New York.

My most vivid memory is the "Wall Of Records". Harold was the one responsible for putting the records on the wall. He would take a record sleeve, cut it in half and print the name of the record, artist and dollar amount before hanging it up on the wall. His handwriting was beautiful. I recall how we would try to duplicate his handwriting. Harold was our "resident artist".

Jerry Greene and Mike (I seem to recall the last name Harris) worked on the side of the store where the records where cheaper. They played the requests from customers on the phonograph. Harold, "Slim" and I worked the side of the store where the "Wall Of Records" was located. Harold was the only full time employee at the time.

My relationship with "Slim" was a friendship although "Slim" wanted it to be much more. He was an older man with power who knew influential people. Times Square Records was the "in" place to be and I wanted to be part of the "magic and mystique". I enjoyed going out on the town with him. "Slim" had a heart of gold. He was very good to me.

"Slim" was the one who gave me the name Genni. My full name is Genevieve. He said we'll call you Jenny and spell it Genni. I do not like the name Jenny. I have an old maiden aunt whose name is Jenny. She is called "Witch Jenny". I prefer to be called Gen.

I was in a group called the Chic-Lets. The other members were my sister Diane, Jeanne Wilowski and her sister Linda. Linda sang with the group on occasion. The majority of the time it was Diane, Jeanne and I who made up the Chic-Lets. We sang on the radio shows and at the Audubon Ballroom Shows. We did record a few demos that Diane still has in her possession. We did not make a record as "Slim" did not feel we were good enough to record.

Originally "Slim" bought time on the Night Train Show which was hosted by Alan Fredericks. Alan Fredericks would come by the shop helping "Slim" go through the records which were to be played on the air. "Slim" decided it was too expensive for time on the radio. He said "he could be just as good" as Alan Fredericks and thus began the radio show with "Slim" at the helm.

I badgered him mercifully to be on the show. He wrote all the scripts himself. One of the lines he wrote was "Irving Rose sat on a stove and Irving Rose". I learned so much working with him on the radio show. It was an enjoyable experience for me; one that I will never forget.

"Slim" had a bad "smoker's" cough. He would make a gesture across his neck when he was coughing to go to a commercial break because he didn't want his audience to hear the cough. I recall that one of the sponsors was Carolina Rice.

I did not know "Slim's" wife Arlene. She never visited the store at either location. I do recall "Slim" telling me a story about the time they went to either Reno or Las Vegas Nevada on a vacation. They were in one of the casinos where "Slim" lost all his money. He went to the manager of the casino to tell him he had no money to get back home. The manager gave "Slim" enough money so they could get home and told "Slim" never to return to the casino.

"Slim" takes the money and instead of leaving he goes next door to another casino where he again loses all his money. On the drive back home it was foggy. "Slim" ran off the road ending up in a backyard. He drove through a clothes line ending up with the clothes on the hood of the car.

I wanted desperately to own a car. Everyone wanted a car when they turned 16...I was no different. My father died when I was very young, leaving my mother to raise Diane and I on her own. Virginia was the oldest out of the three of us. She had graduated high school and was already "trying to find her place" in the world. Diane and I were "wild". My mother had her hands full raising the two of us.

"Slim" and I would discuss my having my own car. In the spring of 1961 "Slim" once again traveled out to Great Neck to meet with my mother regarding the purchase of a car for me. My mother was a "little uneasy" about the idea of my driving back and forth into the city alone in all the traffic and at night. She felt as though this was a "giant step" for a 16 year old. "Slim" again told her he would accept full responsibility for me and the car.

He made a promise to my mother that nothing would happen to me...he would make sure of that.

"Slim" and I went to a dealership in New Rochelle, New York to purchase a car in the spring of 1961. The car was a 1961 white Pontiac Bonneville convertible. The car was only a few months old, with few miles on it and in good condition. "Slim" paid the dealership that day and I had my car.

I wanted to make payments on the car before I actually had it in my possession. "Slim" said no that he would pay for the car upfront and I was to pay him back weekly. We agreed on an amount to be paid back each week. Being a minor at the time, the car was registered to Times Square Records and he put the car on his insurance policy which was also paid by me. My mother knew of this agreement to repay "Slim" and approved. "Slim" always met with my mother to discuss matters that pertained to me or Diane...never doing anything until he met with her and had her permission first. As a matter of fact "Slim" spoke to all the parents. He would take the time to call them to ask how they were or to call and let the parent know their child would be late coming home, etc. That was the type of person "Slim" really was.....

All the paperwork for the car was kept in the cash register. "Slim" kept a log for the both of us to review. Each Friday I would give "Slim" my payment for the car. He would take the paperwork out of the register, note the date and amount and return it to the same spot. The title to the car and registration where kept in the same place as well. Any of the employees had access to the cash register...they also had access to the loan for my car. All documentation was there in plain view in the cash register for them to read. Nothing was ever kept hidden nor was it a secret.

Then came the problem of my age....I had a junior operator's license....requiring me to have a person over age 21 to be with me at all time while driving and I was not able to drive after 9 pm at night.

To make a long story short....I went to Mr. Bird who taught Shop at the high school. I was in my junior year. I told him that I wanted to learn about the mechanics of a car. I badgered him about getting into shop class. I knew if I did this he would offer me driver's education as he taught that as well. Back then you were not able to take driver's education in your junior year. The only possible way to do this was "under special circumstances". Since I did not meet the criteria, I came up with the idea about taking shop classes. Sure enough Mr. Bird gave in and by the end of June, 1961 I had completed my course in driver's education which meant I know would receive a senior driver's license allowing me to drive alone and after 9 o'clock at night.

I was working at the Rolling Hills Summer Day Camp and at the store. I was employed there full time for the summers of 1962 and 1963. My oldest sister Virginia insisted it would be a smart move on my part to have this listed on my resume as I was starting college in the fall of September, 1963 majoring in English. My goal was to be a teacher.

One summer day in 1963 while I was at Rolling Hills, Diane stole my car taking her friends for a joy ride. At the time Diane had no driver's license. She was an under age driver. In New Hyde Park she went through an intersection hitting another car coming the other way totaling out the car. Luckily no one was injured. When the police arrived Diane told them she was eighteen. A police report was taken. Diane was taken to Long Island Jewish Hospital where she was treated and released for minor injuries.

Diane called "Slim" first and told him "Gen is going to kill me". "Slim" asked her why and what had happened. "Slim" then called my mother to tell her about the accident. "Slim" made the arrangements to have the car towed to a garage in New Hyde Park which was located next to a church.

While at work that day, I received a telephone call from my mother informing me of the accident. I immediately went to the garage where the car had been towed. Diane recalls the name of the garage as Rudy's. Both "Slim" and Diane were there waiting for me. When Diane saw me walking towards Rudy's, she ran off into St. Aloysius hiding in the confessional, thinking I wouldn't do anything to her if she was inside a church. I was livid!! My hard earned money used to pay back "Slim" for almost two years gone....my car was a piece of junk!!

"Slim" and Diane went to the police department in New Hyde Park where "Slim" took care of everything. No criminal charges were ever filed against her.

The insurance company paid directly to "Slim" the value of the 1961 Pontiac Bonneville at the time of the accident. When "Slim" received payment from the insurance company, the balance I owed him was paid in full.

"Slim" also purchased a 1961 Blue Plymouth Fury for Martha and Julius Garcia. They were the couple that helped "Slim" raise his son Bobby after Arlene had gone to Detroit. In reality Martha Garcia was Bobby's great aunt meaning Arlene's mother was in fact Martha's sister. Martha and Julius Garcia adopted Arlene at an early age and raised her. "Slim" pampered and spoiled Bobby. He made sure that Martha and Julius Garcia were compensated for helping him.

"Slim" also owned a 1961 Black Plymouth Fury and had a phonograph installed in the car. We all thought it was "cool" that "Slim" had the phonograph in the car. I remember thinking how great it was to be able to go through the tunnels and still hear the music playing.

There was a parking garage on 42nd Street where "Slim" had made arrangements for my car along with his car to be parked during the hours I worked at the store. I don't remember the name of the parking garage. However, I do remember driving my car into a box and having it taken away. To me that was wild!!

After closing the store at night we would go to the French Romanian Restaurant. One particular night "Chubby" went with us. On our way to Brooklyn taking "Chubby" home; "Slim" had the phonograph playing in the car. The song was "Green Onions". "Chubby" and I made "Slim" drive the car to the beat of that song. It was hysterical.

After the store closed one night, Mike, "Slim" and I went to a restaurant a block or so away to have a spaghetti dinner. After dinner we all went to the basement where there was an all night "poker game. I don't remember if this game was planned or any of the details. What I do remember is "Slim" squaring it away with my mother so I could stay all night and watch everyone play cards. I only ever recall attending one of the "all night games" however Mike and "Slim" did it all the time

"Slim" also loved the ponies...the trotters....his favorite track was Roosevelt Raceway. He had a system. By reading the morning line and figuring out different things about the horse "Slim" would then go to the track and bet. Depending on what the final odds paid was the deciding factor on the amount of the bet "Slim" placed on a pony. "Slim" would wait to the very last minute before the race would start, run up to the window and place his bet. This went on for an entire summer.....I don't recall the year, however I do remember "Slim" doing very well. I went many times with "Slim" to the track that summer.

We all were shocked to learn that Jerry Greene was leaving Times Square Records. Diane was in love with Jerry and she was devastated to learn the news. We were told he was leaving, getting married and moving to Philadelphia with Jared Weinstein. No other information was given. No one could understand why the sudden move. Jerry and Jared Weinstein had no friends or family in Philadelphia.

I left Times Square Records in my sophomore year of college. It was becoming increasingly hard for me to commute back and forth from Long Island to Times Square. I tried to stay in touch with "Slim" however lost contact with him once he sold the store.

I have fond memories of "Slim" and Times Square Records. Over the years I have often wondered what ever happened to Irving "Slim" Rose. I am glad to finally have closure to that chapter in my life.

Author's Note Gen Miscavage Snyder was born in Great Neck, New York. She attended Hofstra University in Hempstead, New York where she earned a Bachelor's Degree in English. At the age of 50, Ms. Snyder returned to school where she earned twenty four credits in accounting. She is currently employed by the State Of New York as a Sales Tax Auditor.

Information in this chapter came from several interviews with Ms. Snyder in June, 2006.

The Making Of "There's A Moon Out Tonight"

Three Different View Points

By Al Trommers, Wayne Stierle & Jerry Greene

In this chapter you will read viewpoints of what transpired with the song "There's A Moon Out Tonight". I will present to you each story exactly as told to me. Nothing has been edited for this book. I have been granted written permission from those parties who have shared their viewpoint with me. The reader will be left to drawn their own conclusion. I am merely the storyteller.

View Point One As Told To Me
By Al Trommers

There were/are four partners who bought the Master to "There's A Moon Out Tonight"- Al Trommers, Jerry Greene, Jared Weinstein and Johnny Esposito.

Johnny Esposito, who at the time, was an employee at Times Square Records was out and about looking for records. He stumbled upon ODO Studios. He went inside to inquire about purchasing a few 45's. Among the records purchased was the song "There's A Moon Out Tonight" by the Capris.

After leaving ODO Studios, Johnny Esposito went back to Times Square Records to play the 45's for "Slim". Jerry Greene was working that day and Al Trommers was at the store. Listening to the stack of 45's on the phonograph, the only good song out of the lot was "There's A Moon Out Tonight". "Slim" immediately liked this record. "Slim" wanted this record!! It was taken to Alan Fredericks to play on his Night Train Show.

Immediately Jerry Greene, Johnny Esposito and Al Trommers became partners. According to Al Trommers he is not sure when Jared Weinstein came in on the deal. It was decided between the three of them to go back to Planet Records and purchase one hundred copies to sell to "Slim".

"Slim" purchased the copies and sold them in less than a week. They went back the following week to purchase another one hundred copies and they sold just as fast. The third week they went back to purchase another one hundred copies to find Planet Records did not have any left and had no plans to press more.

At this point a decision needed to be made. It was decided the four of them would buy the master to "There's A Moon Out Tonight" from Planet Records. The cost of the master was $200.00. They were offered to purchase the publishing rights however declined the offer. Hy Weiss would later purchase the publishing rights to the song. The attorney retained for the original master agreement was Jacob Weinstock. (Jacob Weinstock was also "Slim's" attorney). Al Trommers indicates that there was no equal partnership. Johnny Esposito had little money back then. His share was less than the others.

The four of them now own the master. The song is playing on the radio and beginning to take off. They are no longer able to purchase copies of the record to sell to "Slim". It is decided they would start their own label and have the records pressed themselves. Now the four partners need a name for their new label. Jared Weinstein, Johnny Esposito and Jerry Greene could not come up with a name for the record label. Al Trommers already had the name Lost Nite and sketches done as he was going to start his own label. It is agreed to call the label Lost Nite by the four partners.

The original design for the Lost Nite label would include the wavy lines from Specialty, the cocktail glasses from the After Hours, and the musical notes from Red Robin label. Everyone liked the look of the label. The sketches for Lost Nite would never be used as there was not enough time to have the label printed. The first Lost Nite label issued was done using straight print. The color of the label was pink. Included on the label was the address 47 East 44th Street which was the office location for Al Trommers during the day at J. Press Clothing. It was only logical to use this address as the location for Lost Nite Records as Al Trommers had an office along with access to incoming and outgoing telephone calls. Jared Weinstein worked full time during the day at the Brooklyn Navy Yard and both Johnny Esposito and Jerry Greene worked part time at Times Square Records.

The labels were ordered and printed. Al Trommers picked up labels, paid for them and took them back to his office at J. Press Clothing. The record itself was pressed in Spanish Harlem. Al Trommers went to Harlem, picks up the records, pays for them and brings them back to his office. It is indicated by Al Trommers that Jerry Greene, Jared Weinstein and Johnny

Esposito had very little involvement during this time. The year according to Al Trommers is late 1959.

Moving along the time line......"There's A Moon Out Tonight" is taken to Murray the K for air play. Each night Murray the K has a contest where listeners call in to vote for their favorite record. The first night "There's A Moon Out Tonight" is played the Capris win. The Capris would continue to win each night for an entire week.

Sam Weiss is present when Murray the K listens to the song. Sam Weiss liked the record right away and orders 10,000 copies as the story goes.

The four partners did not have the money between the four of them to have 10,000 copies pressed. Sam Weiss suggests to them they contact his brother, Hy Weiss, owner of Old Town Records.

According to Al Trommers he is the one who met with Hy Weiss about leasing the master to Old Town Records. A meeting takes place. Old Town Records signs a contract for "There's A Moon Out Tonight". The Capris sign with Old Town Records. "There's A Moon Out Tonight" became a national hit.

The story does not end here......Many years have now passed.... It is now the mid 1990s.......

Al Trommers is watching late night television....a commercial is on with Time Warner advertising their collection of "Golden Goodies" on compact disc. One of the records listed and playing is "There's A Moon Out Tonight". Al Trommers becomes furious. Years and years have passed by without any royalties from Old Town Records. During this hiatus Jerry Greene continued to do business with Hy Weiss on a regular basis.

Immediately Al Trommers contacts Jerry Greene to ask him if he is leasing "There's A Moon Out Tonight" to Time Warner. Jerry Greene's answer is no...Hy Weiss is the one doing the leasing. Hy Weiss did not own the master to "There's A Moon Out Tonight" therefore had no right to lease it to Time Warner. Several days later Jerry Greene contacts Al Trommers to let him know that Hy Weiss sold Old Town Records along with the master to "There's A Moon Out Tonight" to Music Sales, Inc located in New York City.

The year the sale took place is 1996. By now Al Trommers is enraged and ready to sue.

It is agreed between Jerry Greene and Al Trommers they would sue Hy Weiss. They would use Jerry Greene's attorney at the time, Stuart Levy from the law firm of Archer & Levy. Proceedings commence with the beginning of a lawsuit begins against Hy Weiss. Letters are going back and forth between Stuart Levy and Hy Weiss.

Suddenly all correspondence ends just as fast as it began between all parties involved. Al Trommers receives a call from Jerry Greene advising him that he no longer wishes to proceed with the lawsuit against Hy Weiss. The reason is given to Al Trommers; however this author chose not to disclose it in the book. I am reminded by Al Trommers that Hy Weiss and Jerry Greene continued on throughout the years doing business together.

Al Trommers is on his own now to go after Hy Weiss. He retains his own attorney, Edward Kellman who at the time was located in Manhattan. Once again proceedings commence with a lawsuit against Hy Weiss.

Hy Weiss is served with the paperwork. Realizing now that Al Trommers is serious about getting back his ownership to the master "There's A Moon Out Tonight" and the royalties due him from the onset when original lease was signed between Old Town Records and Lost Nite; Hy Weiss agrees to settle out of court for an undisclosed amount.

It is now somewhere between 1997 and 1998....Al Trommers learns that during the first lawsuit with Hy Weiss using Jerry Greene's attorney, Stuart Levy, two checks were sent to Jerry Greene in the amount of $1,500.00 for royalties. Al Trommers never received his check. Al Trommers also learns that after the original contract was signed with Hy Weiss to lease "There's A Moon Out Tonight" Jerry Greene and Jared Weinstein went to Old Town Records together and received advances in royalties. Years would pass until the time of the lawsuit that Al Trommers would learn about the advancement of royalties.

In closing, Al Trommers has won back his part ownership to "There's A Moon Out Tonight" from Music Sales, Inc. Royalties are remitted on a regular basis directly to Al Trommers not only on "There's A Moon Out Tonight, but the flip side "Indian Girl". According to Al Trommers, Jerry

Greene was annoyed at the time of the settlement between Hy Weiss and himself. All business dealings and communication ended amongst the two of them. Jerry Greene continues to receive royalties from Music Sales, Inc.

Jared Weinstein suffered a massive stroke sometime in the early 90's now resides in a nursing home in New Jersey. Since Jared Weinstein and Johnny Esposito did not come forward regarding their part ownership of "There's A Moon Out Tonight" their shares were automatically transferred over to Music Sales, Inc. The source of this information is from a telephone interview with Philip Black who works in the copyright division of Music Sales, Inc. The interview took place on April 18, 2006.

View Point Two As Told To Me By Jerry Greene

Jerry Greene first heard "There's A Moon Out Tonight" when someone brought it into the store for fifty cents credit. The record was on the Planet Record label. Jerry Greene gave it to Alan Fredericks to play one Saturday night and offered one dollar in credit to anyone who brought the record to the store. Since we did not get one copy that entire week, the next offer went to five dollars in credit for the record. That same week "Slim" also received about a hundred requests for "There's A Moon Out Tonight".

Approximately two weeks later, Jerry Greene received a call at the store from Johnny Esposito. Johnny Esposito was a part time employee Jerry Greene had hired to work at the store. He was calling from a pay phone on 50th Avenue and Broadway outside Planet Records. He told Jerry Greene he had just purchased ten copies of "There's A Moon Out Tonight" for sixty cents each. That afternoon when Johnny Esposito returned to the store Al Trommers and Jared Weinstein were there.

That very same day the three of them put in fifteen dollars each and purchased one hundred copies of "There's A Moon Out Tonight" for sixty dollars. They sold the one hundred copies to "Slim" for one hundred dollars netting themselves a profit of forty dollars. It took a little over a week for "Slim" to sell the one hundred copies of "There's A Moon Out Tonight".

The following week the three of them purchased another one hundred copies from Planet Records for the previous price and sold them to "Slim" again for one hundred dollars. Those copies sold out quickly.

Going back to Planet Records for the third straight week to purchase more copies of "There's A Moon Out Tonight" they hit a snag...Planet Records had no more copies to sell. The owner of Planet Records offered to sell the master of "There's A Moon Out Tonight" for two hundred dollars. For an additional ten dollars, they could purchase the publishing rights. Jerry Greene, Al Trommers, Johnny Esposito and Jared Weinstein would become equals in a partnership to purchase the master to "There's A Moon Out Tonight". Each partner contributed fifty dollars. The partners passed on the purchase of the publishing rights.

According to Jerry Greene as told to me in an interview dated the first week of November, 2006 this is his assumption of how "Slim" felt about "There's A Moon Out Tonight". When the record started to take off and become popular, "Slim" felt "There's A Moon Out Tonight" should have been his record because he was paying for the Alan Fredericks Show. "Slim" felt that anything that pertained to the store or happened at the store should have stayed at the store. According to Jerry Greene, "Slim" had no problem with buying the records from him. "Slim" never came out and said he was angry over the deal with "There's A Moon Out Tonight" to Jerry Greene...however after the success of "There's A Moon Out Tonight" tension grew between the two of them. According to Jerry Greene "Slim's" body language said it all....there were no needs to words....

Jerry Greene did not elaborate on his part in the lawsuit against Hy Weiss.

However, he did relay to me that he was upset with the fact that Al Trommers had spoken to me regarding the lawsuit. Jerry Greene felt as though Al Trommers had no right to discuss the lawsuit.

View Point Three As Told To Me By Wayne Stierle

We had developed ways of tracking down small record companies that no one else had even dreamed of doing. (Donn Fileti and myself, as well as the both of us independently). While others were doing the obvious things, such as looking in the phone book, or calling distributors, we were really going at it like detectives.

This meant going to BMI and ASCAP to track down the address of a publisher. It meant creative things like noticing a writing credit that always showed up on a label, and calling everyone with that last name, in New York, New Jersey, and sometimes Connecticut. (Assuming it was a "New York Area" record). It meant tracking down the vocal group in the same fashion, and even the band, if one was credited. It was long hours of effort, but it made sense.

After re-issuing such records as "Baby Oh Baby" and "Rama Lama Ding Dong", tracking down "There's A Moon Out Tonight" wasn't all that tough. This recording, despite the fact that "Slim" wanted copies, was considered a "weak" record, as it was sung by a white group, and the field was dominated by far better black groups. Still, I found the people who had released it, and they didn't care to lease it to me, but rather wanted to be rid of it, and offered it to me for about $300.00. I couldn't afford it, but I could somehow raise the money in a couple weeks.

Going from that meeting, I proceeded to Times, where I honestly felt that it was understood that whoever was currently working on a record, had "staked out that territory". Furthermore, I felt that "Slim" somehow would be like a cop, and "keep the peace" in that area. I was trusting, fair, and I was wrong. I told "Slim" I would soon have "There's A Moon Out Tonight", and it didn't phase me that Jerry Greene was standing right there listening. "Slim" wanted to know how I had located the master, and I explained the basic processes I used.

Why "Slim" didn't put up the money and go with me that very day and buy the master is still a wonder to me, but "Slim" had not yet heeded my suggestions to start his own label, and was happy to rely on supplies being brought to him. (This was a crucial point in time, because no real hits had come out of Times yet, and though we didn't know it, "Baby Oh Baby" was just about to start breaking big. The point is that the "hit record" perspective did not exist yet).

The story ends here for me. As I went back to Jersey to begin trying to raise the money to buy "There's A Moon Out Tonight", Jerry Greene managed to assemble several guys who hung around Times, and with their pooled monies, he grabbed the master. (The people involved were not told by Greene, anything about my efforts.) It's worth noting that Greene offered no part of it to "Slim", Harold, or me.

By around 1981, when I was still dumb, I assumed we had all "mellowed" with time, and "Slim" had died not long before that. I sent Jerry Greene a note about his father undergoing open heart surgery, and I enclosed excellent copies of my original photos of Times Square Records, that I had taken, for his personal interest. In the 90's, when Jerry Greene released his "Times Square Records" cds, he stole my photos for several cd covers. I wasn't paid or credited. Let me be clear, I took those photos myself, and I own them. I think the moral is clear in this story, but if it isn't, let's just say that no one should swim too near a stingray.

****Author's Note – Hy Weiss passed away March 20, 2007 in Englewood, New Jersey.

Al Trommers viewpoint was provided to me from interviews in the spring 2006.

Jerry Greene's viewpoint was provided from liner notes The Capris Morse Code Of Love CD on Collectibles #5450 and an interview with Jerry Greene on November 10, 2006. He was sent a transcription of the interview on November 13, 2006 for his approval. It was returned to me on November 17, 2006 with his signed approval.

Wayne Stierle's viewpoint was emailed to me the early fall of 2006.

The Strange Saga Of "Stormy Weather"

The Hype...The Baloney & Maybe Even Some Truth

Wayne Stierle

Try to imagine New York City somewhat transfixed by a cosmic treasure hunt to locate a record that no one had ever seen or heard! A record that many people believed didn't even exist! Imagine that mania spreading out to New Jersey, and then the rest of the country. Well, it actually happened.

So HOW did this possible dud of a totally unknown and unheard record become wildly famous? One thing is for sure: Only at Times Square Records could this have happened!

I have both my own opinion, and my facts right from inside Times Square Records on this story. First let's look at what is the basic story that has existed since day one on what became known as "The Rarest Record In History".

The record is a 78 of the classic song "Stormy Weather", as recorded by an unknown group, The Five Sharps, on Jubilee Records in what was believed to be 1952. The Jubilee record number is the infamous Jubilee 5104, which would be burned into our brains for years, whether we wanted it there or not. (The "B" side, "Sleepy Cowboy" was an original song that was assumed to have been written by the group, and like the "A" side, it was a title we wouldn't soon forget.)

"Stormy Weather" by The Five Sharps was a record that no one had ever heard of, and since the song is basically known as a female torch ballad, you could tell without even hearing it, that it probably wasn't much of a "group" record, and could even have been a dreary R&B/jazz recording of no saving grace at all. (Jubilee Records, though a sometimes dependable label, was a "hit and miss" operation and so there was no reason to expect this record to be outstanding, though it was possible). Yet this questionable record became famous for nothing more than having never been heard and for being seemingly impossible to find! (This was totally against the concept of almost all rare records, which are sought after for rarity and quality of the group and the song). There were very few of us, from the original group of record collectors who expected this record to sound particularly good, or even be a genuine "group" record of the type that Times Square Records thrived on.

A collector, Billy Pensabene is credited with having found the record and having brought it in to Times. I knew Billy, and he told a few different versions of the story, over the years. (Perhaps the best known explanation is that the record had been initially found by collectors Sam Wood and Ricky Nelson, in an electronic repair shop somewhere in the lost and confused continent of Brooklyn. Going through piles of 78's, both Ricky and Sam had passed on "Stormy Weather" after playing it. With a second visit to the store they again played and rejected it. After all, the store wanted 25 cents for it! On the third visit, Pensabene came along with Wood and Nelson, and again it was played and not wanted, that is except for Pensabene, who slapped down a full quarter for it, with the blessings of both Nelson and Wood.) No one knows how much time elapsed before Billy brought it to "Slim", who seemed to like it only because of the thunder sound effects in the opening. "Slim" supposedly borrowed the record to play on The Times Square radio show, and rumor has it that he only cared to play it because of the thunder. Considering what I'll tell you later, it's not really likely "Slim" would play a Jubilee record that he didn't have copies of to sell. It cannot be proven if "Slim" did or didn't play the record on the radio. My bet is that he didn't. In fact, it seems that nothing happened at all of any interest that is until the record was broken! (Assuming it wasn't actually cracked right from the start.).

How did the record get cracked? No one really knows, or can prove it either way! The very first story I heard was that Billy had carried it under his winter coat and it cracked. Then the story became that "Slim" put it under his coat and bumped into the door at Times, and it cracked. Then the story changed to "Slim" cracking it as he left the radio station carrying it under his coat. "Slim" seemed to enjoy claiming that Teddy the raccoon had broken it, which was possible as "Slim" said the record was sitting on top of the 45's near the register, and Teddy simply walked over and laid down on it. (The 45's were an uneven surface, and Teddy could easily crack a brittle 78). If "Slim" was taking the record to the radio station, it would have been in a box with the other records he was taking. Would it make sense, or even seem possible, that he was locking up the store, going up the subway stairs, and through the streets of New York carrying the money from the store, and a box of records, plus a 78 under his coat? Is this possible? Maybe...Is it logical? No. Now, assume he broke it when he left the radio station. That still means "Slim" is carrying everything already mentioned. ("Slim" carried the store money from each day in his pocket!). So far, this isn't even a tale worth telling.

Now the story takes wing. Whether or not anything is totally accurate so far, the next thing did happen. "Slim" went on the air and offered a small cash amount for a copy of "Stormy Weather", for the rather dubious reason of replacing the copy Billy had brought in. This isn't like "Slim" at all, for he, more true to character would have paid Billy a few bucks and ended it there. But, he did announce on the radio that he was looking for this particular record. Each week he raised the price a little. This wasn't unusual for Times Square Records, but for no good reason other than dumb luck, the story was written about in a newspaper, and mentioned on a few radio programs, almost as a "semi-news" story. "Slim" raised the price, seeing that he was getting free publicity out of this. As the price of the 78 rose, "Slim" offered even more for a 45 rpm single, which most of us believed had never been made at all. (Jubilee Records didn't press all their releases on 45's in 1952, and when they did, it was with the records that had some life to them, such as The Orioles singles.)

Somehow this "search" hit a nerve with the public. While the original collectors didn't think the record would be any good, we still got involved in the hunt. The regular customers and new collectors seemed to think the record might be fantastic, and they took to it with fevered anticipation. The general public who didn't know a vocal group from a flock of New York pigeons also got involved and interested. "Stormy Weather" seemed to be floating over Manhattan like the Goodyear Blimp. It really became a true happening, and the center of the speculation, both positive and negative, was Times Square Records! The "news" stories kept coming, and "Slim" kept raising the prices. "Stormy Weather" had taken on a life of its' own, and become better known than most of the truly great records that had built Times Records. "Slim" kept raising the price, with the 45 going slowly over time, up to $500.00, and the 78 going up to about half the price of the 45. In the store, "Slim" had even recklessly acted as the gambler he really was and offered $1,000 for the 45, in a statement he didn't repeat on the air. For me, it didn't feel right, and I became more and more positive that somehow "Slim" actually knew for sure that there was no 45 version ever pressed.

Although the "craze" for "Stormy Weather" continued, it was subject to ebbs and flows of interest, and as a "news story" it eventually fell off the radar with the general public. There was an uneasy unreality beginning to build about this, and over time it eventually started to wear out its' welcome, as the "search" continued on for two years before slowing to a crawl! Record collectors and false leads kept the story alive. But, the record was simply not to be found at all.

Stories circulated that the record was phony and never had existed, but would-be reporters found that there really was a Jubilee Records, and Jubilee confirmed that indeed the record was real. It was a counter-balance situation, where "Slim" seemed to non-collectors to be a con artist creating a smoke-and-mirrors trick, and Jubilee Records at the other end of the balancing act, proving it was a legit record company that had actually released "Stormy Weather" back in 1952. The "fake versus genuine" debate kept the story alive, even when record collectors were tiring of the treasure hunt. "Slim" continued to announce his offer on the radio, sometimes accusing the audience of not trying hard enough!

Jubilee Records claimed that several of their masters had been destroyed, including "Stormy Weather", and so the chance of Times Square Records actually causing another odd sales sensation seemed, well, rather slim. (Although the Jubilee story of destruction was weak and self-contradictory, it is almost impossible to think that they wouldn't have released the record if they could have found it, based on what seemed like a ground swell of interest, and the fact that Jubilee was losing steam rapidly as an active record company.)

The whole crazed aura surrounding "Stormy Weather" was the kind of thing that really clicked with the crazies who weren't record collectors at all. As for those unglued record collectors, (and you know who you are), it was a natural for them as well. The phone calls poured into the store about the record, and a million questions were attempted to be tossed at "Slim", who ignored the questions and snapped, "....if ya got it bring it in...if ya don't then go and find it...". Every now and then someone would call and say they found it, and were coming in with it. The first time this happened, we all waited and watched, and even "Slim", jaded as he was seemed to be on the lookout. It was a fake call, naturally, and after that any claims were met with less than belief. It was like "Slim" had created a Halloween prank, and New Yorkers liked the game, and went out of their way to play the same prank in reverse on Times Square Records. "Stormy Weather" was becoming some sort of urban myth that had risen up from the subway and like a ghost it wandered the streets of New York, daring people to find it. Many regular record stores were so sick and tired of being asked about it, that they automatically told their customers it was all a hoax. The truth is that most people could not believe a record made by a record company that was still in business wouldn't be released. Therefore, the assumption was that there was no such record, and that Times Square Records had "invented" the non-existing record for nothing more than a cheap attempt at generating interest for their store. It dragged on so long that there was a certain amount of anger building against Times, although' the regular Times Records customers were simply growing tired of the whole thing, and were waiting for the next interesting fiasco to take its place.

One day in latter 1963 "Slim" tells me he's going to record "Stormy Weather" and call the group The Five Sharps, and put it out. I liked the idea and was hoping it could be done as a real hard core group recording, with a falsetto lead and booming bass voice. I even found that I could get The Shells, The Dubs, or The Royal Kings to record it, for a flat fee, under The Five Sharps name. (The Dubs would do it with Richard Blandon in the background). To my surprise, "Slim" had actually fallen victim to believing his own publicity, and he told me he didn't want to make a great record, but just a cheap recording of "Stormy Weather". My arguments against this fell on deaf ears, and "Slim" told me point blank, ".......if it's "Stormy Weather" by The Five Sharps, it'll sell because everybody wants it......". He really had been seduced by the interest he had created, and while I thought this was a total waste, he managed to make the cheap, boring recording he thought was all that was necessary to sell a ton of records. "Slim" was convinced that no one cared what it sounded like, as long they could just own a copy of this much talked about, unknown and unheard record. To my further horror, "Slim" was not interested in creating a song called "Sleepy Cowboy" to be the flip side. I couldn't imagine changing the flip side title, after all the interest it generated. "Slim" was underestimating the customers that he himself had helped introduce great vocal group recordings to since 1959. It had all the signs of a classic blunder just waiting to happen. On the other hand, Times Records had turned many a blunder into a success.

And so in early 1964, Times Square Records released a less than interesting recording of "Stormy Weather", complete with an opening of thunder. "Slim" backed away from the collectors' possible backlash associated with using The Five Sharps name, by calling the group, The Five Sharks. It wasn't exactly the worst record ever made, but it was among the most unwanted of records.

Directly following this clumsy move, Jubilee Records stumbled in the same way, and released a new recording of "Stormy Weather" by a slightly modern sounding group they called The Five Sharps. (Also with a thunder opening). Jubilee made an even bigger mistake than Times Square Records, for Jubilee not only failed to come up with a "Sleepy Cowboy" song for the flip side, but they pressed it on a new Jubilee label and didn't use the infamous number 5104! Both Jubilee and Times Square seemed to be in a contest for the least needed single of the year, and they may both have deserved the award. (With two years to obtain a lead sheet of their "Sleepy Cowboy" from the copyright office, or most likely, their own filing cabinet, Jubilee hadn't even bothered).

The public was not interested, and hard core collectors were neither impressed nor amused. These two dismal releases had all but destroyed what was left of the "Stormy Weather" craze. The already shrinking balloon had been punctured with a phonograph needle taking the role usually reserved for the fabled pin. (Collectors still sought the supposed pretender to the title of the holy grail of record collecting, but the interest had gone underground, and when "Slim" exited Times in 1965, things got unearthly quiet).

A decade later when a copy of the record finally emerged on a 78, it was the deadly recording many of us had suspected it would be. It was by most standards, a dull demo, with a boring group backed by just a piano. No one knew if Jubilee had actually known about it ahead of time, or had just taken it on after the tape was offered to them. No one knows how many copies were pressed, but the best guess is very few, with many of them, perhaps most of them, going to radio stations in New York, Philadelphia, Baltimore, and Washington D.C., as would make sense by Jubilee promotional patterns. Copies were probably sent to some record reviewers. None of this or any airplay can be truly confirmed. The Five Sharps had only recorded these two songs, and disbanded.

Interesting to note is that in time we were to learn that members of the group were actually far better than they sounded as The Five Sharps, and would emerge in fragments years later as major members of two respected vocal groups. Billy Vera, as you'll see following this paragraph was the person who uncovered the members of the actual Five Sharps! Billy quickly got the story, learning the group was made up of Clarence Bassett, Bobby Ward, Mickey Owens, Tommy Duckett, and Ronald Cuffey on lead vocals. The sole instrument on the record was a piano played by Tommy Duckett. Cuffey and Ward had written "Sleepy Cowboy", but their manager, Oscar Porter, had taken the writing credits for himself.

Billy Vera On His Discovery Of The Actual Five Sharps Group!

Like every other record collector who frequented Times Square Records in the subway, I was familiar with the legend of "Stormy Weather" by the Five Sharps. I'd heard it wasn't very good and didn't put any effort in locating a copy. By the early 70s oldies revival, the subject came up infrequently.

At that time, I was conducting and playing guitar for the Shirelles and several other acts on the circuit. During one short tour of New England, I found myself on the bus, seated next to one of the Cleftones. We were talking about groups that had come from the Cleftones' borough of Queens, specifically Jamaica: the Heartbeats, the Harmonaires. etc., and somehow the Five Sharps name came up. (I don't recall which of us mentioned them).

Herbie or Berman of The Cleftones, I forget which, said that the Five Sharps used to sing in the park where all the groups sang and that Shep, later of the Heartbeats, sometimes joined them. This was pretty big news, as, until that time no collector knew anything about the Sharps.

Cut to a few months later, and The Shirelles and I were doing an oldies show on Channel 13 in New York, along with the Cleftones, the Flamingos and others. The Cleftone I'd ridden on the bus with and I was standing together chatting and, all at once he pointed to a smallish guy with the Flamingos and said, "That's Clarence, he was in The Five Sharps. Want me to introduce you?"

Duh. By all means was my answer. Clarence Bassett laughed with surprise that anybody had ever heard of The Five Sharps. He also had no idea that collectors from around the country were searching for his record and willing to pay stupid prices for it. I thought one of the collector magazines might be interested in publishing his story, so we set up a time for an interview at his home in Queens.

Back in 1952, Clarence, the only member who had a job in the City, met one Oscar Porter, who arranged for the group to record at a small studio in

Harlem. Porter took the recording to Jubilee, who released it in limited quantity. Clarence said they heard the record just twice, once on Dr. Jive's show, and made only one or two appearances, one at the Royal Theater in Baltimore.

I asked if he'd ever seen a 45 of "Stormy Weather" and he thought there was a couple in his mother's attic. A search of Mom's house turned up, not only no 45s, but no 78s, either.

He said that he and Ronald Cuffey, The Sharps' lead singer, later were with the Videos, of "Trickle, Trickle" fame. This, after Clarence's apprenticeship as valet for The Heartbeats.

The funny thing was, I had met Clarence a few times in the 60s, when he was with Shep & The Limelites but, of course, the subject had never come up. And why should it? What self-respecting singer, who'd sung on actual hits, would care about some flop, one that wasn't even that good? Only a record collector, that's who.

Billy Vera

(The release of the real "Stormy Weather" record came about from Bim Bam Boom, a magazine devoted to keeping the spirit of the "Times" era alive. The record that was finally found was cracked and played a loud "click" with every revolution, thus needing to be de-clicked by editing a tape of the record carefully cutting out each click. Today, in digital editing, this is still a long process. The efforts to finally release the record included Ralph Newman, and the optimistic sparkplug of Bim Bam Boom, Marcia Vance).

My Opinion And Facts From The Inside Of Times

This is what I personally saw and know, along with my opinions, and I'm not going to mix facts with opinions. (That's the territory of record collectors and other people who shouldn't be allowed to write).

My Opinion is that the whole thing felt like a stunt to bring publicity to Times. It felt "off-kilter" right from the start. I think "Slim" never told anyone what he ended up really knowing about "Stormy Weather".

The Fact is that "Slim" side-stepped my best questions on this subject, and instead of saying something like "...I don't know that answer..", he was vague where there was no reason to be, unless he was avoiding something.

The Fact is that Jubilee Records handled the distribution of "In My Heart" by The Timetones, which gave "Slim" access to almost any Jubilee information he wanted. Despite the fact that "Slim" was not thrilled with the way "In My Heart" was over-pressed due to Jubilee over-ordering, he nonetheless had more "inside" information on Jubilee Records than any collector could ever have obtained in the early to mid 1960's. Keep in mind that Times Square Records was a store that just might have ended up causing Jubilee to have an unexpected hit record of some sort, as Times had already done several, no pun intended.

My Opinion is that because of the tight ties to Jubilee Records, "Slim" knew there had never been any 45's pressed, and that allowed him to continually raise the offering price. My opinion is that "Slim" knew exactly how many 78's had actually been pressed, or that Jubilee had given him the most likely figure.

My Opinion is that "Slim" never played the record on the air because it was actually a record that had no real attraction, and could be made to seem desirable as long as no one heard it.

My Opinion is that, given the inside Jubilee information, that "Slim" knew almost from the git-go that the masters had been destroyed or lost, long before Jubilee publicly stated that. My opinion is that "Slim" figured the free publicity would go on for a very long time before anyone ever found the record. ("Slim" was right, as the search actually came to a conclusion years after Times Square Records had closed and slipped into rock n' roll history).

This story always was, and still is, my least favorite aspect of the Times Records stories, as it seemed to have a cloud of doom hanging over it from the start. Of all the "trends" that Times Square Records started, this was the one that didn't really last as well and ultimately it was a shame that the record was ever found. Listen, you can hear the ominous thunder in the opening that may have actually been a warning signal.

Like my trip to the race track with "Slim", it was a funny experience, but there were no real winners that day. Similar to the horses "Slim" had bet on,

"Stormy Weather" had failed to cross the finish line, although it had been odds on winner when it started the race. But what a race it was!

****Author's Note – Wayne Stierle emailed this chapter to me on May 25, 2007. The author thanks Billy Vera for his input on the Stormy Weather saga.

"Slim" On The Radio "Live"
From Times Square Records
Wayne Stierle

"Slim" on the radio. Sounds like a crazy idea, and it was, but it came about naturally. Well, as "naturally" as everything else came about at Times, this is to say that most happenings at Times Records were on the other side of the looking glass.

"Slim" did not have any regard for disc jockeys and their vocal quality, or their sometimes-clever phrasings. "Slim" just wanted his records played, and the problem with a show he sponsored was that he could not get all the records played that he wanted to be aired. Although' "Slim" did not really know the music, he liked the truly crazy records, and if one of those happened to sell well, he was pleased to push it on the radio. The problem was that some of these strange records did not fit the program that "Slim" used. "Slim" felt that if he sponsored a show, every record played should be what he wanted played. The line between a commercial and a playlist did not exist for "Slim". He just did not understand the concept of only running a commercial, and letting the show be handled by the disc jockey.

This attitude, and rising ad costs, led "Slim" to doing his own shows. His belief that the point was to play records he had for sale was his only consideration or motivation. After a few very short-lived attempts, "Slim" ended up on the vast wasteland known as FM radio. At this point in time, there was nothing on FM, except classical music, horse races, and a re-broadcast of AM shows that ran on the FM stations owned by an AM station. It was a grim part of a vacant dial filled with static and boredom. In producing his first shows on FM, I produced the first commercial rock n' roll programs ever on FM radio, and "Slim" became the first commercial FM disc jockey for rock n' roll! Who knew that FM would ever mean anything? I n this world of the early sixties, AM was king, and so were good old mono records.

With an additional phone line installed for direct carrier to the station, "Slim" elected to broadcast directly from Times Records. (The "new" or second location we had just moved to.) It may have been insane, but we all took it very normally, as it was just another bizarre happening in a series of seemingly unending strangeness. That first show from the store was a little tense, and "Slim" opted to clear the store for the time the show was on. The table that served as the place for the turntable and mic, and "Slim" himself, was almost in the middle of the store. A crowd gathered outside the door, on the landing that led to the street, or to the subway. The crowd was getting out of hand, as the moment approached, and "Slim" finally relented and let in a few regulars, with the promise that they would remain quiet. The moment arrived, and the show was on the air, except only the intro on the radio told us that it was time, and the radio reception in the subway was really bad. The show stumbled onto the air in typical Times Records fashion, and the reality of it all was lost on us there in the store. There is an odd quiet in the air. We really do not know if the show is on. It is like doing a show in your room and thinking it is on the air. It is like pretend. "Slim", in his usual finesse, says on the air, "Are we on"? The records play, but in the store there is no feeling that they are going out into the airwaves of New York City and beyond. We are feeling the vacuum of being in a fallout shelter and wondering if an atomic war has started above us. We do not know anything. Outside the store, people are starting to knock on the window, and trying to force the door open. It is a form of mutiny, for the store seems open, and yet it is closed, and signs that inform them that there is a radio show in progress do not faze this crowd. This is New York, in the subway, and that is a tough place to expect cooperation for very long.

"Slim" as you must know, was a riot on the air, but funnier, or more to the point, more "Slim" in person, including an amusing side and a dark side. On the air, "Slim" felt he had to be funny, and wrote down his versions of "one liners" to use between records. Everything he wrote was truly "Slim" in personality, but when he rambled away from the jokes, and into a comment that was ad-libbed, things perked up considerably. His mistakes, bad cues on records, confusion, and even anger at some of the recordings are what made the shows what they are known for. I pushed him to toss away the written stuff, but he said he needed it "just in case", but then he ended up using most of it, even when he did not need to. Like his cigarettes, he could not put down the scribbled notes he created, or was handed.

The crowd was making itself heard, right through the door, and records were skipping on the turntable. "Slim" was gesturing the crowd to be quiet, but it looked as if he was shooing them away, and they grew more agitated. Harold was running around, grabbing records, and even trying to work on mail orders during the show. Harold was a perpetual motion machine. I was handing records to "Slim", and setting up the next play, and writing down my own "one liners" and handing them to "Slim". The phone was ringing and we tried to take dedications, but most callers did not know there was a radio show on and wanted information about records. "Slim" was handling the callers with his usual charm, saying things like, "Tell them to call back later", or "Get them off the phone if they don't have a dedication", and "What's wrong with these people?" I was handing him records in a way that paced the tempo of the show, but often he would just grab the wrong record, and play it, with no regard at all to any continuity of flow. His tendency to address the audience as "you people" was actually somewhat endearing, if you watched him doing it, but hearing it on the radio, it became abrasive and borderline offensive. (This was actually a good thing, because that really added the flavor of visiting the store in person)

The show from the store ended that night, with us not knowing if we were really off the air, or if we really had been on the air. The door was opened and the miffed customers poured in, unaffected by wear, but disgruntled. "Slim" was smoking and asking how it had gone, but none of us knew, except it seemed good, because most of the records got played, which was the primary goal. The phone rang continually, but mostly from regular customers, who "Slim" wanted off the phone, so that if anyone who had heard the show called in, he could figure out how far the "reach" of the signal was, and how it had sounded. We called the station and they claimed the show had worked fairly well, but "Slim" doubted it until someone finally called who had actually heard the show. The store was open, but "Slim" eyed the customers warily, trying to see if the show had worked any "magic", which was not going to be obvious, as these were the people who had been locked outside the door for over an hour. "Slim" had asked people to call in and report where they lived, to check the strength of the signal, but only a couple calls confirmed Manhattan, and other calls did not come in with those answers. This was FM radio, and that was a bitter pill to swallow.

After that rocky beginning, "Slim" began retreating behind the counter with the shows, and left the store open for business during a majority of the shows. The most telling thing was that rock n' rollers did not know what FM radio was. Times began trying to sell FM radios, which in an odd way, mirrors the start of satellite radio, especially in 2004, where the only hope for making it "normal" was to hire big name radio stars, in hopes of forcing people to buy the satellite services. In both cases, people do not like buying a special radio just to hear a show or shows, although in time, it does happen. Times

Records was valiantly trying to convert its' customers into "FM Radio" listeners by selling them the radio, which had no use at all, except for that one show. "Slim" figured it was worth it, but he knew better, for you could buy around 50 records for what you would pay for the damn radio, considering "8 records for 5 dollars" and other bargain pricing. To make matters even worse, there was a possibility that you would not be able to pick the show up at all! It was like trying to push a boulder up a steep mountain.

For a time you could wander in on the strange scene of "Slim" on the air, with customers milling around, some not paying any attention whatsoever to anything but looking at the wall of records. You might have thought that "Slim" was making a tape recording, or just fooling around with a turntable and a microphone, and you might have never known it was a "live" radio show. If I was not keeping some level of order in the area where the show was, I was signaling to Harold to kill the phonograph for customers, as the mic was on for the show. When "Slim" played a record on the show, a customer could hear a record they wanted to hear, played in the store, while at the same time a speaker rigged up to hear the show was blaring out another record. "Slim" would be on the air and somebody would walk in and ask to see Teddy. (Teddy was long gone, but his fame lingered). "Slim" thought that customers should buy what he was playing on the air, but he soon accepted the fact that this was not going to the case. There was a distinct distance between the radio audience and the customers right there in the store, which was added to by the subway wanderers who drifted in for no reason at all. It may seem unusual now, but the fact is that the "live" show from the store was not regarded as especially interesting to see in person. Somehow, I guess, Times Records was so off-the-wall, that nothing seemed unusual because it was all unusual.

Harold and I did some announcing on the show, which I liked, and Harold would rather have not done it seemed. There were "live" groups, and groups of kids who were not groups, but got to sing badly for a few seconds, only to be used as the brunt of a "Slim" joke. I did a few full shows from the store myself, which I was both pleased and happy to have done. I remember being on the air and trying to get excitement going about a record, and "Slim" eyeing some shady customers, while chain smoking and coughing, but not following the show itself very closely.

By the time FM Radio had established itself at the end of sixties, both "Slim" and Times Records had exited the scene forever. "Slim" almost made it to the golden age of FM, though not quite. "Slim" and The Times Square Records Radio Show had been there when no one gave a damn about FM Radio, or gave it chance in hell at having any future at all. In retrospect, "Slim" had preceded yet another pop culture phase.

****Author's Note – This chapter was written by Wayne Stierle. He emailed it to me on January 25, 2007.

"SLIM"-ISMS

The Language Of A 42nd Street Philosopher

Wayne Stierle

I think that "Slim" was as close to Yogi Berra as we would ever get in rock n' roll. You know how Yogi has those famous quotes that sound odd, but are actually right on the money. Casey Stengel was the same way. It is a blunt way of saying what you mean in your own "language". It is a "character" thing, where the person speaks like a creation from a book or a movie script, and never elaborates further on the comment.

I played a record for "Slim". It was a record I was about to obtain so I could release it as a Candlelite single. "Slim" listened in his off-handed way of listening, which is to say he did not seem to be listening at all. He never needed to hear much more than 20 or 30 seconds to form an opinion, and even if he decided too quickly, he rarely changed his mind later on. After the record played, I waited for the expected positive opinion, but what I got was a negative wrapped in a "Slim-ism". He said, "...it's a good record...but it's not the kind of record that people want to play...." That took a while to sink in, but I finally realized I was not going to do well at Times with that recording as a new 45, even if I pressed it on red plastic.

Few people talked like "Slim", and the sound of his voice just added to how different his words were. His automatic reaction to situations was usually amusing in some way. One day an adult, who was not a record collector, wandered into the store and screamed "...my God, that's a raccoon..." "Slim", agitated by that, responded immediately, "...that's my pet dog, and you've got a lot of nerve calling him a raccoon...get out of here...". The customer left quickly. "Slim" said, "...the nerve of some people...", and lit another cigarette. In that exchange, "Slim" had sounded similar to Groucho Marx.

I arrived at the store wearing a purple shirt. "Slim" said, "...what's that thing?" I looked behind me, because I thought he was talking to someone else, and he asked again. I just looked at him, and said "what"? He said, "...that thing...", and pulled on his own collar to indicate a shirt. To me, this was a cool shirt, and I replied, "...it's my shirt...". "Slim" said, "...is that what they call it...." I really did not know what to think, but I had learned very early on, not to be insulted by anything "Slim" said, because there was a big difference between his humor and his insults, only you had to know which was which. (A few minutes later, as I was counting out some records, "Slim" said, "...write down the name of the store where you got that thing...I might get one myself...."). Therefore, this had been a compliment that sounded like an insult. (You might be surprised by how many customers were wildly insulted by "Slim", even when he had not actually insulted them. Without even trying, "Slim" had intimidated most people.).

Many of these "Slim"-isms are heard, spoken by "Slim" himself on the companion cd to this book, so I will not repeat them here. Many are jokes jotted down by "Slim" for the radio show, while many are true on-the-spot ad-libs. There was no effort in this pursuit, for "Slim" actually talked that way.

It was the 42nd Street wisdom of "Slim", who demonstrated a truly world weary, odd cross between social commentary and burlesque humor. What made it funnier, and perhaps caused "Slim" to make extra jokes, was that he was surrounded by kids who actually did not understand many of his caustic barbs. "Slim" was doing one-liners that sometimes no one but he understood, and at the same point, he was aware this made it an even more ironic situation, which in turn, gave way to more sardonic humor.

***Author's Note – Wayne Stierle emailed this chapter to me on May 14, 2007.

The "Times" Top 100 Lists

The Dark Side & The Bright Side

Wayne Stierle

"Slim" always had his own view of the world, and a pretty good eye towards how to promote things. He liked it simple, with a touch of the "big time" promotional hoopla. He then mixed in a form of what most people might call insanity. His objective was to amuse and attract record buying kids of all ages, although' Times Records had a large and dedicated following of teenagers.

"Slim" liked lists. Especially lists from record distributors. Seeing exactly what you could get was the no-nonsense type of list he related to, and distributors only listed what they could sell right then and there. He also liked the "hype" of the radio station lists; although he hated the fact that they listed records you either couldn't or wouldn't want to have in your stock. He understood that most record buyers were very interested in lists of records, and very interested in the "hit" charts.

It was quite a good move to combine the aspects of distributors and radio stations into what appeared to be a "chart list" for Times Square Records. The Times Top 100 list was an instant favorite, and few customers ever considered that it was what it wasn't! It was a fun list! You see, it really wasn't a "chart", as it was simply a list of what was available for sale, as a distributor does. However, because the top 15 records were basically the biggest sellers, it did seem to be a "hit chart". So it was both and neither one, at the same time.

Bringing my latest single to Times was a genuine thrill for me, mainly because of the record wall, and the magic of the record hanging by a string from the ceiling that seemed about to collapse any minute. The Top 100 list added to this excitement, because "Slim" would say to Harold, ".......is the list done yet..." If Harold said it wasn't done, then I knew my record would be on the next list! Sometimes when the list was finished but not duplicated yet, "Slim" would take off a record he had only a few copies of, and add my single to the list. (This was in the day of the typewriter, so you didn't just delete something or cut and paste. It wasn't as easy to do as you might assume.)

The list was a selling tool, and customers didn't think about the fact that a record moving up to number 40 from number 70, might actually be a sign that the record wasn't selling so well. The opposite would seem to be the case, but if Times was sitting with 50 copies of a record that wasn't selling as expected, then moving it up the "chart" might give it a boost in sales. The list included the best sellers, to be sure, but it also included the slowest sellers that were hanging around in a larger quantity than needed or wanted.

Some record companies would give "Slim" a box of records for free, just to be on the list. (A "box" was a "25 box", which was 25 singles). If the record was good, it sometimes made the list, and if it missed the list, it ended up on the wall, at the far right side, which was away from the real "action" records that were on the wall in the area of the cash register. If "Slim" was given free records and listed the record, and it sold well, he expected to pay the usual low Times Records price for more copies. If the record company tried to raise the price, he'd throw them out and that was the end for that record at Times.

I was, and am, a one finger typist, but I'm used to writing that way all my life. I typed up some of The Top 100 Lists myself, but I just can't be sure which ones I did. "Slim" typed very slowly and didn't care to correct mistakes, and Harold was pretty fast. "Slim" liked to get one of the girls to do the typing, as they had typing class in school and were generally quicker and better than everyone else. One way or the other, the lists got done, and usually on time or even early. You're probably asking yourself if Genni did any of the typing. She could have, but I never saw her go near a typewriter. I'm not saying she didn't, but I'm not saying Teddy didn't either.

This should have made the list perfect, but there was a dark side that "Slim" hadn't counted on at all. Many of the Times customers came from outside of Manhattan, and were eager to the get the list mailed to them, and looking over the list, they checked off the 45's they wanted, which were all one dollar records. ($1.00 each). Since many of these customers had relatives who worked in or visited Manhattan, the list with the check marks would be given to the adult to take to Times and purchase the records. This was bad. The adult, who was not only somewhat frightened by the store, was also annoyed by the strange music, and therefore a totally non-impulse buyer. If there were 11 records checked on the list, then 11 records were purchased, whereas the actual teenager, who had checked the list, might have easily bought double the amount themselves. Remember that there were new additions to the store that were not on the list, and that fact meant nothing to the adult family member or family friend who was doing the shopping. Sales were soaring at first, and then dropping because of the list! The list that had become popular was sometimes a reverse of what it was intended to be, and there simply was no way around that fact. On the brighter side, the list was a success with people who lived far away, and could only do mail order. However, nothing, and I mean nothing, could top being in Times and hearing those records playing, which almost drove customers to buy records they may not have actually liked that much! There was a "feeding frenzy" caused by some of the records that blasted out into the store, just about causing a riot on some occasions. (That was really great).

Also on the dark side was the fact that some records would sell out and not be readily available again, which meant that some sales couldn't be made, and "Slim" did not like having a record listed that he couldn't sell. To make matters worse, the copycat stores, and stores that had started stocking only a few oldies, would refer to, or duplicate parts of the Times list. This cut into the very sales that the list was promoting for Times. Like almost everything started at Times Square Records, the ripping off of the ideas happened almost as soon as the idea was created. This gets back to something referenced in other chapters, which is that a listing of records that are not "exclusives" will end up causing those records to be sold almost anywhere. It's the "cycle" or "curse" that cannot be controlled.

The Times list did bring in many phone calls at the store, and a multitude of fans who wanted to have long conversations with anyone who answered the phone. "Slim" wasn't your basic friendly phone greeter by any means, and questions about this and that, were met with "Slim" saying things like, "......the store address is on the list, so come in, and stop calling....". "Slim" didn't wait for a "goodbye" as he hammered the receiver down into the phone cradle, and went back to concentrating on his current cigarette. How many callers were insulted or frightened and never came in? Who knows? That wasn't anything that was thought about at Times Records. "Slim" believed a real customer was the one standing in the store, and not the one on the phone. (Generally speaking this is a tried and true rule).

Because of The Times Square Top 100 List, and the radio shows, people calling Bryant 9-3458 expected to talk to "Swinging Slim", the sometimes humorous personality from the radio or the "home grown" lists. But "Swinging Slim" never answered customers calls, and instead they found themselves speaking to Irving "Slim" Rose, who didn't want to gossip with them, and made it clear, very clear.

Times didn't always live up to its' promotional gimmicks, but it always lived up to its' legendary abrasive image. The records that were advertised were there to buy, and there was no fakery about what was being sold or how the credit system worked. People conjured up their own "picture" of what a welcoming place it would be, and given the wonderful music, that's understandable. It's also a fact that most stores that create a "large image" are stuffy and boring, and run by ego-maniacs who promote themselves over the music, unlike Times Square Records, where the music was the focus. Times may not have been Wonderland, but it most certainly was the other side of the looking glass, and The White Rabbit was disguised as a brown raccoon, while The Mad Hatter was a cranky chain smoker, who sometimes morphed into The Cheshire Cat. There was a tea party, but the customers weren't invited.

But everyone looked forward to getting the latest Times Records Top 100 list, either in the mail, or when visiting Times. The list was a hit, and despite its' very basic simplicity, it still conveyed the fact that it came from a truly unique place that defined forever what a real record store could be.

****Author's Note – Wayne Stierle emailed me this chapter on May 23, 2007.

The Story Of Rama Lama Ding Dong
Another Startling Rebirth
Wayne Stierle

It was around Christmas of 1959, and Donn and I were playing records in his cellar, trying to determine what record companies to attempt to locate, with the goal being getting copies to sell to Times Records. We went through hundreds, and a few were added to our very select list. It was the beginning of a process that would cause some local hits to happen, and a few major national hits as well, although' we never guessed anything like that could happen.

Donn put on a single from a tiny label in Arkansas, and I jumped up when I heard the opening, voting to pursue this one. On the Dub International label, it was a group named after a car that soon would become nothing more than a bad joke, the Edsel. The group was The Edsels, and the record was the totally unknown "Rama Lama Ding Dong", a record that had failed to make its' mark and was now gone. It wasn't the greatest group record ever made, but it was delivered with sincerity by a group that seemed very intense. (The flip side, a strange ballad, bore out the strength and devoted credibility of this vocal group).

Tracking down the record wasn't hard, and we got along well the owner of Dub International Records, who sent us sample copies of his records, but he had pressed too many copies of "Rama Lama Ding Dong", and had dumped them all to a warehouse in Los Angeles that dealt with 45's that were of no seeming value. Whatever Dub International had in stock, we bought for 15 cents each, and then went by phone to the place in Los Angeles, where they had thousands of copies. The place was run by Sid Taback, who was easy enough to deal with, and thought we were crazy to buy this "lousy" record. The shipments came in, and we could supply Times Records with "Rama Lama Ding Dong". Like the thousands of records I would eventually supply to Times, I dragged "Rama Lama Ding Dong" through the streets of Times Square. (Down 8th Avenue, and then down 42nd Street). It was great. No profit, but it was great, because it was. It was a quest, in my mind.

The record sold fairly well at Times, and by the hot weather of 1960, it was selling on a very regular basis, with no sign of slowing down. (By this time we were selling many re-issues, but both "Baby Oh Baby" and "Rama Lama Ding Dong" were the steadiest of the group.). Donn left Jersey at the end of August, and I was doing this alone, which aside from dealing with "Slim", began to branch out in other areas. I was actually getting some air-play on "Rama Lama Ding Dong" and other records, but not expecting "hits", and only expecting to keep them "alive" for a longer period of time. In those days you could get to see the disc jockeys if you hung around long enough, although' it usually didn't matter either way. Cousin Brucie was always in a hurry, but friendly and he played your record at least once. Many of the other disc jockeys had their hands out for cash, which I didn't have any of. Clay Cole tossed me out of his office after hearing the opening of "Rama Lama Ding Dong", and then months later when it was a hit, he opened his show by saying "Here's the hottest record in New York City"! (He had thrown it in the garbage when I had played it for him, which was the real barometer of his "musical ear".).

As the summer of 1960 turned to the fall season, "Baby Oh Baby" was getting bigger, and soon Alan Freed, then in Los Angeles, would start playing it. (Freed owned the publishing). The activity associated with "Baby Oh Baby" gave me more influence with "Rama Lama Ding Dong", and it continued to sell, and I continued to make basically no money at all. Sid Taback in Los Angeles was still supplying it to me for 15 cents a copy and it didn't seem as though he was going to run out of it. However, Hy Weiss of Old Town Records had a spy/snitch in Times Records, in the form of Jerry Greene. When Weiss took over 'There's A Moon Out Tonight", as "Baby Oh Baby" broke out in L.A., Weiss got wind of my impending success with "Rama Lama Ding Dong" and moved in on it. Here again, "Slim" was slow to see the value of taking on a master himself, for the label I was trying to get "Slim" to start for himself. I was alone surrounded by a pack of wolves.

I want to point that this record is a serious up-tempo rock n ' roll recording and not a novelty record at all. Most radio stations think it's a "joke" recording or a "novelty". These are the same idiots who won't play "Jingle Bells" after Christmas, because they think a "winter" song is automatically a "Christmas" song. You all know someone with an odd nickname, or maybe you have an odd nickname that some people call you. Well, "Rama Lama Ding Dong" is simply the nickname for the girl that song is about. True, it may be among the odder of nicknames, but that doesn't change the fact that it's a serious rocking vocal group song, and don't you forget that.

Quite simply, heading into early 1961, "Rama Lama Ding Dong" didn't seem like a "hit', but it did seem like a record that was going to keep selling, much like "The Wind", but without any real fanfare. I had gotten permission to put it out myself, from Dub Records, but I was still selling the stock I was getting from Sid Taback in Los Angeles. Unknown to me, Dub Records didn't really own the master, but had leased it from a guy in Ohio. Dub never told me, and Sid Taback claimed Dub was the owner, so it all made "sense". (Taback claimed that Dub Records owed him money, although how that fact played into the final results was never clear.) But, Hy Weiss, tipped off by Jerry Greene had contacted the publisher of the song, who claimed to be the owner, and Weiss made a deal with him to release the record. Meanwhile I was getting air-play for it, which included several New York area stations.

Yet, Hy Weiss wasn't truly sure of who the owner of the master was, for he did something very, very odd for him, when he chose to not release the record on his Old Town label, but rather put it out on what was a non-label, Twin Records. There was no doubt that Weiss was keeping this record away from his Old Town Records label. There was also an un-answered question that I wasn't even aware of, which was how long did Dub Records have control over the master? Was the contract I had to release the record valid? Was The Weiss contract too soon to be valid, and could Dub Records actually legally assign the rights to me, and could the master owner legally assign the rights to Hy Weiss at that point in time?

This all became a moot issue, as the record took off, turning into one of the best remembered singles of 1961, though not a top ten record, its' lasting fame makes it seem in retrospect to have been a #1 record. Billboard Magazine called it a new record in the style of The Marcels "Blue Moon", which was ridiculous as "Rama Lama" was recorded three years earlier, but no one really knew, outside of some of the customers of Times Records. The trade papers and radio stations were just like they are now, musically clueless.

I was still buying copies from Sid Taback, who, for reasons that will never be known, had begun pressing the record himself, even listing Dub Records as being in California, and Sid had begun selling copies wherever he could. With Hy Weiss pressing it on Twin Records, I never put it out on Candlelite, despite believing I had the legal rights. One day Hy Weiss called me, and I wasn't home, and he told my Mother he was going to kill me if I didn't stop selling the record! I knew I wasn't doing anything wrong. but the low-life bastard that he really was, despite the good records he made sometimes, had upset my Mother for no reason. Instead of going to the police, I went to "Slim". To his credit, "Slim" was really mad, and he never told me what he did, but Weiss called my Mother and apologized, and he never called me again. (Somehow I ended up speaking to Weiss in the latter 90's, and he wanted to know why I had never done any business with him over the decades, and I told him why, in no uncertain terms. He immediately blamed the threats on his brother, George Weiss, who also worked in a form of the record business. Within a few minutes, Weiss was telling me he had killed people with his bare hands in World War Two, so this creep was still trying to instill fear into people. He was, I admit, interesting to talk to and a legendary character, but I never let myself forget what a bastard he was.)

The pressure of all these re-issued records taking off, as well as my constantly pushing "Slim", had finally gotten him to start his own label, and in a strange twist of fate, The Timetones on Times Square Records, with "In My Heart", hit the national charts at almost the exact time as "Rama Lama Ding Dong" did, in the glorious spring of 1961. It was a magical time.

I stopped buying "Rama Lama" from Taback, because it was all over the place. I received permission from Dub International Records to pursue legal action against Hy Weiss, but I didn't have a clue how to do that. Looking back on it, I can see now that it's possible Dub International had their rights to the record run out by that point. However, what has never been proven to me are the exact dates that the rights changed hands and the extent of the rights actually controlled by Dub International. This remains a gray area, and I accept that.

Over the years, the phrase "Rama Lama Ding Dong", and sometimes "Lama Rama Ding Dong" manages to pop up in sitcoms and movies, and indeed the title itself is more a part of the pop-culture than is the record itself. The title even became a surfers "hello" greeting in California in the 90's, and characters in shows refer to their boss as "the head Rama Lama", etc. Most people think it was a number one record, but in truth it peaked at number twenty on most charts nationally, although it was top ten in some cities. The highest it got was on The Times Records Top 100, which was the original goal to start with. If any of these records come on the radio, I don't listen, and I grew to learn the full wisdom of the old saying "Ignorance Is Bliss".

****Author's Note – This chapter was written by Wayne Stierle. It was emailed to me the first part of April, 2006.

The Cast Of Characters
Remembering The Employees
Shandy Hnetinka

The year was either 1960 or 1961 when I discovered Times Square Records. I was ten or eleven at the time and my brother Steve was fifteen or sixteen. We would tune in each week to listen to Alan Frederick's Night Train show on the radio. Steve and I would take our wish lists along with five or ten dollars to that packed little call box of a store. At the time we both thought there was nothing strange...the small space...the crowds...a raccoon named Teddy. It just seemed like a great place to buy records and we always went home happy. Remembering now, it really was a strange place to be.

I loved Teddy. His favorite foods were grapes and chocolate cookies. Teddy became "famous" when a passerby took a picture that landed in one of the newspapers as a human interest short. Animal control got wind of it. During those years, you needed a special permit to have a raccoon, which "Slim", did not have and did not meet the qualifications on the application. "Slim" always claimed he took Teddy to a farm. I always doubted this story, as farmers do not like raccoons.

There seemed to be a revolving cast of characters behind the counter. When I was a customer, I just remember "Slim" and Harold. "Slim" always reminded me of Ichabod Crane. He was so gaunt and did not look healthy. I am sure always having a cigarette in his hand was not helping the constant cough he had.

They were always very nice to me and "Slim" on many occasions seemed surprised by my unusual choices. Most likely because there seemed to be no female collectors and I was the youngest customer I ever saw there. When I would see another female I would always try to strike up a conversation about the music, but it always turned out that they were "along for the ride" with their boyfriends and had no real interest themselves. "Slim" had a sign above the door in both stores that read, "Through these portals pass some of the most beautiful women in the world". I used to think to myself what women, where? It was lonely for a young girl collector. The people refused to take me seriously, however "Slim" did.

One day while he was ringing up my records, he asked if I would like to work in the store for him. I was both thrilled and crushed. Having a job working with this music at my age; which was twelve in 1962, would be my idea of a dream job. I figured once "Slim" learned my real age I would not be hired....this is something I would learn later that this was typical of "Slim". His fast reply to me was "I don't care." I worked only a short time in the first store before we moved to 42nd and Sixth subway arcade, across from Bryant Park.

The new store definitely had its special funky charm, however as a worker, the new store was much more comfortable to be in and there was so much more customer and "hang out" space. It was also much cleaner and put together. I always thought the old store would cave in on us if "Slim" coughed too hard! The only drawback for me was the restroom. I had to enlist one of the "guys" (never an employee) to escort me, it was that scary, and I was never one to scare easily. You had to travel through a door several yards outside the store that opened onto a large, deserted (seemingly) shipping maze. A few scattered, dim, bare bulbs did little to shed any light.

If memory serves, the minimum wage as $1.25. I made a dollar and a record an hour off the books, no deductions. A government worker came in one day and asked "Slim" if he had any underage workers and he told him he did. I coasted until I was thirteen and got my working papers. That man never came back.

I got along with "Slim", but it was not always easy. He once told me "I don't pay you to think". I quickly replied, "You don't pay me to show up". The customers cracked up, so I felt avenged. "Slim" offered me extra money for certain "favors", which I refused several times. He was not threatening or pushy in anyway, it was strictly a business proposition to him. He also offered me a hundred dollars (a huge sum at the time), to take his five or six year old son Bobby to Palisades Amusement Park, which was a popular place in New Jersey at the time. This would include meals and taking Bobby on the rides. Again, I declined, but I did meet Bobby at the store once. He was a cute little guy.

I saw "Slim" as a typical Times Square minor hustler, but he could have his good moments. One time an old black man came into the store.... He did not pretend to be a customer. He was crying because he said he was a drunk and he wanted to quit. "Slim" let him call his sister in Baltimore and talk for a long time. In addition, “Slim” had a favorite restaurant on the Lower East Side.....Sammy's Romanian. It is still there. He would take Wayne, Charlie "Chance" and me to dinner on occasion. We always had a great time.

I never knew about the jewelry/record business that “Slim” had prior to Times Records. I was aware of his "girlie" bookstore business, which seemed more his style. He had some sort of promotional card we would hand out. It was two-sided, but I only remember what it said on one...."With this card and one token, ride the subway free". It was typical of his humor. Some customers actually came in to complain that it did not work!

The over priced records were kept in a locked built-in box toward the back of the store and on the wall over it where “Slim” usually sat. “Slim” handled all these sales. I thought the lock was somewhat amusing and referred to it as "The Vault". My job was to fill the large orders. I no longer remember how many records or sales I filled back then. They were the regular run records, nothing over priced. I loved this since I was to work with that one customer only and it kept me busy in an interesting way. Since these customers never seemed to bring a wish list big enough to fill, I could make suggestions because I could see their taste at a glance. It was more involved and one-on-one...not just ringing up and bagging.

I met “Genni” only once at the second store. She was very pretty and sophisticated to me. She was just beginning college at Hofstra and was pledging to a club/sorority called "Wreath and Foil". She had to carry an increasing number of bricks with her around campus and present them when asked. Do not ask me why I remember this, but I do. It disappointed me that she did not have much knowledge or interest in the music. I thought she would finally be the female collector I could share my love of music, however, maybe she just moved on. I could not imagine her associating with “Slim” in any context whatsoever, it was far fetched and I never found the nerve to ask.

I saw Harold as “Slim's” right-hand man. I do not remember him ever not being at the store. I know his salary was ninety dollars a week, but I do not know if he told me this or if it was “Slim”. I would never have asked, but it seemed reasonable for the time and for “Slim”. Harold lived in Brooklyn. I met his wife, Rosalie, once. I am not able to claim to have known her, but you could not help liking her right away. She was as sweet and warm as could be. Harold would always handle any customer who went too far with me. All I had to say was "Harold, you take him" and he knew just what I meant, no questions asked. I always appreciated that.

I met Ricky Nelson during the brief period I worked at the first store. He was working there at the time too. He had a wonderful "to die for" collection. We had the same taste in music; however, what he collected was way out of my price range. We dated for a while and he gave me a wonderful reel-to-reel tape (no cassettes then), that I still have along with the transcription my brother Steve made for me later. He now resides in California as my brother has been in touch with him. I do not remember him working in the second store, but he was definitely a "hallway guy". I bought a terrific reissue from him the names escapes me. There was wheeling and dealing outside the store, as well as singing.

Wayne Stierle was probably the nicest person I met at Times. He certainly was the best one I worked with. He was normal where no one seemed so, but unique in being a young man with his own label, Candlelite. He looked young enough to have his own paper route. The first time I saw him, my impression was "This boy looks like he just got off the bus....I'll have to look out for him". Nothing could have been further from the truth, which I found out in our first conversation. He never lost that appearance of a wide-eyed innocent boy. I used to tell him it was a good thing he was a gentleman, because he could get away with anything having that face. He ended up looking out for me. Not obvious, but I always knew and appreciated it. He was always so unassuming; it took him forever to tell me "Well, I don't actually work for "Slim." I never got the real picture of how much he was involved. He also considered my opinions about music. Chauvinism was rampant in this area, so it was nice to have his ear. Guys who did not have half my knowledge would be dismissive of me. I am glad to know he has stayed true to his love of music.

Anita "worked" at the second store with me for a short time. This consisted of helping herself to the cash register, with "Slim's" permission, to go on petty shopping sprees. The rest of her day consisted of flirting with her many "admirers". I liked that it gave me a break from some of the "creeps". Anita attracted so many, I had to fight off the over flow. Guys would come in looking for her, not evening knowing what she looked like, just by reputation. When I told them I was not her and nothing like her, they almost wept with disappointment. I will admit I enjoyed doing that very much. She was a sweet girl though, without a mean bone in her body that I could see.

Charlie "Chance" (for his love of the Chance record label) worked with me for a short time in the second store. He came from Mill Basin in Brooklyn and had an Italian last name. He was a nice guy.

Shari Halpern worked with me also. We became friends. I had the feeling she was slumming. She came from Port Washington, Long Island and was very artistic. She liked writing up the record sleeves because that was about as close to artistic as you could get in that store.

Her favorite song was "Pizza Pie" by Norman Fox and the Rob Roys. I would give her this record as a present for her birthday. She left to attend Boston College. A few years later, I would receive a card in the mail announcing that she was married and living in England.

These are the best recollections of the many employees. So many came and went in a blur. Maybe some of them did not actually work there, just happened to be behind the counter for some reason. Others were dubious young "girlfriends" of "Slim's". After all, that is how it was.

My favorite customer was Louie Silvani. I do not remember him actually ever buying anything, but he always seemed to be in the store, like a permanent installation of some strange kind. He was very funny. Unfortunately, he did not remember me as we spoke several years ago on Danny Romanello's radio show on WFUV. In my opinion, many things were a blur to him back then. When he bought the store across from Times, I went in to see him. The store was completely empty as there had been a police raid the day before and the police had helped themselves to the cash register. I felt bad for him as that store must have been his dream and he did not look too happy.

Dominick D'Lia was another regular I remember, mostly for beating up his younger brother in the hallway for hitting a wrong note. I called him to task for it, and people thought I was insane for going up against "Crazy Dominick", but I could not take it anymore, even if his brother could. He always had radar for protecting me, even though we were not friendly. If someone would give me a particularly nasty time, he would appear out of nowhere and then disappear like the Lone Ranger. I never figured out how he did it. Several years ago, I got a chance to talk to him, again on Danny's radio show.

Billy Shibilski was another nice customer, a Fordham guy. His good manners made him stand out. He also floored me by giving me a 78 of "I Cover the Waterfront" by Sonny Til and the Orioles, one of my favorites at the time and unattainable for me. I will never forget his kindness in doing that, no strings attached. He went on to have the very popular "Polka Party" radio show on WFUV that lasted over thirty years. We both were to meet again at the telephone company in the late 1960s or early 1970s. We worked in different departments. He saw my picture in a company magazine and was nice enough to stop by my department to say hello.

There was a very unusual, nervous customer whose name escapes me. I called him "Hit It In The Middle", because when you played a record for him you had to start dead center and he kept repeating that phrase over and over. He was challenged in some way. His "collection" revolved around records that had picture sleeves so he could put them on this wall. The music seemed to be "beside the point". He came in almost weekly.

****Author's Note – Information in this chapter came from several emails from Shandy Hnetika in the late summer/early fall 2006 and January, 2007. This chapter was revised by Ms. Hnetika on April 9, 2007.

The Long Fade Out....

The Ending Of An Era

Wayne Stierle

"Slim" lost the lease at the original store. After all, the store was under the Times Building, in Times Square, the building from where the ball falls on New Years Eve. Looking back, it's hard to believe that the space was even available! (Yes, that's why it was called Times Records. The Times, the New York Times owned the building, and they objected to the name of the store, which led "Slim" to using the name "Times Square Records".). Over the years, it seems that most people automatically use the latter name, "Times Square Records".

It's impossible to know how long the Times Records "magic" may have gone on, had the old store remained as it was, but I personally believe it had another 1 1/2 years of "magic" before an overhaul of some type would have been necessary. I knew, and I felt, long before the new store opened that an era was closing. I could sense it in the air. Sure, it was exciting to be moving the old store in shopping carts, in the heart of New York City, but I knew it wasn't ever going to be the same. "Slim" had a strong dislike for photos, but he relented enough for my taking those photos that you've seen. I always wondered if he pondered this passage, and maybe feared it as I did. I never asked him. I don't think he did see it as era ending at all, and I hope that's correct.

Looking at it from the view of "Slim" himself, here he had created an icon of a store, and was rightfully moving to a bigger store, and on to bigger and better things. Having no choice but to move, he was staying as close to the old address as he could, and he was staying underground, down in the subway. This was remaining true to the image, and providing more space for the customers. When you think about it with logic, then it makes perfect sense. Ah, but logic had nothing to do with the success and the almost mystical magnetic attraction of Times Records. This move had the feeling that would later come when Coca-Cola changed their formula. It was wrong, and it doesn't matter why it's wrong. Some things are meant to be.

If you built a movie set to capture the original store, no one would believe it. It just was what it was, and it was a place filled with records that rumbled with the subway vibrations, and maybe was only a heartbeat away from falling down on our heads. It didn't pretend to be great. It was great because it was what it was. I'm telling you this because any fancy five-syllable description would miss the point. This was genuine Americana, only a few years after the birth of rock n' roll. You can't top that.

Even in the early days "Slim" would tell me that he wanted to have a store that sold everything for 39 cents. Nothing would cost more or less. He was, in 1961, predicting something he would never see, "the dollar stores". He asked me if I wanted to manage one, while he ran the main location. He saw it as a "chain" operation. This made me nervous, because I needed to think of "Slim" as the guy with the rare records, and all the other craziness that was Times Records. It took me years to understand, and even now, it's not something I dwell on, because I believe in the musical part of the story. It's easy to understand that dealing with each rare record, one at a time, would eventually become very difficult for "Slim", whereas selling items you don't have to know the history of would be appealing. "Slim" had come from quick sale retail, and it was what he related to in a natural way.

But, attitudes and styles were changing not so slowly. The re-issued singles becoming new "hits" had almost stopped by mid-1963, as "Slim" was moving the store. Stores copying Times Records had sprung up in major cities, and in smaller cities in key places such as New Jersey. While these stores all owed their very being to Times Records, they sought to corner their own market, and in doing so they undercut "Slim" in what were sometimes very unkind moves. "Slim" had painted a target on his back, and there were people aiming at the target. It was a natural evolution, but it wasn't necessary. The original vocal groups of the fifties had almost all disbanded, or changed drastically, and those few that remained were getting too mild. The new groups weren't really singing as "groups", but were relying on the commercial aspects of the productions that were geared to a more "solo" feeling. New and really weak white groups were mere mimics of the black group sounds of 1959, and all the while the new black groups were going in a different direction, away from true vocal group sounds. It wasn't a "plan" actually, but it seemed like a scheme to water-down what had initially been so bold and powerful. It was mid-1963 and we didn't know that in only months, President Kennedy would be killed, and the nation would plunge into a morbid, more adult atmosphere. Furthermore, only a half year after Times Records moved, the benefactors of the darkness that held sway over radio in the month following the Kennedy killing, would be the Beatles, who, in early 1964, gave little kids a break from the serious tone that prevailed. Radio was fast becoming the enemy, in its' greed and total uncaring attitude toward the music that had helped establish the very format of the stations. This was the worst time for Times Records to have moved. Even if there had been a chain of Times Records stores, it would have been terribly wounded by what was coming. The stores that survived the rest of the sixties, did so by also selling current popular records, and that was not a concept that would have worked with the Times image. Everything was knocked out of kilter, and nothing would ever put humpty-dumpty back together again. This was probably the main reason not to move the store. (Day by day we move into the future, whether we like it or not).

In the early days of Times Records, even the known oldies were hard to find in stores, because they were not being re-pressed. They were gone. It may seem hard to believe now, but records such as "Deserie", "Florence", "Chapel Of Dreams", and all the others that are considered "standards", could only be found in quantities at Times Records. If you really wanted to add "People Are Talking" or "A Thousand Miles Away" to your collection, you needed to head to Times Square, and drop in at Times Records. There was a whole audience of "oldies" buyers who were not "collectors" and these people just wanted the records, and didn't care about the trappings of strange surroundings. Before "Slim" knew it, stores were starting to stock the main "oldies", and people from the suburbs didn't have to trek into the city, if all they wanted was a standard oldie. The Times Records customers were the remaining, and newly converted collectors, and all those extra people that created long lines outside the store had vanished. Gone were those golden days of only letting two people into the store when two people left and the subway stairs being crowded with anxious customers chomping at the bit, no matter how bad the weather. There had been the feeling of being let in to a rare place, where few got to go, and it was also similar to the stories of trying to get into Studio 54, or other nightclubs that only let a handful of people in. This paragraph is another reason why Times moving to a new location was not a good thing.

"Slim" had tried valiantly to stem the tide of losing customers to other stores who only stocked a handful of oldies. He tried to get "exclusives" on re-pressings of 45's. I gave him exclusives on what I was doing, and so did a few others, but for the most part it was a losing battle. Sometimes he got an exclusive for a week or two, in return for playing the record on his radio program. Soon it was obvious that the only real "exclusives" he could count on would be his own releases, which worked pretty well for awhile, but tapered off as the quality of the releases became run-of-the-mill group sides, which were good records, but wouldn't draw you in from out of town. When "Slim" had trouble getting certain records, he began trading his releases with stores in return for the records he needed, but this was counter-productive, in that the competing store now had his "exclusive" records in their stock. It was a spiral that could not be controlled, no matter how it was configured. Times Records was no longer "the only game in town", but it was still the one and only original store. And yes, this is yet another graphic reason why moving the store was not the thing to do.

The original store was a nightmare to any "normal" customer, even by New York standards. People would wander in and look around, in shocked disbelief, and leave mumbling to themselves. Adults stopping in to purchase a record for their children would stare at the high prices on the wall, and not understand that these were older records. The most usual happening was the funniest though, and that was the non-record customer who was looking for chewing gum or a newspaper, or a subway schedule, and left dazed and confused by the unreality of the world they had stumbled into. The Twilight Zone of Times Records. I loved it. What was not to love about it?

There was a time that you could drive through small towns and out of the way cities, and actually find record stores that no one knew about. It was exciting. It was intoxicating. I mean there were stores that had started in the latter forties or early fifties, and had benefited by what rock n' roll had brought them, and they were still around in the dawning days of the sixties. These were classic stores, with listening booths. By any yardstick you apply, Times Records was the new kid in town, and yet because Times was 100% devoted to rock n' roll vocal group records, it became the main hub of stores, around which all others would revolve in orbit. Times Records assumed the role of being new and old at the same time. Times were tacky and lurid, like a New Jersey boardwalk on a hot, edgy night. How could you resist that?

So, what had "Slim" really done? Don't stores go out of business every day? Doesn't the "hot location" in any area of the country eventually become old news? And, wasn't "Slim" just trying to make a buck as any store owner does? He hadn't invented selling records. He hadn't invented selling used items. Yet, something about the "rummage sale" aspect of this, applied to "group" records, was attractive and addictive. (The old time "rummage sales" became called "garage sales", "yard sales", "swap meets", and "flea markets".

With the internet it is best known in its' electronic form as Ebay). He had done a lot of things by accident, and not everything done on purpose made sense. So what was the big deal?

I'll tell you what the big deal was. "Slim" had, by luck, and strange fortune, done for us what we hadn't done for ourselves. In the confusion, and the chaos of Times Records, he had created a shrine to vocal group recordings, and its light shown like a beacon in the night, guiding us to it's' source. Times Records restored our faith that this kind of music meant something, even if the damn radio stations chose to diminish and ignore it. Those of us, who had never wavered in our faith, were nonetheless inspired by the glow that we felt, even when we couldn't see it. Times Records kept the dream alive, and underscored the fact that the New York area was the home of hard core vocal group rock n' roll and R&B. It was the right thing, at the right time, in the right place. It was a magic store without the tricks. It was home to the heartbeat of the city as personified in the very music it presented. It was on many levels, a part of us all. Even if you never were there, you should thank God that once upon a time, such a place existed. We are all the better for it.

****Author's Note – This chapter was written by Wayne Stierle. He emailed it to me in February, 2006

The Final Years...
"Slim" After Times Square Records
Tony D'Ambrosio

On or about the year 1971, on a Friday night I accompanied my Cousin Vinnie to work. We went from place to place and nothing eventful was happening. While he dealt with the various managers of the shops, I occupied myself by checking the merchandise, etc and then it happened. We went to a place on 42nd Street between 6th Avenue and Broadway. It was there that I heard over the loudspeaker, an unmistakable voice that could only be the voice on one man......"Slim" Rose.

I immediately looked around and saw that the person broadcasting over the loudspeaker was indeed "Slim" himself. My cousin had just finished business with him ("Slim") and he ("Slim") was back to hustling customers. I grabbed my cousin and said "Do you know him"? His answer was "Who, Irving"?

We then proceeded back to "Irving" and I confirmed that he was in fact "Slim" from Times Square Records. I was no longer collecting records at this time, but of course I had to ask him the question if he was the same "Slim" from Times. He somewhat hesitatingly confirmed that yes he was "Slim" from Times. I then proceeded to ask him what he had done with all those records.

At first, he did not answer me. I had to ask again about the records. His reply to me was "he could do me a favor because of my cousin". He pulled out a book and gave me a phone number of someone by the name of "Lloyd". He told me to call him and mention, "Slim sent me".

Now remember I had mentioned that I really was not collecting records in 1971. I put Lloyd's number in my wallet, never expecting to really call him. About a year later, I had started collecting records again. I still had Lloyd's number so I gave him a call. At that time Lloyd was an employee of the Chelsea Hotel. I think he was a porter or something similar. When I asked him about the records and indicated to him who had referred me, he replied that "he had some that I needed to pay cash on delivery and no checks". I proceeded to meet Lloyd at the Chelsea Hotel. There I found an old man. He took me to his room which was half filled with boxes full of records. The labels were Josie, Jubilee and Port. It seems he had worked for Jay-Gee (Author's note it was Cosnat Distributors he worked for, the parent company of Jay-Gee, Jubilee) records and when they went out of business he ended up with a lot of their stock. Lloyd only wanted five (5) cents a record provided I bought $20.00 worth. I purchased them all. There were approximately 5,000 records in total. Most were second pressings, for example the Ravens on Jubilee, Cadillacs on Josie and all of the Port recordings. There were a few originals such as "Peek A Boo" by the Cadillacs, "The Bell" and "I Love You" by the Volumes along with others.

As we were concluding our deal, Lloyd asked me how I knew "Slim". I told him from the days of Times Square Records and more recently my meeting with him on 42nd Street. Lloyd mentioned that "Slim" was a "Times Square Guy". Lloyd knew him from the area many years ago. All the years that Lloyd knew "Slim" he always referred to him as a "Times Square Hustler".

Shortly thereafter, while the "Doo Wop Revival" was in full swing I tried to find "Slim" again. My cousin Vinnie was still in the same business as in 1971, however, he had not seen "Slim" in months.

I checked out every adult retail place in the Times Square area and "Slim" was nowhere to be found. Yes, I did ask about him in a few places, however I soon learned that even though they knew "Slim" they would not talk about him.

I eventually ran into someone who also had run into "Slim" in the 1970's. He told me that "Slim" was still working in retail in the Times Square area.

****Author's Note – This chapter was written by Tony D'Ambrosio. He emailed it to me February, 2006.

It Had To End Sometime...

"Slim" Decides To Sell

Eddie Gries

Within the words of this chapter, I will tell you how Eddie Gries became involved with "Slim" and Times Square Records. The time line will take you from the early days where Eddie is listening to radio in his bedroom, to working part-time at Sam Goody at the same time attending classes at Montclair College, to working for Apex-Martin Record Sales, to opening the Relic Rack and eventually purchasing the inventory and masters from Times Square Records. I will use a time line for this chapter keeping it smooth and simple, yet to the point.

The year is either 1960 or 1961. Eddie Gries learns there is a great place located at 42nd and Broadway to buy records. The store is in a subway basement that has exposed pipes, low ceilings and is decrepit in looks. Eddie and a friend travel to New York seeking out this store. They both are amazed at what they find.

Within the walls of this store are records that hang from the ceiling with string, lists with the Top 100 hits and a cute little furry critter named "Teddy" that is a raccoon. Located on the left side of the store is a "wall of records". On this "wall" are record sleeves written with the title of the record, the artist name and the record amount. The sleeves have been pinned to the wall. The records range in price from $2.00 each to as high as $20.00 or $30.00.

The "cast of characters" at the store are Harold who is a skinny little Jewish kid who waited on customers. "Genni" (according to Genevieve Miscavage "Slim" is the one who came up with the spelling of "Genni") is a cute blonde-haired person that stands around doing nothing. Mike who seems to be in his 30s or 40s is a friend of "Slim's". Jerry Greene is working behind the counter. He is nasty to everyone that comes into the store. (Eddie Gries has known Jerry Greene for over forty-five years. He is a tough competitor and a smart businessperson. He has great respect for him. He is a survivor of the oldies business. Now and then Eddie Gries will see Jerry Greene out in public. The two always exchange friendly greetings). Then there is "Slim". He is a tall skinny person who wore glasses and had a moustache. He looked like "Andy

Gump". He wore "long johns" all year long and had a bad smoker's cough that would eventually turn into emphysema.

Eddie Gries starts to compile a list of the records that "Slim" has hanging on the famous "wall of records" at the store. At the same time, Eddie is listening to the Alan Frederick's show compiling a list of what to buy.

Eddie Gries is working part-time at Sam Goody in Paramus, New Jersey His starting hourly rate at Sam Goody is $1.00 an hour that would increase to $1.10.

Eddie Gries decides to set up a record display on the counter at Sam Goody. The display will hold approximately one hundred records. He calls the display "Oldies but Goodies. It is not long before he has a hit with the records. His boss is elated.

To quote Eddie Gries "he begins to perform a shell game".

Eddie Gries would travel to the Sam Goody Distribution Warehouse (also known as Good One Stop or Goody One Stop) located at 49th Street on the second floor in New York to pick up one hundred to three hundred records at a time for the Paramus store. Leaving Sam Goody, he would stop home to exchange records from his own collection. He would bring out "stuff" he thought the "kids" would like.

Once the "Oldies but Goodies" sold out or became "stale", Eddie Gries would start his "shell game" again. Back to the Goody Distribution Warehouse in New York he would go, stopping home first to "switch out" the records and back to Sam Goody. He would do this many times while employed with Sam Goody.

Eddie Gries is also going to Woolworth's, Grants and Kresge's buying records for fifteen or twenty-five cents a piece. Eddie begins to take his records to local diners in the area selling them in the parking lot from the trunk of his car. He is charging one dollar a record. He now is making as much as seventy cents profit on a record.

His record collection is now growing leaps and bounds. Eddie divided his collection into two different sections. The "switch out" records were stored in his bedroom or his mother's attic. The over selling stock was stored on shelves in the basement.

At the same time, Eddie Gries is taking advantage of the credit system that "Slim" has to offer at Times Square Records. "Slim" is giving fifty cents credit toward any dollar record he had at the store. Eddie Gries begins to ask "Slim" for multiple copies of records. There came a time when he had racked up $500.00 in credit with "Slim". "Slim" was having trouble keeping up with the high credit slips. Eddie Gries was wiping out the stock at Times Square Records. "Slim" decides to give him fifty cents in cash when he brought in quantities of records instead of credit.

Eddie and "Slim" now have a good business relationship. "Slim" relied on Eddie for certain labels such as Fury, Fire, Gone, Ivy and Jamie to name a few.

Moving along the time line...It is now June 1961. Eddie Gries has graduated from Montclair College. He is certain he does not want to become a teacher.

He loves the "music" too much. He is now gone from Sam Goody.

Enter Apex Martin Record Sales ....Eddie Gries began working at Apex-Martin in June 1961 right out of college. Apex-Martin was located at 347 Washington Street Newark New Jersey. Joseph Martin is the owner of the company. He tells Eddie that he cannot afford to hire him at $1.50 an hour. Jerry Cohen would be the one to convince Joseph Martin to hire Eddie. Eddie Gries would begin with a salary of $60.00 a week. Eddie Gries started out as a stock boy, became a sales representative eventually working his way up to a buyer for Apex-Martin. This is a working relationship that would last seventeen years.

Eddie Gries arranges the first live show "Slim" would sponsor at Palisades Park, New Jersey. This show took place in 1961.

Appearing "live" on stage are the Avons, the Willows, the Summits, the Timetones, the Chic-Lets, Bobby J and the Laddins. In the past all artists lip sync to the music. A record player would be hidden back stage playing the records.

There was free admission. "Slim" paid all the artists that appeared on stage. "Slim" also advertised the show in the newspaper and on the radio. The owner of the park, Irving Rosenthal was elated to have the artists perform, as there would be no out of pocket expenses for him.

"Slim" had his son, Bobby on stage with him. Bobby was three or four at the time. Eddie also was on stage with "Slim". This would become an important moment in his life. A place in time he would never forget.

According to Eddie Gries, there are no photographs of the show in existence.

Moving along the time line…"Slim" is now relying on Eddie Gries more and more for records. Fortune Records is now at Apex-Martin. Eddie Gries is the sales representative for Fortune Records at Apex-Martin.

"Slim" makes the decision to start a record label. "Slim" wanted records that would be exclusive to the store. Looking back Eddie Gries feels it was a fatal error on "Slim's" part to have exclusives only and not share them with other stores.

Enter The Relic Rack…..Eddie Gries now wants to branch out and start his own store. Joseph Martin would finance Eddie Gries. The creation of the Relic Rack name came from George Tucker who was a DJ on the radio that played group sound oldies. The name of the oldies radio show was Relic Rack.

Relic Rack opened November 1962. Eddie Gries would use his basement stock for inventory. The location was 116 Main Street in Hackensack moving to 136 Main Street in 1963. The controlling interest of shares went to Joseph Martin. Eddie Gries had twenty-five or thirty-three percent of stock shares. Jerry Cohen along with his niece would write the checks.

The Relic Rack is now officially "Slim's" competitor in the New York area. The kids in New Jersey no longer had to travel outside their area to buy records. They were now saving money on gas so they can afford to purchase more records. Since "Slim" was keeping the exclusives, it was next to impossible for Eddie Gries to get the records he needed. This was a tough time for him as customers were asking for the records that "Slim" would not give up. Eddie however did continue to do business with "Slim".

Eddie develops a plan that will help him to get the records needed from "Slim". He buys ads on WNJR, The Danny "Katman" Stiles show. The show aired five nights a week at either eleven or twelve o'clock. Eddie Gries supplied the exclusives.

Now the customers in the New York City area are hearing records that are on the Relic Rack label that Eddie Gries has in stock. Things have now turned around for Eddie as he has exclusives that "Slim" needs. They begin to trade exclusives. Now Eddie has what "Slim" has and vice versa.

Eddie Gries is now buying out other record labels. The first two labels purchased were Milo and Onyx.

Again moving along the time.....The Relic Rack is growing. Business is good. Eddie Gries decides it is time to buy out Joseph Martin. Along with Donn Fileti and Stan Krause, the Relic Rack now is a corporation of three.

Stan Krause's father fronted the money for the buyout.

The first release to come out on the Relic Rack label was "I Love You" by the 4 Most. He purchased the master from Joe Flis who at the time had two "vanity" labels Milo and Cool. The record sold roughly 1700 copies. Joe Flis also owned Milo Studios. Milo Studios was the recording studio. The location of the studio was in Harrison, New Jersey.

Stan Krause decides it is time for him to move on. He leaves Relic Rack to open Journal Square Records on Kennedy Boulevard in Jersey City. His label was Catamount Records.

The year is 1965.... Eddie Gries receives a call from "Slim". He lets him know that he has learned he and Donn Fileti are looking to rent a store in the midtown Manhattan area.

"Slim" makes it very clear from the beginning that Harold Ginsburg is included in the package deal. "Slim" wanted to secure a place for Harold, as he had been a loyal employee almost from the onset of Times Square Records back in 1959/1960.

I will now list the facts in order. Please refer to the "Slim" Archives for the photo documentation.

Times Square Records sold on or about March 15, 1965.

Purchase amount was $4,500.00. There would be 45 weekly installments of $100.00.

Included in the purchase price were all available inventories in the store such as fixtures, cash register, records, etc.

Also included were the master recordings, which recorded on the Times Square Records label that "Slim" still held the rights too. Please note that "Slim" did not sell the name Times Square Records, Inc. He retained the name of the corporation for himself. The State Of New York Corporate Division dissolved Times Square Records, Inc. on December 15, 1969 for being non-active.

Hyman Ginsburg, Harold's father put up the initial investment.
The name would change to Times Square Music, Inc.
There were stock certificates.
Harold Ginsburg was the President. He and his father held fifty percent of stock shares.
Eddie Gries was Secretary and Treasurer. He held nineteen percent of stock shares.
Donn Fileti held nineteen percent of stock shares.
Dennis Arakelian held twelve percent of stock shares.

The closing of Times Square Music, Inc......The details of the closing are not clear to this author. Although Harold Ginsburg was located and contacted several times, he failed to contact this author.

Donn Fileti and Dennis Arakelian are both in the military. Eddie Gries is running the Relic Rack.

Harold Ginsburg is alone to run the store. Eddie Gries is there long enough to sign checks for Harold and then exits. Sales are way down with cash flow being next to nothing. The Relic Rack is supplying inventory to Times Square Music, Inc. The Internal Revenue Service begins to make daily visits taking money out of the cash register due to non-payment of withholding taxes.

The date when Harold Ginsburg made the decision to close the doors and walk away from the business is not known. What is known Harold Ginsburg gave what was left of the inventory to Lou Silvani. The inventory included the fixtures and cash register. There were no records included in the inventory. Lou Silvani had been a long time customer/collector that Harold Ginsburg had known for several years.

Since Times Square Music, Inc. owed money to the Relic Rack, Eddie Gries went to Harold Ginsburg requesting payment in the form of all the original masters that were purchased from "Slim". Harold Ginsburg gave the original masters to the Relic Rack as payment in full. The corporation stayed intact.

To lay the rumor to rest....Lou Silvani never purchased Times Square Music, Inc. or Times Square Records. He was given the fixtures and cash register only. It is not known whether an agreement was made between Lou Silvani, Harold Ginsburg and the owner of the building regarding the lease.

Harold Ginsburg was left owing the Internal Revenue Service. This author does not know if a settlement was made with the Internal Revenue regarding the back taxes owed.

Eddie Gries continued to work for Apex-Martin until 1978.

***Author's Note – Harold Ginsburg was located in Brooklyn, New York. Mr. Ginsburg was contacted by mail several times notifying him about the book. Mr. Ginsburg failed to contact me. This author respects his privacy.

The information in this chapter came from an interview with Eddie Gries during the month of October, 2006. Mr. Gries was given a hard copy of the transcribed interview. This author reviewed the interview with him by telephone the first part of February, 2007. A few changes were made and Mr. Gries gave his approval to print this chapter.

Memories Of My Dad...
A Son Remembers...
Robert Rose

My dad always loved cats. Growing up we always had one or two around the house. He fed all the "alley" cats outside the apartment. I remember he would always put food in foil and bring it to them. If dad saw a cat on the street, he would find a store, buy cat food and feed the cat right there on the street.

My dad's favorite restaurant was the French Romanian. We ate there all the time. Dad would send me downtown to a bakery or eatery to buy cheese bagels. I do not recall the name, however I do know it was the only place that carried "his cheese bagels".

Dad was a good person. He was kind to everyone.

He had a very close friend back then. His name was Sal. I do not remember his last name.

Dad also loved to take me to Palisades Park. Dad would also rent a car and take me to Florida on vacation. We also took a trip to Canada. Dad loved to travel.

He spoiled me as a child. He treated me as though I was a "little king". All I had to say to him that I wanted this or that and before I knew dad would go out and buy it for me. He also saw to my education. He sent me to private school. I never wanted for anything growing up. He was a very good father.

I remember one day we were out and I wanted to go to the toy store. Dad took me to the store and let me purchase as many toys as I wanted that day. We took a cab home. Dad left a few of the packages inside the cab by mistake. Dad being the kind of "dad" he was...was not going to let me lose my toys...he called the cab company right away letting them know what had happened. As soon as the "cabby" came into the garage, they sent him back to the house with my toys.

I also remember when dad bought me my "Schwin" bike. I was eleven years old at the time. I told my dad how much I wanted this bike. The name of the bike was "pea picker" and the color was green. Dad went right out and bought it for me. It was the best bike out at the time. Dad knew that I really had wanted the "apple crate model"; however, I did not want to wait for it.

Dad was a "home body" person. He loved television. His favorite show was the Johnny Carson show.

I have many wonderful memories of my dad.

Robert Rose
Summer, 2006

Prominent Dates

Birthdates:

Irving "Slim" Rose: Born January 17, 1913 Died April, 1979
Exact date of death is unknown.

Arlene Rose: Born April 22, 1939
Maiden name Fallon

Robert Rose: Born April 25, 1956 in Los Angeles, CA

Facts of Interest

"Slim" and Arlene married June 7, 1954. Arlene was 15 and "Slim" was 41. They were married in Newark, New Jersey. They spent their honeymoon at Palisades Park. They resided at 53rd and Lexington Avenue. They divorced September 21, 1960. "Slim's" attorney for the divorce was Jacob Weinstock.

"Slim" never remarried.

The surname was changed from Rosenzwieg to Rose by "Slim".

The social security number issued to him was 079-03-9106.

"Slim" loved cats.

His favorite restaurant in Manhattan was the French Romanian.

His brother's name was Nathan Rosenzweig. Nathan was born in 1903 and died December 19, 1959 at the age of 56. Whether or not "Slim" had any other siblings is unknown.

"Slim's" address from approximately 1957 up until his time of death was 321 East 26th Street.

Times Square Records was incorporated. The date of the filing was May 12, 1960 in New York County. The registered agent was Jacob Weinstock, Esquire whose address was 55 West 42nd Street, New York 36 New York. The corporation was dissolved December 15, 1969.

He banked with Chemical Bank New York Trust Company.

"Slim" moved to Los Angels, CA with Arlene five months before Robert was born. The approximate date was December, 1955 or early January, 1956.

He obtained a Chauffeur's License driving for Yellow Cab Company.

His address was 454 Figneroa Street, Los Angeles. He would later move to 833 1/2 West 84th Street in Los Angeles.

Summing It All Up....

My Final Thoughts

Nadine DuBois

Throughout the entire book I have been your storyteller. The words you have read are not my own...they are the words of those who were there...who experienced or witnessed an event. Over the years many rumors have surfaced about "Slim". My sole purpose is to bring closure to days gone by....to put all the rumors to rest. These words are to honor Irving "Slim" Rose. To remember what time has forgotten...

I have remained neutral throughout the entire book. Any conclusion that you, the reader comes too.... will be one of your own accord. I have remained unbiased with my investigative journalism and continue to remain unbiased.

I regret that I was not able to include Harold Ginsburg's memories. Although I did locate him and I did contact him he failed to contact me. I respect his privacy.

My journey started back in January 2006. Although there have been detours I can truly say this journey has been a once in a lifetime for me. It is a journey that will remain near and dear to my heart.

It saddens me that I did not have the opportunity to meet "Slim" and the "gang". I am quite sure I would have fit right in at Times Square Records.

There is so much more to "Slim's" story that has not been told within these pages. I continue to be contacted by those who have a memory or two.... or a story to share.

Should you have any questions or would like to comment on the book, please feel free to email me at timessquarerecords@yahoo.com. There is also the Times Square Records website. The link to the website is http://www.timessquarerecords.org.

I apologize to you the reader for any misprint typing errors. I have since revised the book several times changing all the errors as they are brought to my attention.

The information in this book is factual to the best of my knowledge. I have substantiated this information with photo documentation when possible.

Should there be any disagreements regarding what has been written within the pages of this book, please contact the person whose name is associated with the chapter. I have stated from the beginning I am only the storyteller.

There is only one more thing left to say and I quote "Slim".......

"IT HAD TO END SOMETIME"

Irving "Slim" Rose

And so it did March 15, 1965

The "Slim" Archives....
A Photo Gallery

Arlene & Bobby Rose In California 1956...In the background is the cab that "Slim" drove while in LA....

Arlene Rose Pool......Today

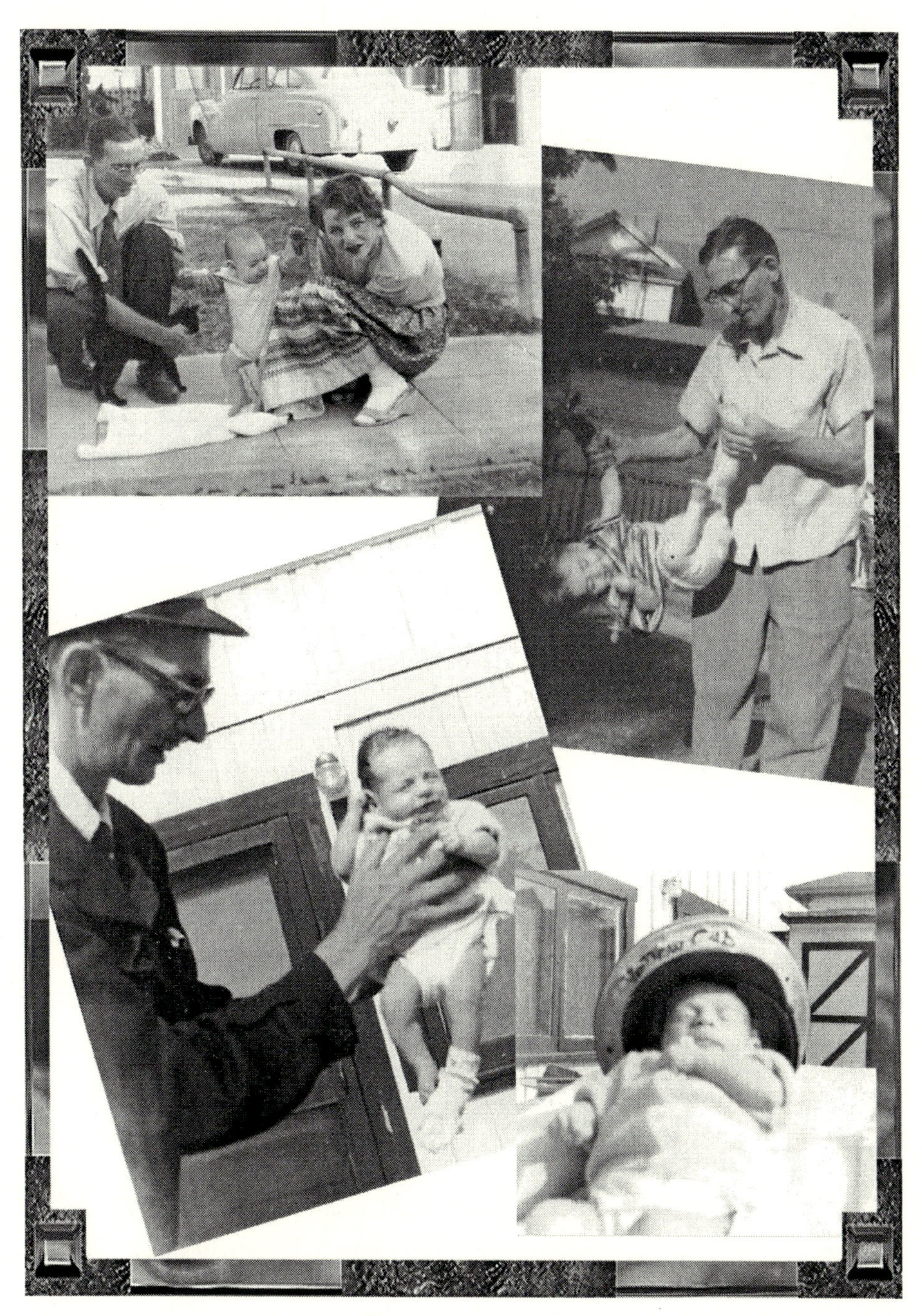

Family Photos In Los Angeles, CA....1956.....Note Little Bobby Is Wearing "Slim's" Yellow Cab Company Cap....

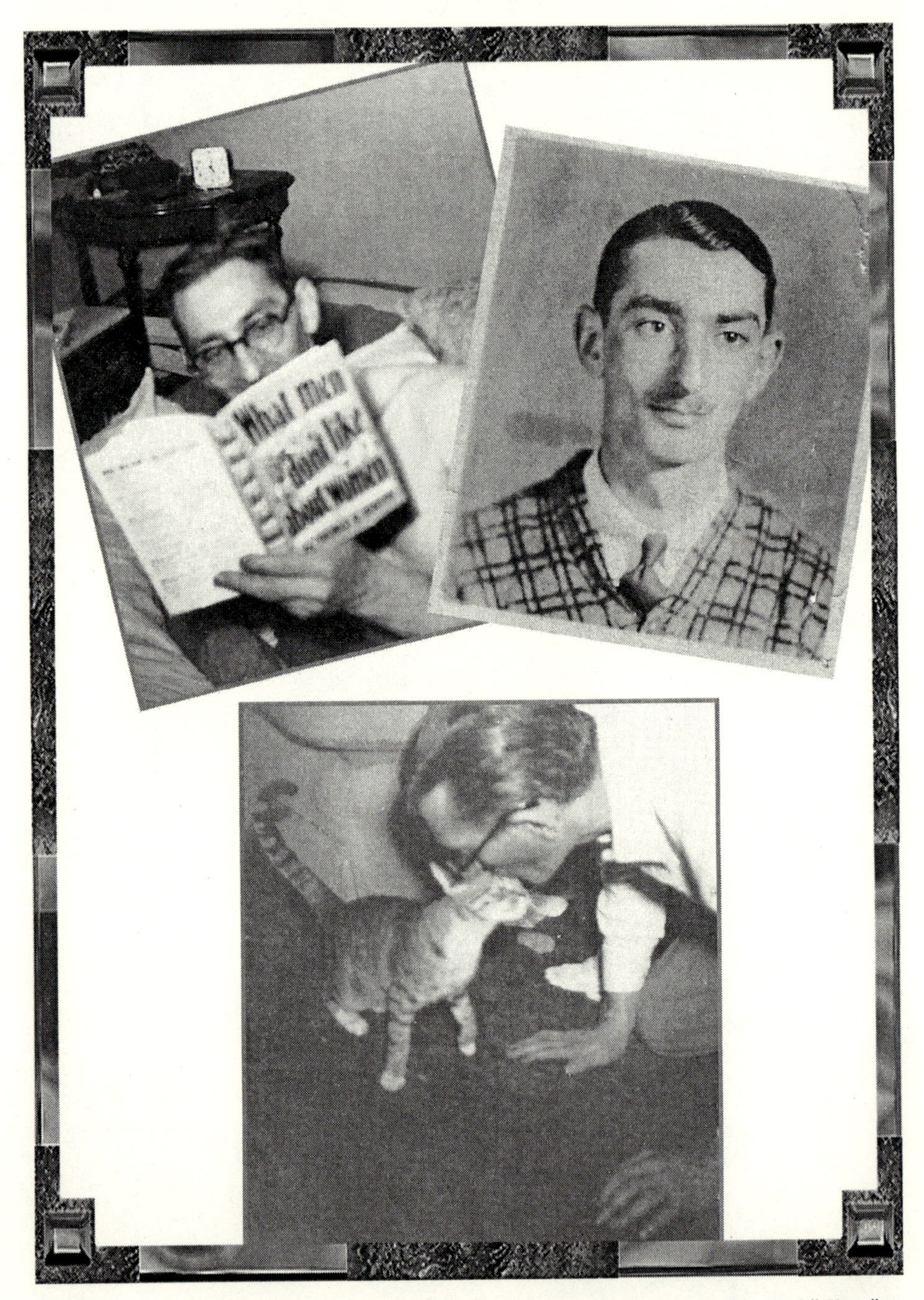

"Slim" Loved Cats....Here He Is At Home With Mausy....Early Photo Of "Slim" circa late 1930s...."Slim" Reading....Note The Title Of The Book...."Just Like "Slim".....

"Slim" Takes A Vacation.....In Florida.....

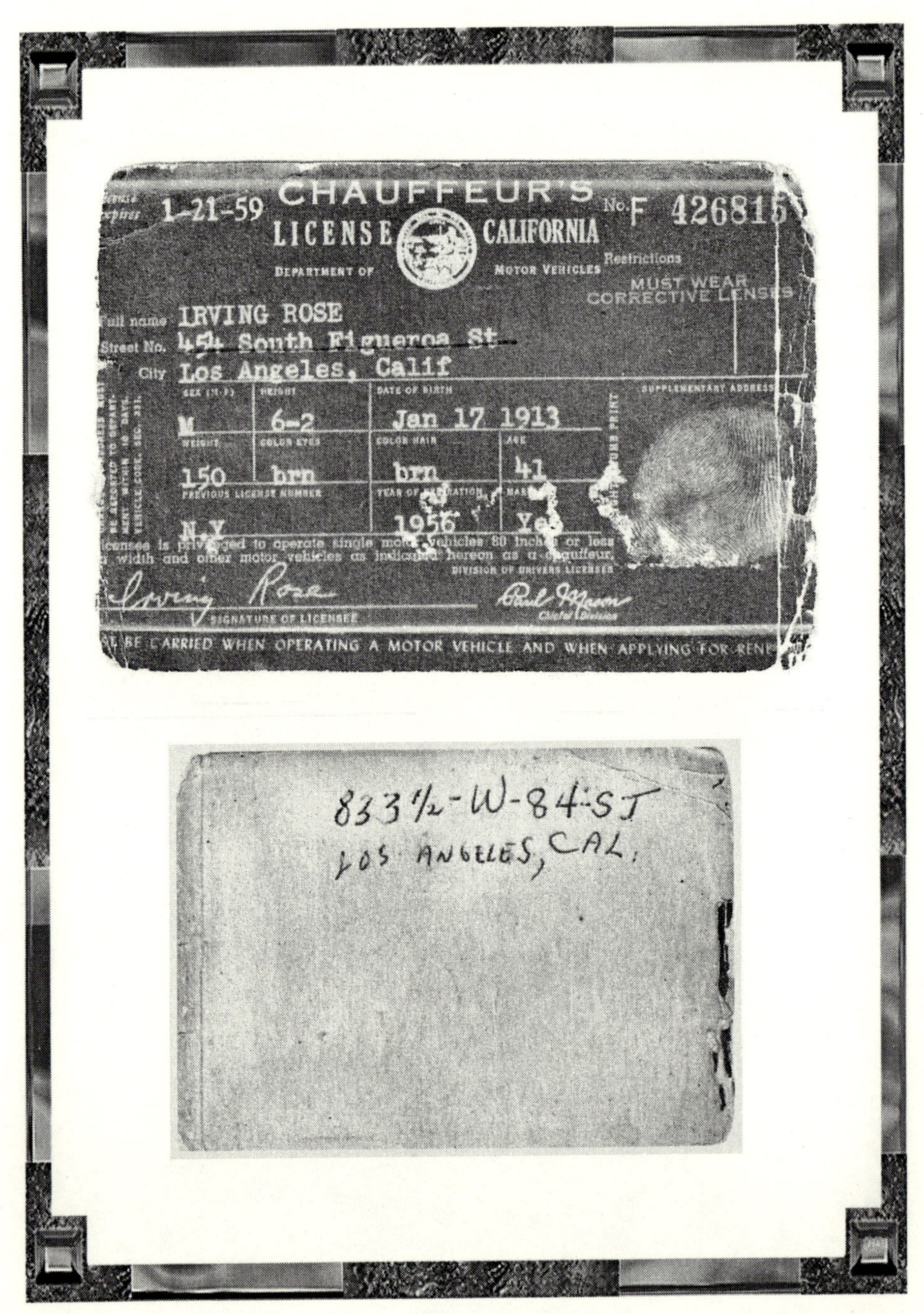

1-21-59 CHAUFFEUR'S No. F 426815

LICENSE CALIFORNIA

DEPARTMENT OF MOTOR VEHICLES

Restrictions

MUST WEAR CORRECTIVE LENSES

Full name IRVING ROSE

Street No. 454 South Figueroa St

City Los Angeles, Calif

SEX	HEIGHT	DATE OF BIRTH	
M	6-2	Jan 17 1913	
WEIGHT	COLOR EYES	COLOR HAIR	AGE
150	brn	brn	41
PREVIOUS LICENSE NUMBER		YEAR OF	
N.Y.		1956	Yes

SUPPLEMENTARY ADDRESS

in width and other motor vehicles as indicated hereon as a chauffeur.

DIVISION OF DRIVERS LICENSES

Irving Rose

SIGNATURE OF LICENSEE

Chief, Division

BE CARRIED WHEN OPERATING A MOTOR VEHICLE AND WHEN APPLYING FOR RENE

833½-W-84 ST

LOS ANGELES, CAL.

"Slim's" CA Drivers License....Contrary To The Rumors..."Slim" Did Drive....Note The Date 1956

"Slim" In Uniform....According To Arlene Rose Pool
"Slim" Served In The Army....

DAILY NEWS, FRIDAY, DECEMBER 9, 1960

A Li'l St. Nick Surprises Santa

By SALLY JOY BROWN

Record retailer Irving Rose of 1475 Broadway phoned the other day, saying he had a "surprise for Santa." He appeared at Sally Joy's Christmas Toy Chest yesterday with his 4-year-old son, Robert, dressed like old St. Nick. But that was only half if it.

To start off, junior Claus man Robert presented Santa with a piggy bank "filled with over 1,000 pennies that I put in myself." Then, with a "Look Santa, I'll show you how this works," Robert handed over some 200 toys, including banjos, dump trucks, jack-in-the-boxes, 3-D cameras and—to top it all off—600 candy canes.

How about YOUR youngster?

The Forgotten Child

Has he or she a shiny new toy to brighten Christmas morn for some otherwise forgotten child?

Bring both youngster and gift to Santa at THE NEWS today.

And remember, not having something to give is no reason for staying away!

We've a holiday display in our newly enlarged lobby that'll pop the youngster's eyes. There's a 57-foot simulated Christmas tree brightened with bells, bulbs, horns and other ornaments. And you'll want to take a look, too, at our famed revolving globe, maps and weather instruments.

Santa's Schedule

As for Santa—he's on duty 9 A.M. to 6 P.M. weekdays and 10 A.M. to 6 P.M. Saturdays and Sundays. If you can't see him, you can leave your gift with a Santa's Helper 6 to 7 P.M. Mondays through Fridays.

Santa's beautiful blonde elf, Twinkletoes, will personally see to it that all of Sally's donors receive a Christmas button and Santa Helper Certificate, and that they have their names published in THE NEWS.

(NEWS foto by George Mattson)

Santa meets Santa as Robert Rose, 4, presents toys to Sally Joy Brown's Christmas Toy Chest yesterday.

How to Aid St. Nick

Bring your gift to THE NEWS lobby, 220 E. 42d St. If you would like to contribute, but haven't time to shop, Sally Joy Brown will shop for you. Simply make your check or money order payable to Sally Joy Brown's Christmas Toy Chest, THE NEWS, 220 E. 42d St., New York 17, N. Y. Donations are tax deductible.

Carol Weissman, Phyllis O'Neill, Sharon Wasserman, Idalia Delgado, Kathy and John DeBaun, Patricia Elvir, Julie and Mark Baron, Diane Levine, Amy and Wendy Pesin, Kenny Rappolla, Jacob Nahmias, Deborah Conchon, Cheryl, Gregory and Diane Powell, John Keappock, Bradly Walsh, Joyce Smith.

Pam, Terry and Bernard Beldo, Pauline and Debbie Sanoritano, Carol Munoz, Peter and Gregory Jeswski, Suzanne Steren, Bernard Thombs, John Stratrcakis, Gwendolyn, Elliott and Bruce [illegible], Laryne Wolliey, Brunilda Roja[illegible], Marie Pezzi, Josephine Izzi, Joseph and Phillip Femoyer, Vincent and Barbara Auleta, Barbara, Anthony and Frank Ferrante, Kathy, Adeline and Francis Rattigan, John, Gregory and Lisa Orolino, Charles Fischer, Stephen Scotto-Lavino.

Pauline Forsrave, Angela and Joseph Minissi, Augusto Baraohe, Jane [illegible]son, Kenny Himmel, Moreen Downing, Stephanie Fanelli, Floyd Esauri, Susan and Richard Younger, Raymond Durert, Linda and Frank Gall, Johnny Tori, Keith Wilson, David Peraza, Arthur Ippolito, Ralph and George Mayer, Lester, Lee and Pamela Saltzberg, Larry Samson, Erika Dobbelaar, Paul Lewis, Patrick and Sean Forkins, Elizabeth Church, Joseph Cosentino, Danny [illegible]

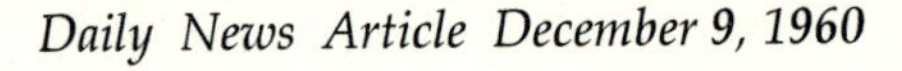

Daily News Article December 9, 1960

"Slim's" Son Bobby....Graduating....His Current Wife Joanne

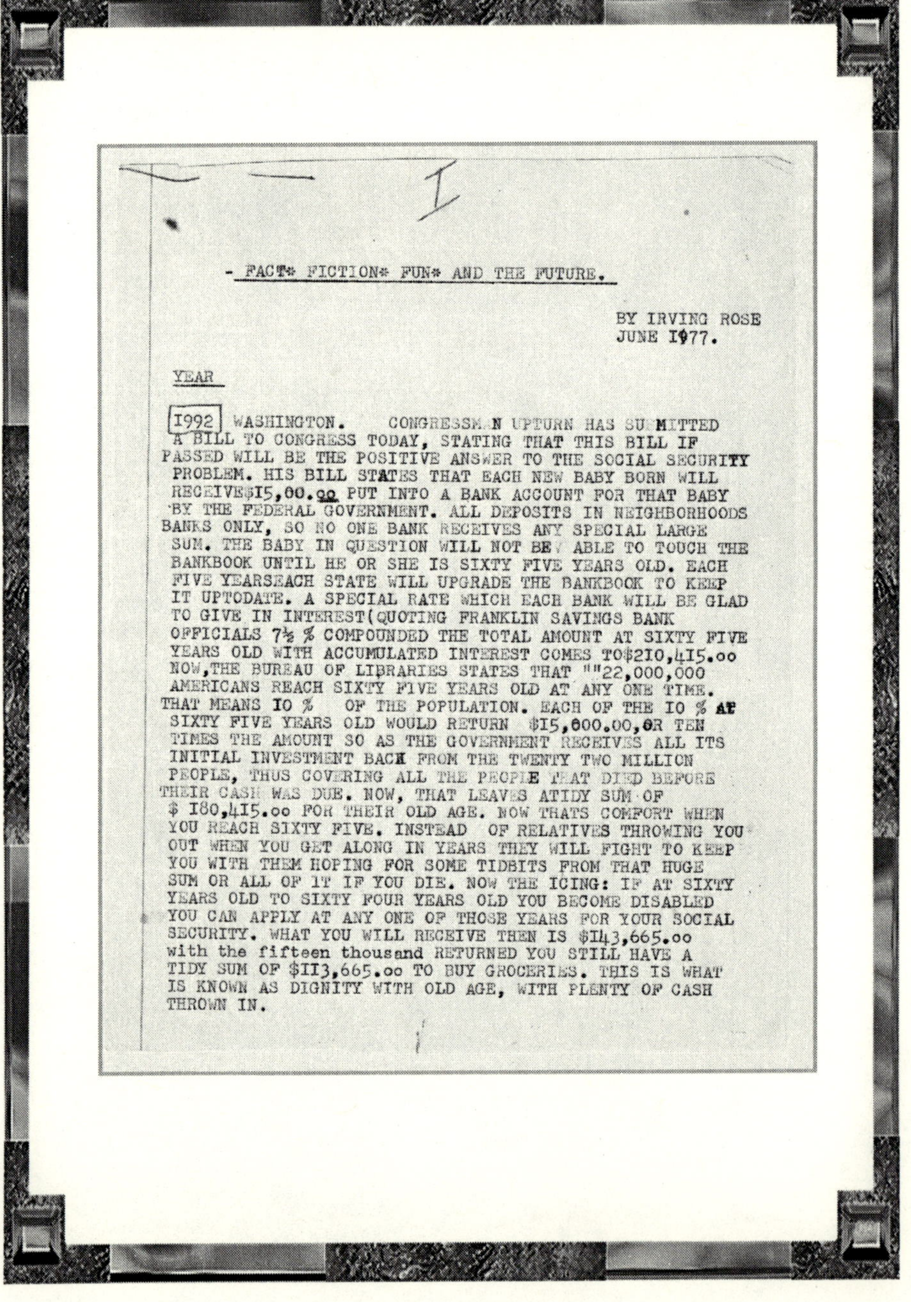

I

- FACT* FICTION* FUN* AND THE FUTURE.

BY IRVING ROSE
JUNE I977.

YEAR

1992 WASHINGTON. CONGRESSMAN UPTURN HAS SUBMITTED A BILL TO CONGRESS TODAY, STATING THAT THIS BILL IF PASSED WILL BE THE POSITIVE ANSWER TO THE SOCIAL SECURITY PROBLEM. HIS BILL STATES THAT EACH NEW BABY BORN WILL RECEIVE$I5,00.00 PUT INTO A BANK ACCOUNT FOR THAT BABY BY THE FEDERAL GOVERNMENT. ALL DEPOSITS IN NEIGHBORHOODS BANKS ONLY, SO NO ONE BANK RECEIVES ANY SPECIAL LARGE SUM. THE BABY IN QUESTION WILL NOT BE ABLE TO TOUCH THE BANKBOOK UNTIL HE OR SHE IS SIXTY FIVE YEARS OLD. EACH FIVE YEARSEACH STATE WILL UPGRADE THE BANKBOOK TO KEEP IT UPTODATE. A SPECIAL RATE WHICH EACH BANK WILL BE GLAD TO GIVE IN INTEREST(QUOTING FRANKLIN SAVINGS BANK OFFICIALS 7½ % COMPOUNDED THE TOTAL AMOUNT AT SIXTY FIVE YEARS OLD WITH ACCUMULATED INTEREST COMES TO$2I0,4I5.oo NOW,THE BUREAU OF LIBRARIES STATES THAT ""22,000,000 AMERICANS REACH SIXTY FIVE YEARS OLD AT ANY ONE TIME. THAT MEANS IO % OF THE POPULATION. EACH OF THE IO % AT SIXTY FIVE YEARS OLD WOULD RETURN $I5,000.00,OR TEN TIMES THE AMOUNT SO AS THE GOVERNMENT RECEIVES ALL ITS INITIAL INVESTMENT BACK FROM THE TWENTY TWO MILLION PEOPLE, THUS COVERING ALL THE PEOPLE THAT DIED BEFORE THEIR CASH WAS DUE. NOW, THAT LEAVES ATIDY SUM OF $ I80,4I5.oo FOR THEIR OLD AGE. NOW THATS COMFORT WHEN YOU REACH SIXTY FIVE. INSTEAD OF RELATIVES THROWING YOU OUT WHEN YOU GET ALONG IN YEARS THEY WILL FIGHT TO KEEP YOU WITH THEM HOPING FOR SOME TIDBITS FROM THAT HUGE SUM OR ALL OF IT IF YOU DIE. NOW THE ICING: IF AT SIXTY YEARS OLD TO SIXTY FOUR YEARS OLD YOU BECOME DISABLED YOU CAN APPLY AT ANY ONE OF THOSE YEARS FOR YOUR SOCIAL SECURITY. WHAT YOU WILL RECEIVE THEN IS $I43,665.oo with the fifteen thousand RETURNED YOU STILL HAVE A TIDY SUM OF $II3,665.oo TO BUY GROCERIES. THIS IS WHAT IS KNOWN AS DIGNITY WITH OLD AGE, WITH PLENTY OF CASH THROWN IN.

"Slim" Liked To Write......

2

1982---WASHINGTON **** SENATOR ROBERT BAGMAN WAS SUSPENDED TODAY FOR SMOKING A MARAJUANA CIGARETTE WHILE THE SENATE WAS IN SESSION. HE IMMEDIATELY INTRODUCED A BILL IN CONGRESS MAKING MARAJUANA LEGAL.

1981**** NEW YORK****ASS. PRESS**********ALL T V WEATHER FORECASTERS WERE ARRESTED TODAY FOR FRAUD. DISTRICT ATTORNEY HEAVES ANNOUNCED THE ARRESTS TODAY. THE INDICTMENTS CHARGE THAT ALL THE WEATHER FORECASTERS DISCRIMINATE BY NOT GIVING ANY WEATHER FROM EAST TO WEST. DISTRICT ATTORNEY HEAVES SAYS, HE IS SURE THAT OREGON AND WASHINGTON STATE DO RECEIVE WINDS AND STORMS FROM THE EAST. (CHECK YOUR WEATHERMEN)

2001***HOUSTON,TEX.
DINA SAUR FIRST LADY ASTRONAUT TO FLY IN SPACE HAS SENT A SIGNAL BACK TO THE HOUSTON GROUND CREW THAT SHE WAS RAPED IN SPACE AND WHAT TO DO. HER ANSWER CAME IN A QUESTION, WERE THE CAMERAS ON THEN? BRING THE MOVIES BACK SO WE ALL CAN BE SURE.

2407**UNMATED PRESS
THE STURGEON GENERAL HAS ANNOUNCED TODAY THAT SMOKING CIGARETTES MAY CAUSE CANCER, SO PLEASE STICK TO MARAJUANA.

2011 **QUEERSVILLE TEXAS
AT 6PM LAST NIGHT THERE WAS A BIRTH IN THIS SMALL TOWN. NOTHING UNUSUAL EXCEPT THAT THEY WERE SIAMESE TRIPLETS. DR CUTTER MADE A STATEMENT. HE SAID THEY ARE SO MIXED UP HE DOESNT KNOW IF THEY ARE GIRLS OR BOYS.

1986---N.Y.C.
THERE WAS A HYJACKING LAST NIGHT. SOMEONE MADE OFF WITH THE STATEN ISLAND FERRY. THERE WAS A COUPLE INVOLVED. THEY DEMANDED TO GO TO CUBA(FURTHER DETAILS LATER.

ERIES ONE

I

IRVING ROSE
JUNE 1971

LITTLE THOUGHTS OF THE PAST.-

Sleeping in the small waiting rooms with the pot bellied stoves on the 2d or 3d ave. elevated train stations(With no worrys).----
Women using Chanel #5, just enough to drive men wild.----
The unemployment agencys and beanieries on 6th ave. between 42d st. and 50th sts.-----
Nuts, shooting a cannon at the U. N. Building from long island city, and coming up short.------
Listening to the first radio called a crystal set and the only program was a church choir four blocks away(A wonder at the time though.-----
Sleeping in Central Park at night with the only worrywhether it wpuld rain or not. -------
WHEN the Daily News and Daily Mirror were 2 cents each and riding the subway was 5 cents.-----
Listening to Mayor La Guardia read the comic strips over the radio on Sundays.-----
Spending the whole night eating at the Bird In Hand Restaurant on Broadway and 52th St.(Talking Mostly)-----
Many women wearing full size bathing suits and still looking beautiful.(Thats why you are here today)-----
When Babe Herman in Ebbetts Field tried to catch a fly ball with his head.-----
Lefty Gomez pitching for the Yankees in a world series game tie score, bases loaded, nobody out,he stops to watch an airplane overhead pulling a streamer which read,keep cool.---
The great food in all the Automats, those days.-----
Florsheim Shoes priced at $4.98------(YOUR - PICK - IN - STORE)
Cars with homemade trunks on the back, usually Fords, also running boards on sides to stand on.-----
Solid cars in their day, STUTZ MOON CHANDLER.-----
In the winter when theres a heavy snow, only men with shovels are used, as they pry open the sewersand shove the snow down in

"Slim's" Brother Nathan.....Julius & Martha Garcia In The Car "Slim" Purchased For Them....Bobby Standing In Front Of The Car....Note The Date...November, 1960

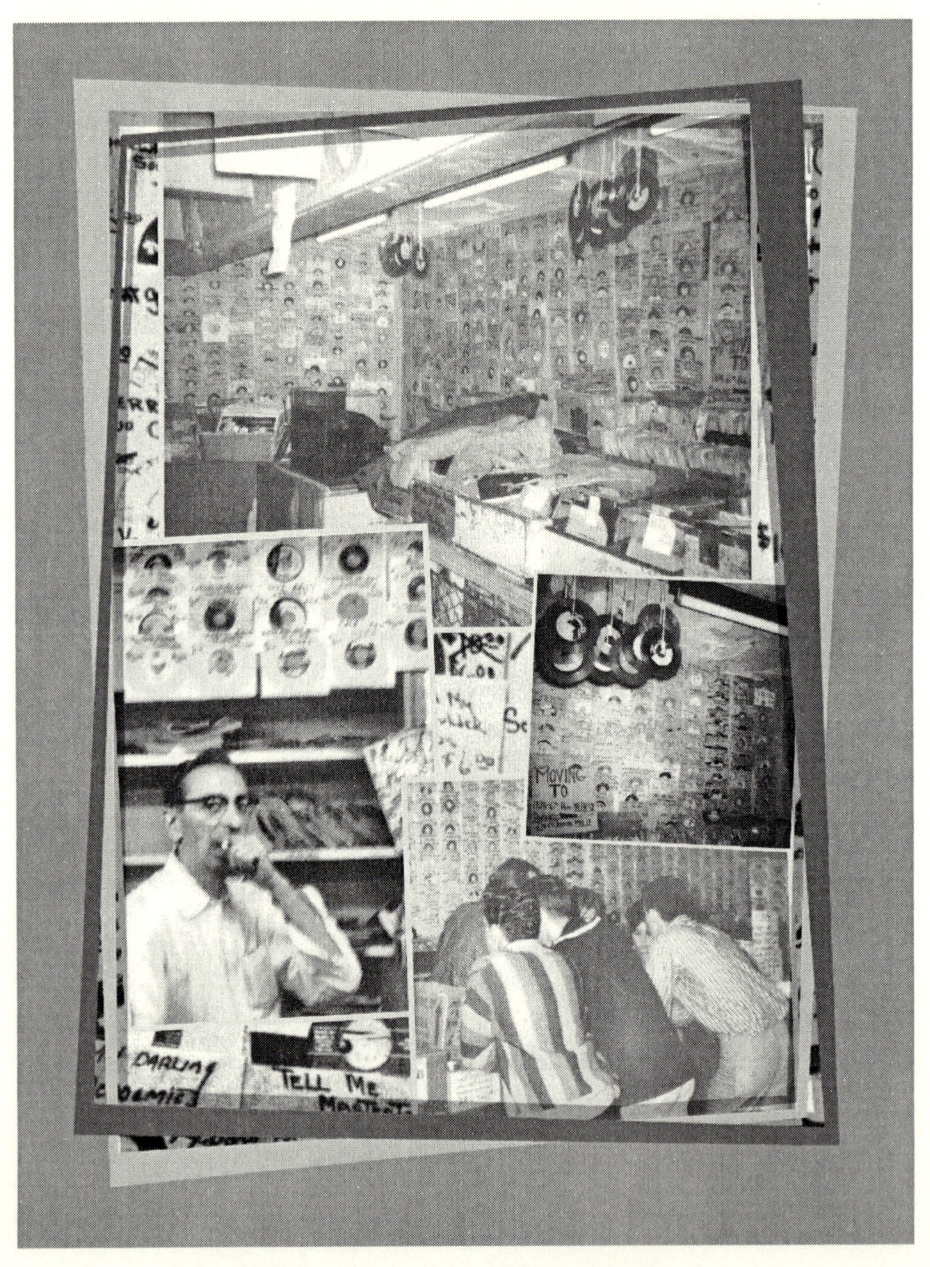

The Beginning Of Times Square Records.....

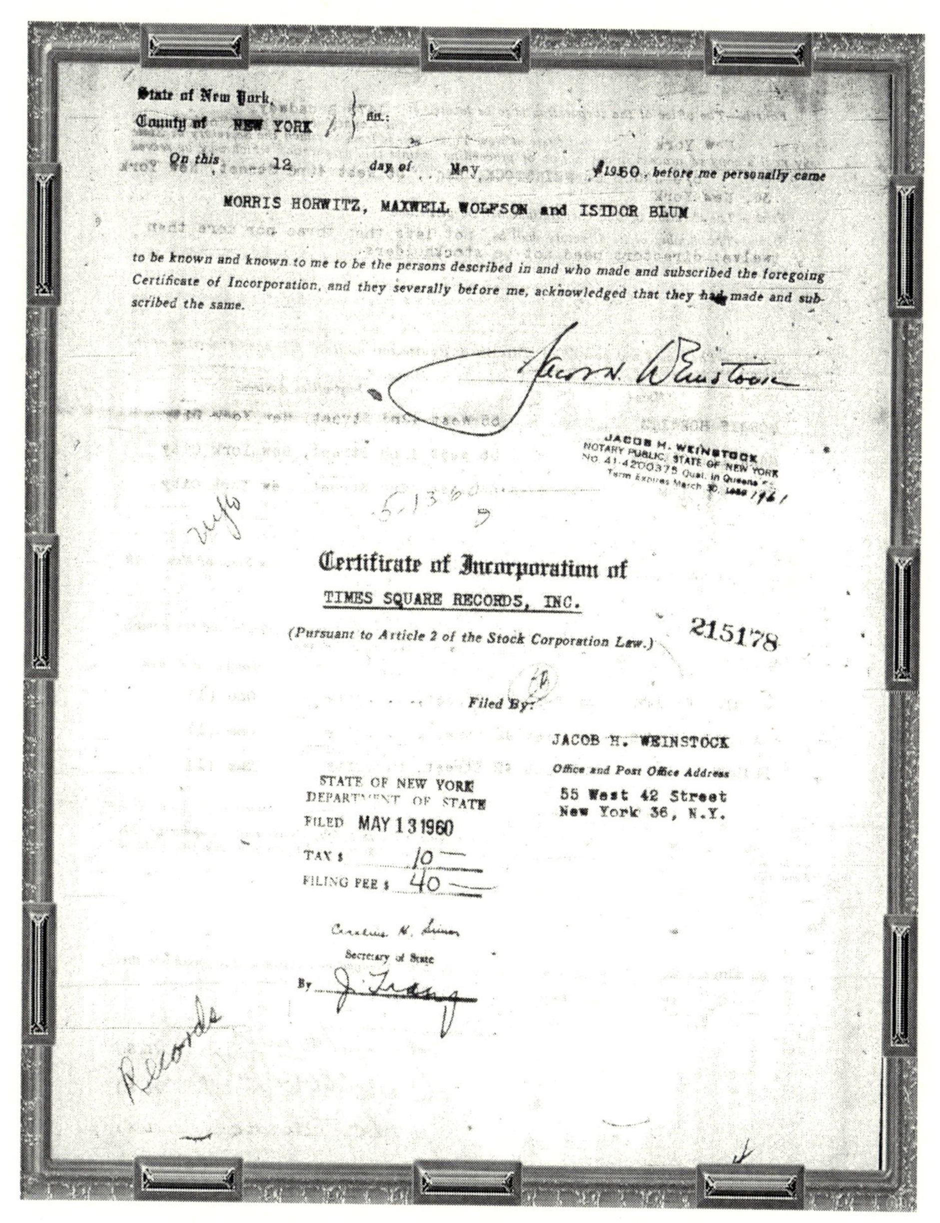
State of New York,
County of NEW YORK } ss.:

On this 12 day of May 1960, before me personally came

MORRIS HORWITZ, MAXWELL WOLFSON and ISIDOR BLUM

to be known and known to me to be the persons described in and who made and subscribed the foregoing Certificate of Incorporation, and they severally before me, acknowledged that they had made and subscribed the same.

Jacob H. Weinstock

JACOB H. WEINSTOCK
NOTARY PUBLIC, STATE OF NEW YORK
No. 41-4200375 Qual. in Queens Co.
Term Expires March 30, 1961

5-13-60

Certificate of Incorporation of
TIMES SQUARE RECORDS, INC.

(Pursuant to Article 2 of the Stock Corporation Law.)

215178

Filed By:

JACOB H. WEINSTOCK
Office and Post Office Address
55 West 42 Street
New York 36, N.Y.

STATE OF NEW YORK
DEPARTMENT OF STATE
FILED MAY 13 1960
TAX $ 10
FILING FEE $ 40

Secretary of State

By

Records

I Obtained An Original Copy Of The Corporate Records…..

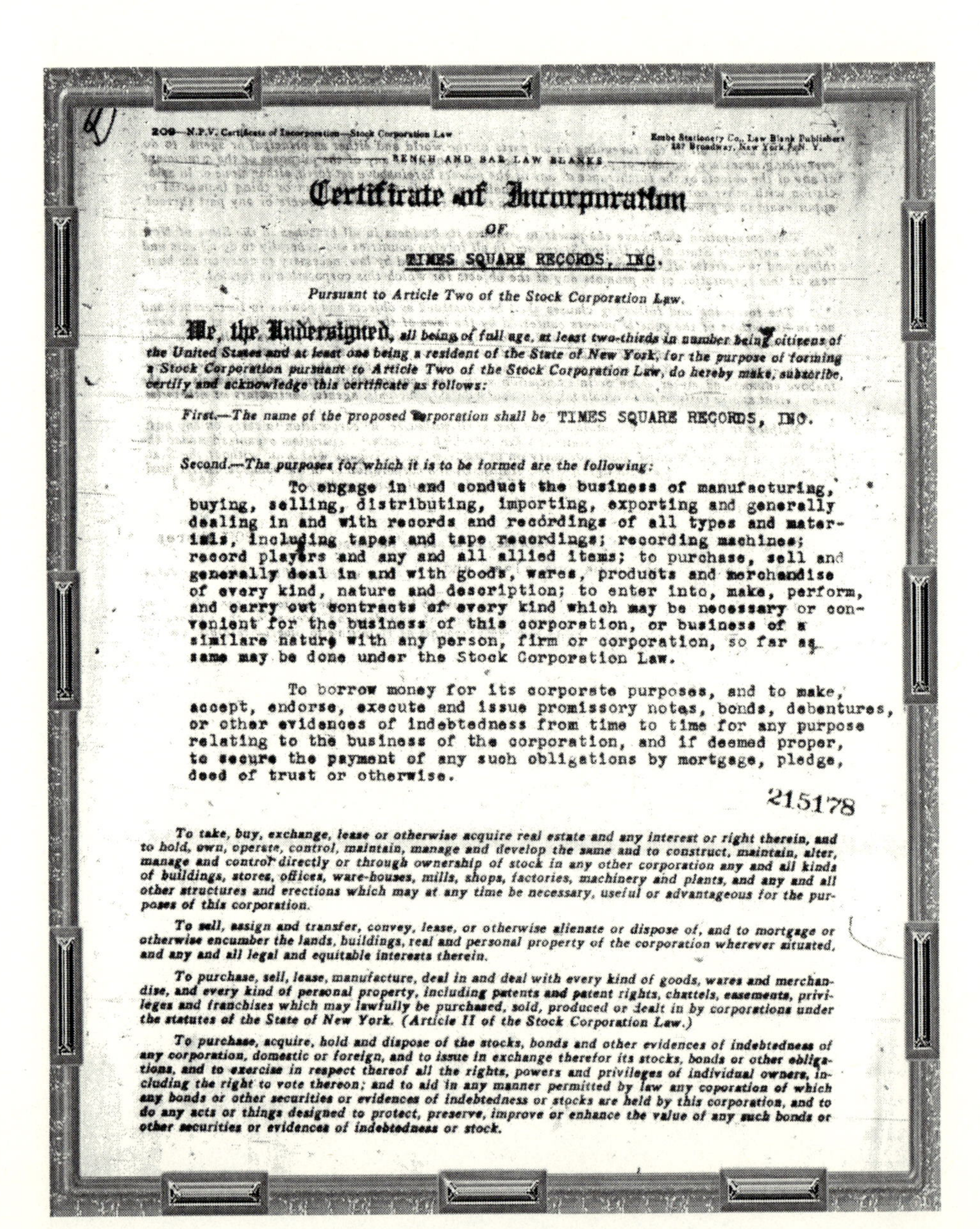

209—N.P.V. Certificate of Incorporation—Stock Corporation Law

Embe Stationery Co., Law Blank Publishers
187 Broadway, New York, N. Y.

BENCH AND BAR LAW BLANKS

Certificate of Incorporation

OF

TIMES SQUARE RECORDS, INC.

Pursuant to Article Two of the Stock Corporation Law.

We, the Undersigned, *all being of full age, at least two-thirds in number being citizens of the United States and at least one being a resident of the State of New York, for the purpose of forming a Stock Corporation pursuant to Article Two of the Stock Corporation Law, do hereby make, subscribe, certify and acknowledge this certificate as follows:*

First.—The name of the proposed corporation shall be TIMES SQUARE RECORDS, INC.

Second.—The purposes for which it is to be formed are the following:

To engage in and conduct the business of manufacturing, buying, selling, distributing, importing, exporting and generally dealing in and with records and recordings of all types and materials, including tapes and tape recordings; recording machines; record players and any and all allied items; to purchase, sell and generally deal in and with goods, wares, products and merchandise of every kind, nature and description; to enter into, make, perform, and carry out contracts of every kind which may be necessary or convenient for the business of this corporation, or business of a similare nature with any person, firm or corporation, so far as same may be done under the Stock Corporation Law.

To borrow money for its corporate purposes, and to make, accept, endorse, execute and issue promissory notes, bonds, debentures, or other evidences of indebtedness from time to time for any purpose relating to the business of the corporation, and if deemed proper, to secure the payment of any such obligations by mortgage, pledge, deed of trust or otherwise.

215178

To take, buy, exchange, lease or otherwise acquire real estate and any interest or right therein, and to hold, own, operate, control, maintain, manage and develop the same and to construct, maintain, alter, manage and control directly or through ownership of stock in any other corporation any and all kinds of buildings, stores, offices, ware-houses, mills, shops, factories, machinery and plants, and any and all other structures and erections which may at any time be necessary, useful or advantageous for the purposes of this corporation.

To sell, assign and transfer, convey, lease, or otherwise alienate or dispose of, and to mortgage or otherwise encumber the lands, buildings, real and personal property of the corporation wherever situated, and any and all legal and equitable interests therein.

To purchase, sell, lease, manufacture, deal in and deal with every kind of goods, wares and merchandise, and every kind of personal property, including patents and patent rights, chattels, easements, privileges and franchises which may lawfully be purchased, sold, produced or dealt in by corporations under the statutes of the State of New York. (Article II of the Stock Corporation Law.)

To purchase, acquire, hold and dispose of the stocks, bonds and other evidences of indebtedness of any corporation, domestic or foreign, and to issue in exchange therefor its stocks, bonds or other obligations, and to exercise in respect thereof all the rights, powers and privileges of individual owners, including the right to vote thereon; and to aid in any manner permitted by law any coporation of which any bonds or other securities or evidences of indebtedness or stocks are held by this corporation, and to do any acts or things designed to protect, preserve, improve or enhance the value of any such bonds or other securities or evidences of indebtedness or stock.

Times Square Records Had Stock Certificates

To do any or all of the foregoing in all parts of the world and either as principal or agent; to do everything necessary, suitable or proper for the accomplishment of any of the purposes or the attainment of any of the objects or the furtherance of any of the powers hereinabove set forth, either alone or in association with other corporations, firms or individuals, and to do every other act or thing incidental or appurtenant to or growing out of or connected with the aforesaid business or powers or any part thereof.

This corporation shall have the power to conduct its business in all branches in the State of New York or any other State of the United States and in all foreign countries and generally to do all acts and things and to exercise all the powers, now or hereafter authorized by law, necessary to carry on the business of this corporation or to promote any of the objects for which this corporation is formed.

The foregoing and following clauses shall be construed as objects and powers in furtherance and not in limitations of the general powers conferred by the laws of the State of New York; and it is hereby expressly provided that the foregoing and following enumeration of specific powers shall not be held to limit or restrict in any manner the powers of this corporation, and that this corporation may do all and everything necessary, suitable or proper for the accomplishment of any of the purposes or objects hereinabove enumerated either alone or in association with other corporations, firms, or individuals, to the same extent and as fully as individuals might or could do as principals, agents, contractors or otherwise.

Nothing in this certificate contained, however, shall authorize the corporation to carry on any business or exercise any powers in any state or country which a similar corporation organized under the laws of such state or country could not carry on or exercise, or to engage within or without the State of New York in the business of a lighting or a transportation corporation or in the common carrier business, or to issue bills, notes or other evidence of debt for circulation as money.

Third.—The total number of shares which may be issued by the corporation is 200 shares all of which are to be one class and all of which shall be without par value.

The capital of the corporation shall be at least equal to the sum of the aggregate par value of all issued shares having par value, plus the aggregate amount of consideration received by the corporation for the issuance of shares without par value, plus such amounts as, from time to time, by resolution of the Board of Directors, may be transferred thereto.

2

Available Were Two Hundred Shares

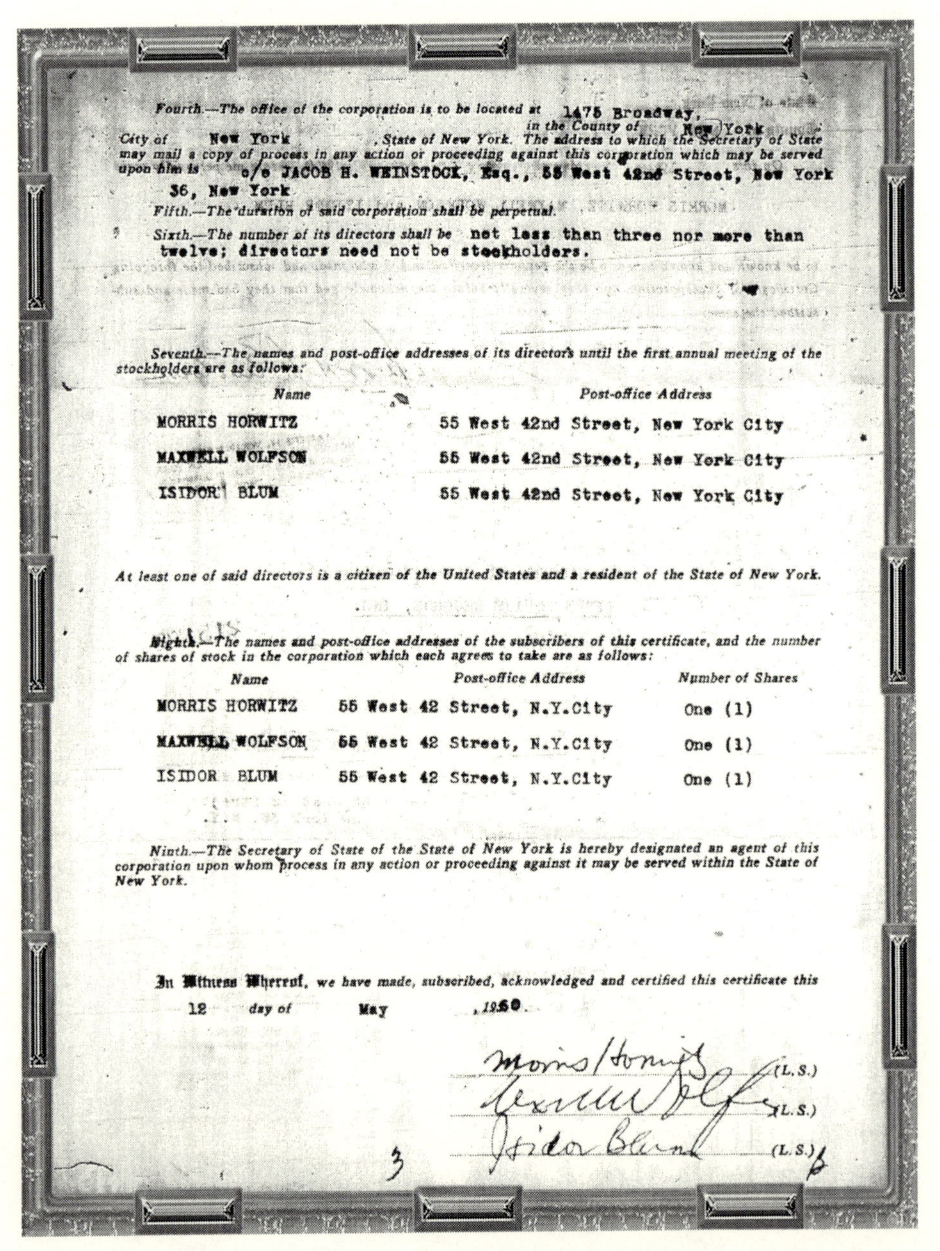

Fourth.—The office of the corporation is to be located at 1475 Broadway, in the County of New York City of New York, State of New York. The address to which the Secretary of State may mail a copy of process in any action or proceeding against this corporation which may be served upon him is c/o JACOB H. WEINSTOCK, Esq., 55 West 42nd Street, New York 36, New York

Fifth.—The duration of said corporation shall be perpetual.

Sixth.—The number of its directors shall be not less than three nor more than twelve; directors need not be stockholders.

Seventh.—The names and post-office addresses of its directors until the first annual meeting of the stockholders are as follows:

Name	Post-office Address
MORRIS HORWITZ	55 West 42nd Street, New York City
MAXWELL WOLFSON	55 West 42nd Street, New York City
ISIDOR BLUM	55 West 42nd Street, New York City

At least one of said directors is a citizen of the United States and a resident of the State of New York.

Eighth.—The names and post-office addresses of the subscribers of this certificate, and the number of shares of stock in the corporation which each agrees to take are as follows:

Name	Post-office Address	Number of Shares
MORRIS HORWITZ	55 West 42 Street, N.Y.City	One (1)
MAXWELL WOLFSON	55 West 42 Street, N.Y.City	One (1)
ISIDOR BLUM	55 West 42 Street, N.Y.City	One (1)

Ninth.—The Secretary of State of the State of New York is hereby designated an agent of this corporation upon whom process in any action or proceeding against it may be served within the State of New York.

In Witness Whereof, we have made, subscribed, acknowledged and certified this certificate this 12 day of May, 1960.

Morris Horwitz (L.S.)
Maxwell Wolfson (L.S.)
Isidor Blum (L.S.)

3

List of Stockholders

The "Cast Of Characters"..."Slim" & His Employees

Customers....Billy Haines (Deceased)...Val Shively center....Frank Devaie and Marcia Vance. The name of the girl in the upper right corner is unknown.

Val Shively...Bobby Campbell....Note The Newspaper Hanging On The Wall..."Slim" Selling Pretzels.....Val Shively Was Always Playing Tricks On "Slim"...

Lou Tavani Sang With The Contenders....Val Shively Holding His First Expensive Purchase..."Miss You"...."Crows"...."Rama"..." Red Wax"...Price $30.00 Circa 1964

"Slim" Behind The Counter......

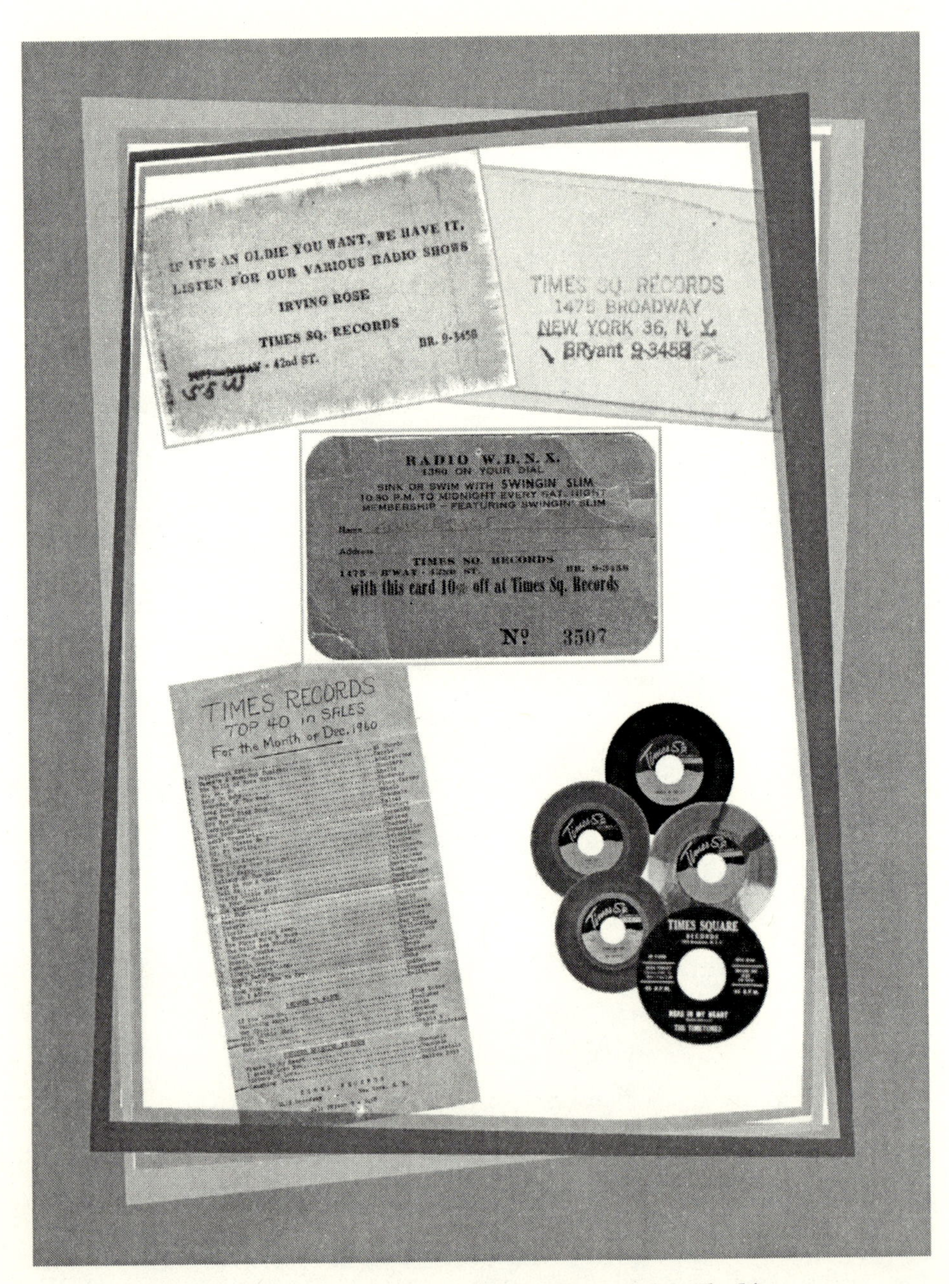

The Business Card....Fan Club Card....The Label & The Lists.....

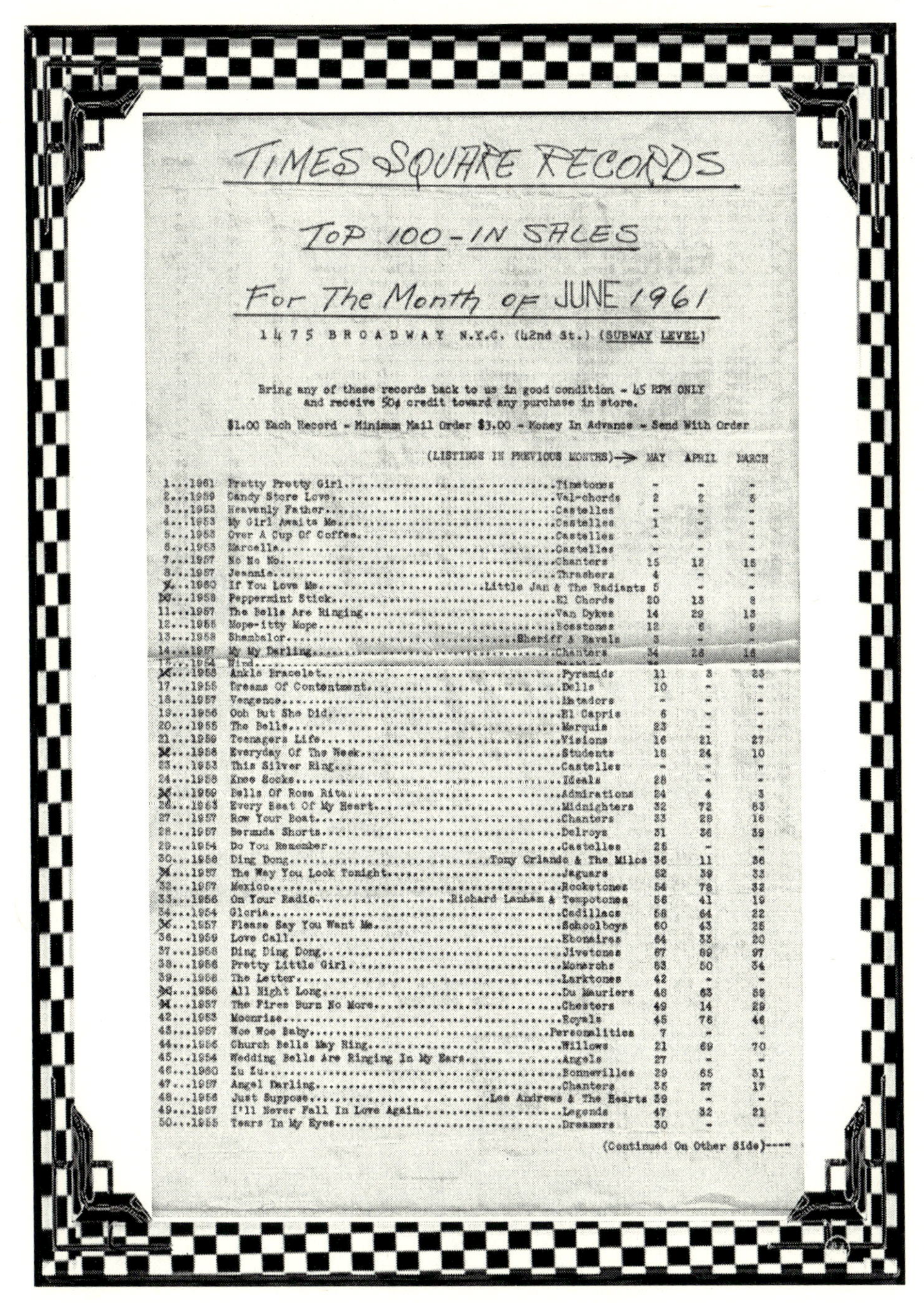

TIMES SQUARE RECORDS

TOP 100 - IN SALES

For The Month of JUNE 1961

1475 BROADWAY N.Y.C. (42nd St.) (SUBWAY LEVEL)

Bring any of these records back to us in good condition - 45 RPM ONLY
and receive 50¢ credit toward any purchase in store.

$1.00 Each Record - Minimum Mail Order $3.00 - Money In Advance - Send With Order

No.	Year	Title	Artist	(LISTINGS IN PREVIOUS MONTHS)→ MAY	APRIL	MARCH
1	1961	Pretty Pretty Girl	Timetones	-	-	-
2	1959	Candy Store Love	Val-chords	2	2	5
3	1953	Heavenly Father	Castelles	-	-	-
4	1953	My Girl Awaits Me	Castelles	1	-	-
5	1953	Over A Cup Of Coffee	Castelles	-	-	-
6	1953	Marcella	Castelles	-	-	-
7	1957	No No No	Chanters	15	12	18
8	1957	Jeannie	Thrashers	4	-	-
9	1960	If You Love Me	Little Jan & The Radiants	5	-	-
10	1958	Peppermint Stick	El Chords	20	13	8
11	1957	The Bells Are Ringing	Van Dykes	14	29	13
12	1955	Mope-itty Mope	Bosstones	12	6	9
13	1958	Shambalor	Sheriff & Ravels	3	-	-
14	1957	My My Darling	Chanters	34	28	16
15	1954	Wind	[illegible]	[illegible]	[illegible]	[illegible]
16	1958	Ankle Bracelet	Pyramids	11	3	23
17	1955	Dreams Of Contentment	Dells	10	-	-
18	1957	Vengence	Matadors	-	-	-
19	1956	Ooh But She Did	El Capris	6	-	-
20	1955	The Bells	Marquis	23	-	-
21	1959	Teenagers Life	Visions	16	21	27
22	1958	Everyday Of The Week	Students	18	24	10
23	1953	This Silver Ring	Castelles	-	-	-
24	1958	Knee Socks	Ideals	28	-	-
25	1959	Bells Of Rosa Rita	Admirations	24	4	3
26	1953	Every Beat Of My Heart	Midnighters	32	72	63
27	1957	Row Your Boat	Chanters	33	28	16
28	1957	Bermuda Shorts	Delroys	31	36	39
29	1954	Do You Remember	Castelles	26	-	-
30	1958	Ding Dong	Tony Orlando & The Milos	36	11	36
31	1957	The Way You Look Tonight	Jaguars	52	39	33
32	1957	Mexico	Rocketones	54	78	32
33	1956	On Your Radio	Richard Lanham & Tempotones	56	41	19
34	1954	Gloria	Cadillacs	58	64	22
35	1957	Please Say You Want Me	Schoolboys	60	43	25
36	1959	Love Call	Ebonaires	64	33	20
37	1958	Ding Ding Dong	Jivetones	67	89	97
38	1956	Pretty Little Girl	Monarchs	63	50	34
39	1958	The Letter	Larktones	42	-	-
40	1956	All Night Long	Du Mauriers	48	63	58
41	1957	The Fires Burn No More	Chesters	49	14	29
42	1953	Moonrise	Royals	45	76	46
43	1957	Woo Woo Baby	Personalities	7	-	-
44	1956	Church Bells May Ring	Willows	21	69	70
45	1954	Wedding Bells Are Ringing In My Ears	Angels	27	-	-
46	1960	Zu Zu	Bonnevilles	29	65	31
47	1957	Angel Darling	Chanters	35	27	17
48	1958	Just Suppose	Lee Andrews & The Hearts	39	-	-
49	1957	I'll Never Fall In Love Again	Legends	47	32	21
50	1955	Tears In My Eyes	Dreamers	30	-	-

(Continued On Other Side)----

Top 100 Hits....June 1961...Front

#	Year	Title	Artist	MAY	APRIL	MARCH
51	1957	Coralee	Teenchords	59	68	75
52	1957	Why Do You Make Me Cry	Cubs	65	92	52
53	1958	My Weakness	Capris	70	-	-
54	1957	Lamplight	Deltas	76	79	60
X	1959	Let It Please Be You	Desires	68	20	64
56	1961	Wear My Ring	Creators	97	-	-
X	1959	To Make A Long Story Short	Eddie & The Starlights	92	74	91
58	1957	My Love Is Gone	Ladders	80	25	11
59	1958	I Remember	5 Discs	79	22	6
60	1954	God Only Knows	Capris	73	67	71
61	1957	Sweetest One	Crests	57	57	28
X	1959	Shout	Isely Bros.	51	17	88
63	1956	Bluebird of Happiness	Lee Andrews & The Hearts	37	-	-
64	1959	Bad Girl	Miracles	40	51	32
65	1959	Chapel Bells	Fascinators	43	5	2
X	1958	Bye Bye Baby	Channels	46	30	12
X	1957	The Legend Of Love	Legends	26	38	50
68	1956	Our Love Will Never End	Avons	72	-	-
69	1957	Honey Honey	Teenchords	55	58	78
70	1957	I'll Make You Understand	Performers	52	81	65
71	1958	Summer Is Here	Pals	63	-	-
72	1957	You I Adore	YoungTones	66	67	98
X	1957	Let's Go For A Ride	Collegians	66	44	30
74	1958	I See A Star	Roulettes	8	54	80
75	1960	Cruise To The Moon	Chaperones	41	55	88
X	1954	Smoke From Your Cigarette	Mellos	17	16	66
X	1957	Dont Ask Me	Dubs	50	-	-
78	1957	Can I Come Over Tonight	Velours	9	40	28
X	1958	Two People In The World	Little Anthony & Imperials	98	88	44
80	1956	Mary Lee	Rainbows	96	97	-
81	1958	Money	Miracles	82	-	-
82	1954	Hoping You'll Understand	Strangers	71	-	-
83	1957	Be My Girl	Videls	75	90	93
84	1957	Ding-A-Ling-A-Ling	Troys	77	-	86
85	1959	Over The Rainbow	Little Butchie & The Vells	88	-	-
86	1955	My Heart's Desire	Wheels	[illegible]	[illegible]	[illegible]
	1957	Baby	Avons	59	95	[illegible]
	1954	Tell The World	Platters	84	80	[illegible]
	1956	Get Yourself Another Fool	Tempo-tones	87	84	[illegible]
	1956	Dear I Swear	Plants	74	-	[illegible]
	1960	My Imagination	5 Classics	81	10	[illegible]
	1959	I'm Alright	Little Anthony & Imperials	95	-	[illegible]
	1954	Paradise Hill	Embers	85	-	[illegible]
	1957	Forever I Vow	Chestnuts	78	-	[illegible]
	1959	Wedding Bells	Tiny Tim & Hits	94	100	[illegible]
	1958	Kathaleen	Adelphis	91	71	[illegible]
	1956	My Mother's Eyes	Softones	93	77	[illegible]
	1955	Lonely Room	Lee Andrews & The Hearts	-	-	[illegible]
	1959	Babalu's Wedding Day	Eternals	-	-	[illegible]
	1957	Zoom Zoom Zoom	Collegians	-	-	[illegible]

RECORDS RECEIVING NATION WIDE ATTENTION THRU THE EFFORTS OF TIMES SQ. RECORDS

Title	Artist	Label
Pretty, Pretty, Girl	Timetones	Atlanticords
No No No	Chanters	DeLuxe-King
X If You Love Me	Radiants	Vim
Every Beat Of My Heart	Midnighters	DeLuxe
The Bells Are Ringing	Van Dykes	DeLuxe
X Rama Lama Ding Dong	Edsels	Dub
My My Darling	Chanters	DeLuxe

S I N K   O R   S W I M - - - - - - - - W I T H   S W I N G I N'   S L I M

Times Square Record Show — PRIZES EVERY WEEK — Various Contests

Radio WBNX - - 1380 on your dial - - 10:30-12:00 PM - - - Radio WBNX

WATCH FOR THE NEW RECORD by THE SUMMITS

T I M E S   S Q U A R E   R E C O R D S

(First Subway Level)

1475 Broadway - 42nd St. New York, N. Y.

(beneath Walgreen's Drug Store)

Tel: BR 9-3458

Top 100 Hits...June, 1961 Back

The Artists...Youngones....Nicky & The Nobles...Lytations Back Then...Lytations In 1996....Decoys & Timetones

MEET THE ARTISTS

The LYTATIONS

Group Members
Jack Strong - Lead Singer
Frank Torpey - First Tenor
Ken Harper – Baritone
Billy Gianguillo – Bass
Bob Bintliff - Second Tenor

The Lytations formally became a group in 1962 in Ardmore, PA. The group took its name from a combination of The Ly-Dells & the Quotations. Members of the group were Jack Strong, Frank Torpey, Ken Harper, Bob Bintliff and Billy Gianguillo. Billy Gianguillo passed away October 15, 1996.

Jack, Frank, and a friend, J.T., went to high school together where they formed a group called The Violators. They sang at various frat parties and coffee houses. Frank knew a guy named Bob Bintliff from his neighborhood who, at the time, was singing with Billy Gianguillo, Ken Harper, and Don Nickleson.

Jack had been exposed to the recording studio playing guitar on a dub by the Crystals recorded at RECO-ART in Philadelphia. The songs were "While Walking" and what would be titled "You're Mine" ("We Belong Together"). Some members of the Crystals would soon become the Ly-Dells.

Bob Bintliff attended business school with a guy named Val Shively and the two collected group sounds, although Val was already amassing a great collection. The records Jack heard at Bob's house definitely talked to him. Such records were "Life Is But A Dream" and "Ala Men Sy".

Jack had never heard the sound that was on the records, although he thought he knew a lot about music. One day, Bob took Jack to Val's house to check out his sounds. It was there that Jack heard the Nutmegs "Let Me Tell You" on the "Times Square Records" label.

The idea that you could sing without music and sound like that knocked Jack out and still does to this day.

The first session produced "Dreaming Of You", "I Know Somewhere", "Hetta" and "The Girl That I Love".

Other than Bill Whitney, the drummer, the rest of the band member's names are unknown. Billy had gotten them together for the session.

The second recording session produced "Over The Rainbow", "Look Into The Sky", "Stormy Weather", Let Me Tell You, "Little Star" and "Sunday Kind Of Love".

It is unknown why "Dreaming Of You" backed with "I Know Somewhere" was re-recorded by the Lytations as the Kaptions on Ham-Mil Records at Virtue Recording Studio in Philadelphia, Pa. Billy played saxophone so well at this recording session.

Without financial backing and the influx of love affairs, jobs, and growing up; rehearsals became fewer and fewer to the point where the group broke up and everyone went their own way.

In 1966, Jack joined the Navy and the group disbanded. Jack later became a carpenter, Bill went into renovations, Bob became an accountant, Ken got into the roofing business and Frank became an auto mechanic.

The TIMETONES

Group Members
Rodgers LaRue Lead
Claude "Sonny" Smith Bass
Glenn Williams First Tenor
Thomas DeGeorg
Thomas Klozek

Rodgers LaRue began his singing career in gospel music.
Rodgers LaRue passed away on January 14, 2005 in Harrisburg PA
Claude "Sonny" Smith was born in Chicago. He returned to Chicago after the group disbanded and was killed in the late 1960s.
Glenn Williams was born in Maryland. He returned to Maryland after the group disbanded. He has since passed away.
Tom DeGeorg and Tom Klozek presently live in Glen Cove, New York and have remained friends all these years.
It was while the group was performing in Long Island they were given

Clarence Johnson's business card. They were told to contact him. The group contacted Clarence Johnson who set up an appointment with them for an audition at his apartment. Clarence Johnson liked what he heard, contacted "Slim" who also liked the "sound" which would lead to "Slim" signing a contract with them to record on the Times Square Label. They recorded "In My Heart" at the Beltone Studios located at 31st Street.

Speaking with Tom DeGeorg in a telephone interview he indicated to me that Clarence Johnson and "Slim" were wonderful to the Timetones. It would only be a year or so that "Slim" would sell the group's contract to Atlantic Records. He also indicated to me that group made between $700.00 to $800.00 which had to be divided five ways. Although the Timetones were around for a short time, Tom DeGeorg said "It was a heck of a time while it lasted". He has wonderful memories that remain with him to this day.

The Timetones would try to make a comeback in the early 1980's. Rodgers LaRue wanted to do something special to commemorate the Bi-Centennial. This time the group would be made up of three of the original members, Rodgers LaRue, Tom DeGeorg, and Tom Klozek, along with newcomers Johnson Hicks and Michael Martino. They would record "Don't Make America Cry"/I'm Your Captain" on the Greenstone Label, however the record never received any air play on the radio.

The EL SIERROS

Group Members
Barry "Wolf" Edelman Lead
Phil Rudnicki First Tenor
Casper "The Ghost" Sierra Second Tenor
Joe "Cat" Philips Baritone
Chuck Aaronson Bass

The EL SIERROS were a group of five "guys" from the Lower Eastside of Manhattan. The group formed in 1963. To help them stay out of trouble a few of them got together and started singing "group harmony" on the street corners, subways and in Washington Square Park Greenwich Village.

The original name of the group was going to be the Sierras, after "Casper" however, there was another group already using the name. Instead, they agreed upon a Latin version of the second tenor's name coming up with the "EL SIERROS.

During this time, they were only interested in making records. Our managers, Peter Schekeryk and Ed Hitt had us put together some original material along with a few oldies. We recorded a string of demos at 254 West 54th Street studio, which was the home of CBS and would later become the "infamous" Studio 54.

Peter Schekeryk took the demos to "Slim" Rose at Times Square Records. "Slim" liked he heard. "Slim" turned our demos into masters and into distribution.

Chuck recalls the first time he heard the first recordings on the Alan Fredericks Night Train Show. Alan Fredericks played "Love You So" backed with "Valerie". All of us were "blown away" at what we heard.

Subsequently, "Slim" released their recordings one after another on his Times Square Records label in 1964. Later on that year, they recorded their only doo-wop record on the Yussels Label. It was "Daddy's Coming Home" backed with "Sunday Kind of Love".

Although this record did not sell many copies, it is now very collectible in near mint condition on green plastic and books for $75.00 in the Kreiter's Guide. The Times Square recordings have also increased in value over the years. In addition, the EL Sierros recorded "This Is The Night" as the Palisades on the Relic Label.

The group disbanded in 1965 when Joe Phillips and Chuck Aaronson went into the Army.

The EL Sierros Discography On The Times Square Records Label:

* Indicated Original Material Written By The EL Sierros

1. Sometimes I Wonder*	LP Sound Of The City	201
2. Love Is A Vow*	LP Sound Of The City	201
3. Glory Of Love*	LP Sound Of The City	201
4. This Is The Nite	LP Sound Of The City	201
5. Over The Rainbow	LP Sound Of The City	201
6. Walking Alone	LP Sound Of The City	201
7. Picture Of Love	45 RPM	36B

8. Love You So*	45 RPM	29A
9. Valerie	45 RPM	29B
10. Pretty Little Girl	45 RPM	101B
11. Life Is But A Dream	45 RPM	101A

The YOUNGONES

Group Members
Eddy "Smiley" Naveras
Joey Leon
Eddy Hernandes
Steve Barrentas
Phil Rudnicki

The Youngones were a Spanish group from Brooklyn. They sang a different kind of harmony.

Phil Rudnicki first met the Youngones in 1962 or 1963 while they were singing on 11th Street and 1st Avenue in Manhattan. At the time he was living at 1st Avenue and 11th Street. Back then the group was made up of four members. Phil Rudnicki would later join them as a fifth member in late 1965-1966.

The manager of the group was Peter Schekeryk. During this time he was married to his first wife Marie. He wrote the song "Marie" for his wife. The Youngones and the Harps would record "Marie".

"Slim" purchased the demo recordings, turned them into masters on the Times Square Records label and distributed them.

Phil Rudnicki would meet two of the Timetones at "Slim's" second store located at 42nd Street and Broadway in 1964. He does not recall which members of the group he met or the exact date of the meeting.

The Youngones performed at Palisades Park in New Jersey with Cousin Brucie, Danny Stiles' record hops in the Bronx and New Jersey and with Jerry Blavatt in Atlantic City and Camden New Jersey. There were photos taken at the concerts and record hops. Phil Rudnicki stored the photos at his mother's home. It was while he was serving in the military his mother's home would be destroyed by fire. All photos of the Youngones were lost in the fire.

Phil Rudnicki also sang with the EL Sierros, which recorded "Love You So" and "Valerie".

After serving eighteen years in the military, Phil Rudnicki retired and moved to Florida where he continues to reside.

The CHIC-LETS

Group Members
Genevieve ("Genni") Miscavage
Diane Miscavage
Jeanne Wilowski
Linda Wilowski

The Chic-Lets were put together by "Slim". He wanted his own group. They took modern dance classes from a small studio on Broadway. "Slim" paid for the classes. He wanted the Chic-Lets to have a finished polished look while performing live on stage.

Genevieve "Genni" and Diane Miscavage were sisters as well as Jeanne and Linda Wilowski. They performed live shows and on the radio.

Most of the performances were with "Genni", Diane and Jeanne. Linda did not perform full time with the group.

The Chic-Lets did record a few demos however nothing was ever recorded and distributed by "Slim".

REMEMBERING

Courtesy photo

Rodgers L. LaRue Sr., bottom left, became a member of the doo-wop group the Timetones after graduating from high school.

Rodgers L. LaRue Sr. 1938-2005

Singer left large legacy of doo-wop, soul songs

BY TOM BOWMAN
Of Our Lebanon County Bureau

When the lead singer of the doo-wop group the Timetones died last month, he left behind listeners who are still discovering the group's music.

"They really have that '50s doo-wop sound that I like," said Bruce Blanchard, an engineer at WSCL-FM in Salisbury, Md., who first heard the Timetones on Internet radio station Live365.com.

Rodgers L. LaRue Sr., 66, of Harrisburg, died Jan. 14, ending a career that had started early in his life. He began singing in a Maryland gospel church with his mother and his brothers, said his brother Clarence, 62, of Medford, N.Y.

"We were raised in the church," Clarence LaRue said. "We were singing on radio station WASA, Annapolis, Md., when we were just 4 or 5 years old."

Rodgers LaRue formed a group in high school in Havre de Grace, Md.

After graduating in 1959, Rodgers LaRue headed for New York City and a recording contract. A short time later, Clarence followed him.

Tommy DeGeorge, 62, of Glen Cove, N.Y., one of two surviving Timetones, said you can hear Rodgers LaRue's gospel roots in some of the Timetones' songs.

"Especially his soul songs," DeGeorge said. "The [gospel] songs, the ones that were popular, they weren't slow. You play the other side of the record of 'My Love' and 'I Got a Feeling,' you can hear it."

Rodgers LaRue "was a tremendous guy with a tremendous voice," DeGeorge said. "He loved the music. He wrote a lot of stuff, a lot of stuff that never even got heard. He must have written 100 songs."

Old loves, new loves, lost loves. They're the subjects of doo-wop songs, always with harmony that carries the words. Even in the songs about hurt, the singers seem to be having fun.

"It was fun. You'd sing in hallways and bathrooms," DeGeorge said. "You always went where there was an echo. You always need an echo. A bathroom, a hallway, anything where there was an echo."

DeGeorge and the others took the train from Long Island into New

Please see LARUE on Page B7

TIMETONES SONGS

- "I've Got a Feeling"
- "House Where Lovers Dream"
- "My Love"
- "Pretty, Pretty Girl"
- "Get Hold of Yourself"
- "I'm the Captain"
- "Don't Make America Cry"

LARUE: Lead singer's music is still getting discovered

Continued from Page B1

York to the Times Square Record Shop, where they first recorded.

Today, DeGeorge and Tommy Glozek, 63, the other remaining member of the Timetones, live in Glen Cove and work at Glen Cove High School.

The Timetones' racial makeup was unusual at the time. DeGeorge said they were one of the first two integrated groups in the nation.

"Us and the Del Vikings," DeGeorge said. "We knew all of them. We sang with all of these groups."

The Del Vikings were about two years ahead of the Timetones. In 1957, the Del Vikings hit with "Come Go With Me."

Two years later, DeGeorge and Glozek met Glenn Williams, a black first tenor. Williams introduced them to LaRue, who had just moved to New York City.

The Timetones had two big hits: "In My Heart," written by LaRue, and "Pretty, Pretty Girl," written by Glozek.

Some day while they are working at Glen Cove High School and the school is empty and quiet, DeGeorge and Glozek plan to get together and harmonize in an empty hallway to commemorate Rodgers' life. They'll sing the old songs and remember their lead singer, Rodgers LaRue.

"I get together with Tommy," DeGeorge said. "We have some fun."

TOM BOWMAN: 272-3759
or tbowman@patriot-news.com

	The Discography	
Record Number	**Title**	**Artist**
421	Here In My Heart/ My Love In My Heart/ My Love	Timetones
422	Go Back Where You Came From / Times Square Stomp	Summits
6201	Pretty, Pretty Girl / I've Got A Feeling	Timetones (Atco Label)
1	Poor Rock 'N' Roll / Ting-A-Ling	Nobles
2	No One To Love / Wish She Was Mine	Crests
3	Did It / Now You're Gone	Laddins
4	All Mine / Rose Mary	Five Satins
5	Crying For You / Oh Darling	Centuries / Jaytones
6	Let Me Tell You / Hello	Nutmegs
7	Your Tender Lips / Praying For A Miracle	Syncapates
8	It's Going To Be All Right / Oh Baby	Decoys / Bel-aires
9	So You Will Know / Don't Cry Baby	Paragons
10	Union Hall / Forever And Ever	Montels / C Notes
11	Let's Go For A Ride / Heavenly Night	Collegians
12	Crime Don't Pay / Darkness	Nobles
13	Patricia / By The Candleglow	Youngtones

Times Square Records Discography

14	The Way Love Should Be / Wide Hoop Skirts	Nutmegs
15	Betty / Ride Away	Centuries / Revlons
16	The Chimes / Voodoo Woman	Shades
17	I Love You / I'm Really Too Young	Nobletones
18	Who Cares About Love / Calypso Baby	Nobletones
19	Down To Earth / Coo Coo Cuddle Coo	Nutmegs / Admirations
20	I've Searched / Mixture Of Love	Heartspinners / Admirations
21	Paradise On Earth / Monkey Business	Five Satins / Pharotones
22	Why Must We Go To School / Ink Dries Quicker than Tears	Nutmegs / Volumes
23	Tell Me Why / Where Are You	Bel-airs
24	Give Me A Chance / Butterball	Chanells / Butterballs
25	Santa Town U.S.A. / Bells in The Chapel	Lonnie & The Crisis
26	Sunday Kind Of Love / Angels In The Sky	Timetones
27	Down In Mexico / My Sweet Dreams	Nutmegs
28	Gloria / Just Two Kinds Of People	Young Ones
29	Love You So / Valerie	El Sierros
30	I've Got The Right / Baby Please	Moonglows
31	I Do / Day Train	Youngones / Blasters
32	Dance Girl / That's My Baby	Camelots / Suns

Times Square Records Discography

33	Why Be A Fool / The Search	Nobles
34	The House Where Lovers Dream / Get A Hold Of Yourself	Timetones
35	Stormy Weather / If You Love Me	Five Sharks
36	Sweeter Than / Picture Of Love	Young Ones / El Sierros
37	School Bells / Schoolday Crush	Nicky & the Nobles
1	Pretty Baby / Let's Rock	Cupids
2	I'll Never Let You Go / Darling I Love You	Gents / Teen Five
4	Island Of Love / Till The End Of Time	Gents / Teen Five
6	Baby / I Love You So	Crests
9	Tomorrow / I Want Only You	Decoys
11	Darling You're My Angel / Will I	Memories
101	Life Is But A Dream / Pretty Little Girl	El Sierros
102	A Lovely Way To Spend An Evening / Walking My Baby Back Home	Flamingos
103	Your Crying / Wa Do Wa	Nutmegs
104	I Only Want You / Over The Rainbow	Young Ones
105	The Storm (So Blue) / Fall In Love	Vi-Tones
106	Chapel Of Love / Marie	Donnie & The Styles
107	Over The Rainbow / Look Into The Sky	Lytations

Times Square Records Discography

Genevieve "Genni" Miscavage.... At The Empire Hotel
"Genni" sang with the Chi-Lets. She was also an employee.
She had her own radio show called "Swingin" With "Genni" which aired every Wednesday night at 9pm. Her show premiered the summer of 1962. She had her own fan club.

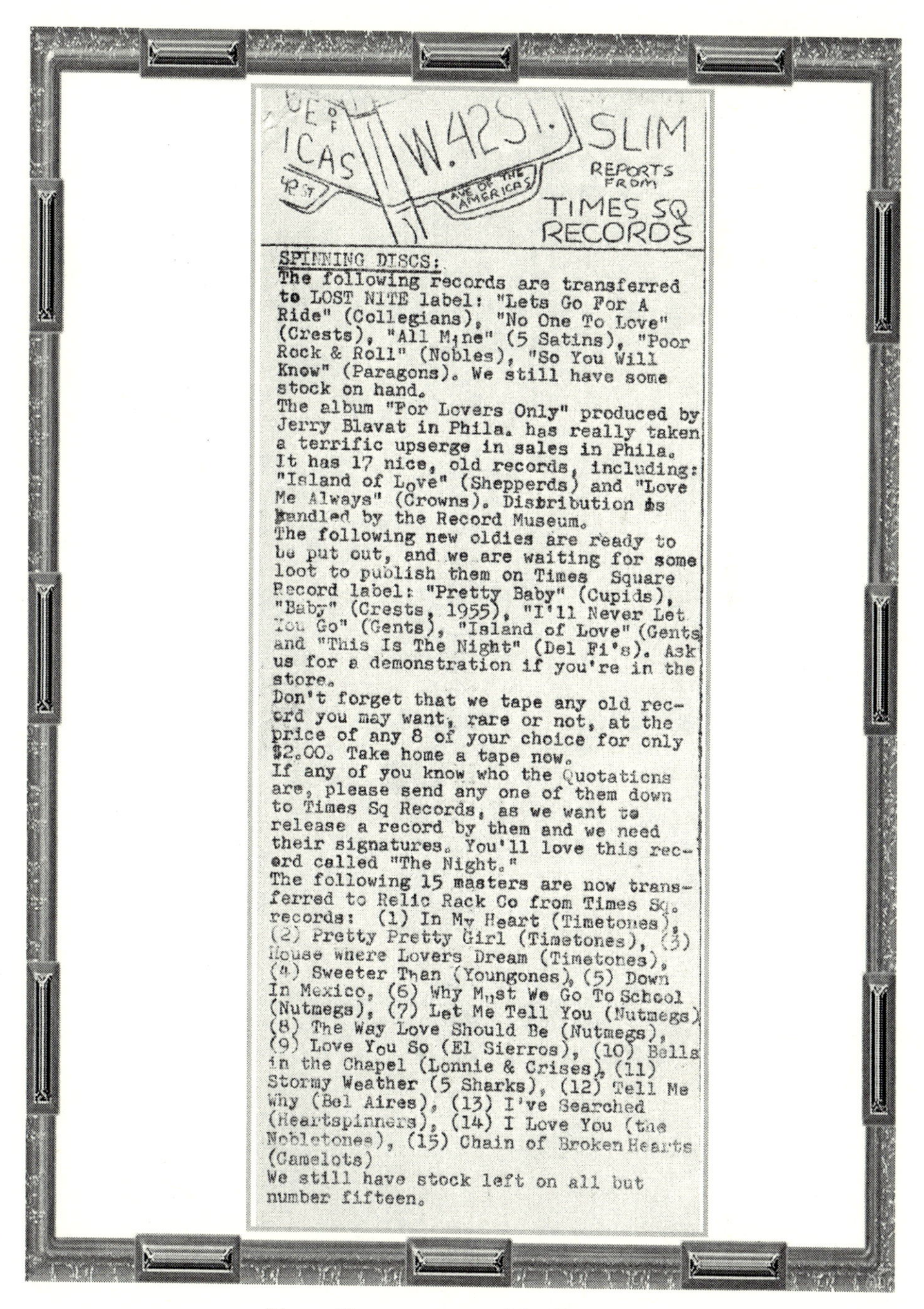

SPINNING DISCS:
The following records are transferred to LOST NITE label: "Lets Go For A Ride" (Collegians), "No One To Love" (Crests), "All Mine" (5 Satins), "Poor Rock & Roll" (Nobles), "So You Will Know" (Paragons). We still have some stock on hand.
The album "For Lovers Only" produced by Jerry Blavat in Phila. has really taken a terrific upserge in sales in Phila. It has 17 nice, old records, including: "Island of Love" (Shepperds) and "Love Me Always" (Crowns). Distribution is handled by the Record Museum.
The following new oldies are ready to be put out, and we are waiting for some loot to publish them on Times Square Record label: "Pretty Baby" (Cupids), "Baby" (Crests, 1955), "I'll Never Let You Go" (Gents), "Island of Love" (Gents) and "This Is The Night" (Del Fi's). Ask us for a demonstration if you're in the store.
Don't forget that we tape any old record you may want, rare or not, at the price of any 8 of your choice for only $2.00. Take home a tape now.
If any of you know who the Quotations are, please send any one of them down to Times Sq Records, as we want to release a record by them and we need their signatures. You'll love this record called "The Night."
The following 15 masters are now transferred to Relic Rack Co from Times Sq. records: (1) In My Heart (Timetones), (2) Pretty Pretty Girl (Timetones), (3) House where Lovers Dream (Timetones), (4) Sweeter Than (Youngones), (5) Down In Mexico, (6) Why Must We Go To School (Nutmegs), (7) Let Me Tell You (Nutmegs), (8) The Way Love Should Be (Nutmegs), (9) Love You So (El Sierros), (10) Bells in the Chapel (Lonnie & Crises), (11) Stormy Weather (5 Sharks), (12) Tell Me Why (Bel Aires), (13) I've Searched (Heartspinners), (14) I Love You (the Nobletones), (15) Chain of Broken Hearts (Camelots)
We still have stock left on all but number fifteen.

Harry Hepcat sent me this clipping....

SWINGIN SLIM REPORTS FROM TIMES SQ

More Transfers: TO RELIC RACK RECORDS:
Dance Girl (Camelots), Gloria (Youngones)
TO CANDLELIGHT RECORDS:
Down To Earth (Nutmegs), Go Back Where
You Came From (Summits), Crime Don't
Pay (Nobles), Why Be A Fool (Nobles)
More on Transfers later.
We may get a large shipment of oldies
in soon. Watch for it. First come, fir
sold.
There's a fairly new music magazine ou
now that is great for the price. It's
only 25¢. It's called MUSIC BUSINESS.
It's sold at most record shops. Weekly.

Went fishing on the holiday weekend and
a fish had the laugh of its life. I was
half sitting on my fishing rod to eat
sandwich and (BOOM) the rod flew from
under me over the boat, and out of
sight in he water All in a few seconds
It didn't even say "Thank You."
Our six new "oldies" are going like crazy
They are in order of sales: (1)I911
Never Let You Go (Gents) (2)Pretty Baby
(Cupids-Acappella) (3) Island of Love
(Gents-Acappella), (4) Tomorrow (Decoys)
(5) Baby (Crests-Acappella), (6) Darling
Your My Angel (Memories-Acappella)
Thanks for your liking them so much.
Since I introduced this Acapella bit,
other companies are trying it too. Record
Museum in Phila has purchased a Camelots
record called Don't Leave Me Baby, which
is acappella: they are doing terrific
with it. It's number one with the oldie
lovers out there.

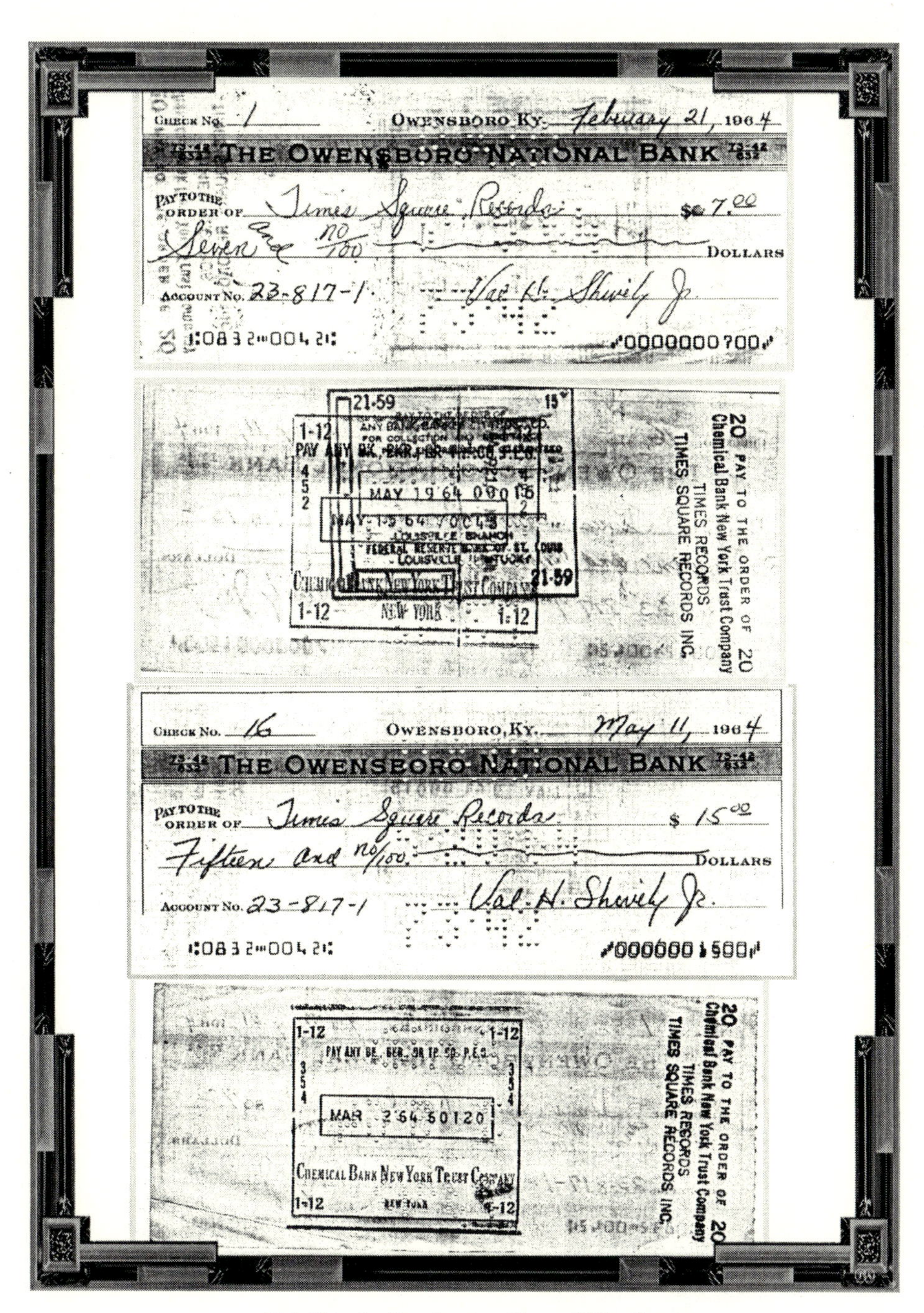

Check No. 1 — Owensboro, Ky. February 21, 1964

THE OWENSBORO NATIONAL BANK 73-42/832

Pay to the order of Times Square Records $7.00

Seven and no/100 Dollars

Account No. 23-817-1 — Val H. Shively Jr.

⑆0832⑈0042⑆ ⑈0000000700⑈

20 Pay to the order of
Chemical Bank New York Trust Company
Times Square Records
Times Square Records Inc.

21-59 — May 1 9 64 — Louisville Branch Federal Reserve Bank of St. Louis, Louisville, Kentucky — 21-59

1-12 Chemical Bank New York Trust Company New York 1-12

Check No. 16 — Owensboro, Ky. May 11, 1964

THE OWENSBORO NATIONAL BANK 73-42/832

Pay to the order of Times Square Records $15.00

Fifteen and no/100 Dollars

Account No. 23-817-1 — Val H. Shively Jr.

⑆0832⑈0042⑆ ⑈0000001500⑈

20 Pay to the order of
Chemical Bank New York Trust Company
Times Square Records
Times Square Records Inc.

1-12 Pay any bk., bkr., or tr. co. p.e.g. 1-12

MAR 2 64 50120

Chemical Bank New York Trust Company 1-12 New York 1-12

Val Shively Purchasing From "Slim"....

"Slim From Times" Ad..... Appeared in the March - April Issue Of Bim Bam Boom 1973...

"SLIM" RETURNS!

East Rutherford, New Jersey — Those attending the United In Group Harmony Association (UGHA) meeting on March 27th were surprised to find Irving "Slim" Rose, the legendary founding father of group record collecting, chatting with many of his customers of nearly 15 years ago. In one of record collecting's better kept secrets, the Association presented Slim as a guest speaker, who recalled the "good old days" as he fielded avid questions from the audience. After many years of far-flung rumors concerning Slim's fate, it was indeed a treat to find him alive and well and with him memory substantially intact. A great time was had by all, and we look forward to the Association's future contributions in the field of record collecting.

"Slim" Returns...His Last Public Appearance...UGHA... March 27, 1979

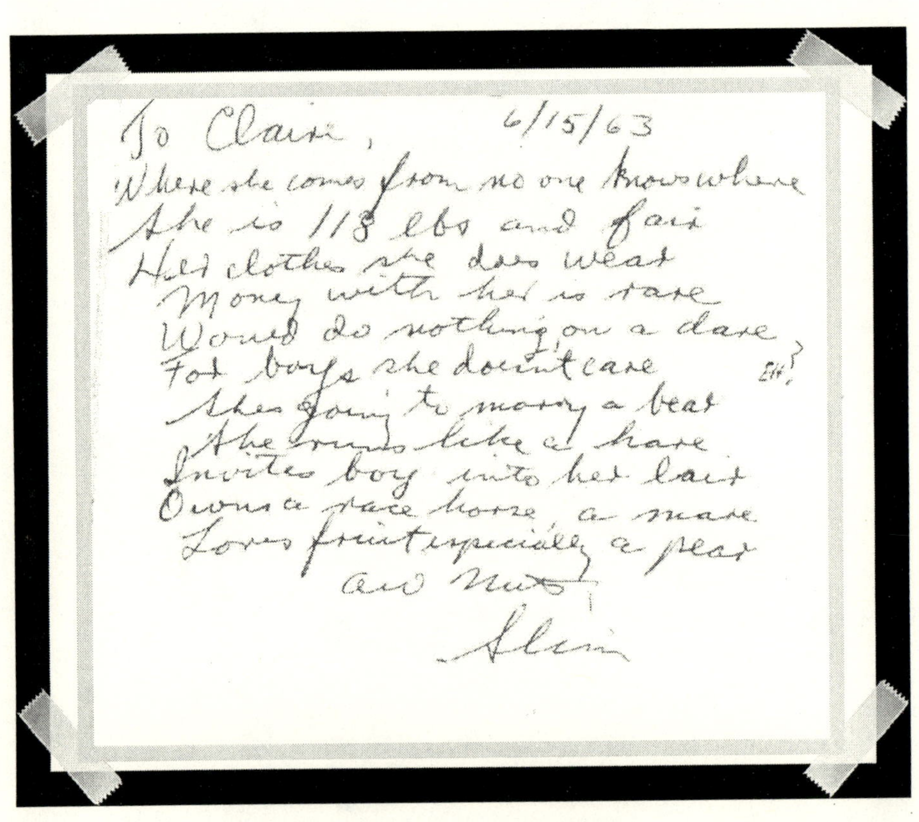
To Claire, 6/15/63
Where she comes from no one knows where
She is 118 lbs and fair
Her clothes she does wear
Money with her is rare
Would do nothing on a dare
For boys she doesn't care Eh?
Shes going to marry a bear
She runs like a hare
Invites boy into her lair
Owns a race horse, a mare
Loves fruit especially a pear
and Nuts!
Slim

"Slim" Writes A Note To Shandy.....

Jerry & Nina Greene On The Left....Jared & Dorothy Weinstein On The Right...At The Record Museum 1962

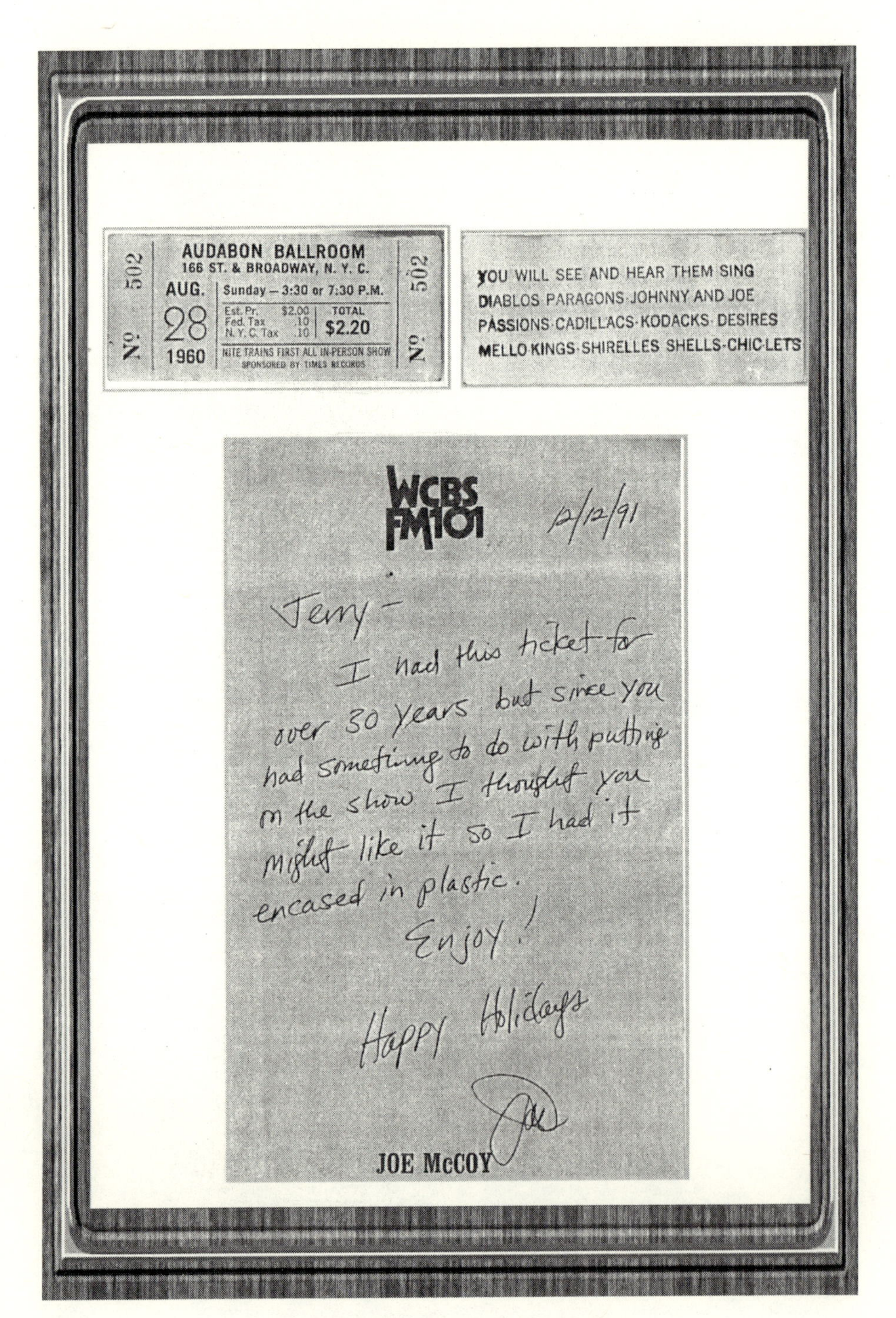

Nº 502

AUDABON BALLROOM
166 ST. & BROADWAY, N. Y. C.

AUG. 28 1960

Sunday — 3:30 or 7:30 P.M.

Est. Pr.	$2.00	TOTAL
Fed. Tax	.10	$2.20
N. Y. C. Tax	.10	

NITE TRAINS FIRST ALL IN-PERSON SHOW
SPONSORED BY TIMES RECORDS

Nº 502

YOU WILL SEE AND HEAR THEM SING
DIABLOS·PARAGONS·JOHNNY AND JOE
PASSIONS·CADILLACS·KODACKS·DESIRES
MELLO KINGS·SHIRELLES·SHELLS·CHIC-LETS

WCBS FM101

12/12/91

Jerry –

I had this ticket for over 30 years but since you had something to do with putting on the show I thought you might like it so I had it encased in plastic.

Enjoy!

Happy Holidays

Joe

JOE McCOY

Original Audubon Ballroom Ticket

CARL'S DIGGINS
HOUSE OF JAZZ
735 NO. MAIN ST., PROV., R.I.

carl's diggins

~~xfoxtwxtonxxandall~~ street, providence, r. i.
735 No. Main

November 4th, 1960

Gentlemen:- foward this letter to the person it concerns.

A few weeks ago I was in Times buying records. You in turn asked me if I could get a certain record played in the R. I. area. I then told you there was only one d. j. out here that would play r&b and I would give the record to him. (Joe Thomas of WPAW)

As of today we have received a number of call for the record and would like it shipped to us immidiately. You stated that you would sell me .40¢ per copy. I'm in not possition to distribute for you. You'll have to sell it to my boss (Carl Henry) in care of (Carl's Diggins).

He would like you to send him 25x special delivery on open account. He won't accept COD.

If you can spare 2 copies for d. j. purposes, I have two other d.j. in mind that <u>might</u> play it.

Joe Thomas had a "Make It Or Break It" on his show and the telephone calls for it were <u>48 to make</u> it and 2 to break it.

The record I'm talking about is <u>"There's A Moon Out Tonight" by The Capris on Lost Nite.</u> Our phone number here is MAnning 1-9077 if you have any questions.

Jim Daigle

CARL'S DIGGINS--Carl Henry

jd

gaspee 1-8027

carl henry — w r i b

Letter Regarding "There's A Moon Out Tonight"

The following are the terms of a binding contract between Donn N. Fileti, 1 Belgrade, West Orange, N.J. and Wayne Stierle, 410 Main St., West Orange, N.J. taking effect as of the above date. A general partnership shall be enacted between the aforementioned principles, in which the initail capital sum to be invested is $350.00. $78.75 of this sum shall be supplied by Donn N. Fileti and $271.25 by Wayne Stierle. The initial amount shall be used to buy 1000 copies of MY HEART'S DESIRE (phonograph record) which will be sold to various retailers in the N.Y.-N.J. area. These records will be purchased from Saul Weinstein, Transdisc Corp. of Boston , 615 Albany St., Boston, Mass., who has agreed to supply the purchaser with copies at 35¢ per copy. The following are the terms of the $271.25 investment by Wayne Stierle:

a- All moneys received from the sale of copies will be given to Wayne Stierle until the initial investment of $271.25 is paid back. Then, the next $78.75 will be paid to Donn N. Fileti. All profits realized after the initial capital will be divided in this proportion : $120.00 to Wayne Stierle and $30.00 to Donn N. Fileti. These profits are subject to change depending on expenses of the company. This division will be on the sale of the aforementioned 1000 records alone.

b- If such records (the first 1000) arrive broken, Donn N. Fileti will see that all are replaced.

This general partnership will be known as General Record Distributors or General Record Distributing Co. and officers will be as follows:

Pres. - Donn N. Fileti
Vice Pres.-Wayne Stierle
Sec. - Wayne Stierle
Treas. -Donn N. Fileti

Company policy will be decided on the vote of the officers. Profits will be shared equally after the sale of the first 1000 records (MY HEART'S DESIRE). Losses will also be shared equally after the sale of the first 1000 records. Officers will be elected yearly at an annual meeting, the first time to be held on Friday, September 2, 1960 at the offices of the company, 1 Belgrade in West Orange, N.J. at 10:00 AM, when an annual statement will be made. The above is agreed upon as of 6 PM, May 16, 1960.

Wayne Stierle
WAYNE STIERLE

Donn Fileti
DONN N. FILETI

General Record Distributors Contract

B-W MUSIC, Inc.

PUBLISHERS (B-M-I) and PRODUCERS (B-W RECORDS)
P. O. BOX 337
WOOSTER, OHIO
HO 2-1241

DANA T. BURNS
President
BEREA, OHIO
BE 4-6808

QUENTIN W. WELTY
Vice Pres. - A & R
Member:
A. F. of M.
N. A. R. A. S.
N. A. B.
D. J. A.

August 2nd, '60

Donn N. Fileti
GENERAL RECORD DISTRIBUTORS
#1 Belgrade
West Orange
New Jersey

Dear Donn:

Many thanks for your recent letter and your interest in our B-W release, #601-2...."NO PARKING!" AND "DOUBLE ROCK" This is, strictly, a traditional rock or r & b coupling, and got a lot of play in this area of Ohio.

We never attempted to go national with this, our first release, as we immediately went into session with several other records.

However, I feel that with the right distributor on this record, It could go well in your major metropolitan area.

I have sent, under seperate cover, fifty (50) promo copies of this B-W-601. Also am sending some info-promo sheets that might be of help to you. Please note that I have sufficient stock to immediately supply any orders that you might want.

Also, we have two brand new releases to hit the markets this month and next. A modern-pop sound with three great new singers; typical Teen-Age record. And also a terrific Country-Western group. Please advise if you can use either of these.

Thanks again for your interest...the fifty promos are in-the-mail, and let me know what you can use.

Most cordially,

Quentin W. Welty
Gen. Mgr.

QWW:ns

"Good Music is Good Business"

B&W Music.....Letter To Donn Fileti

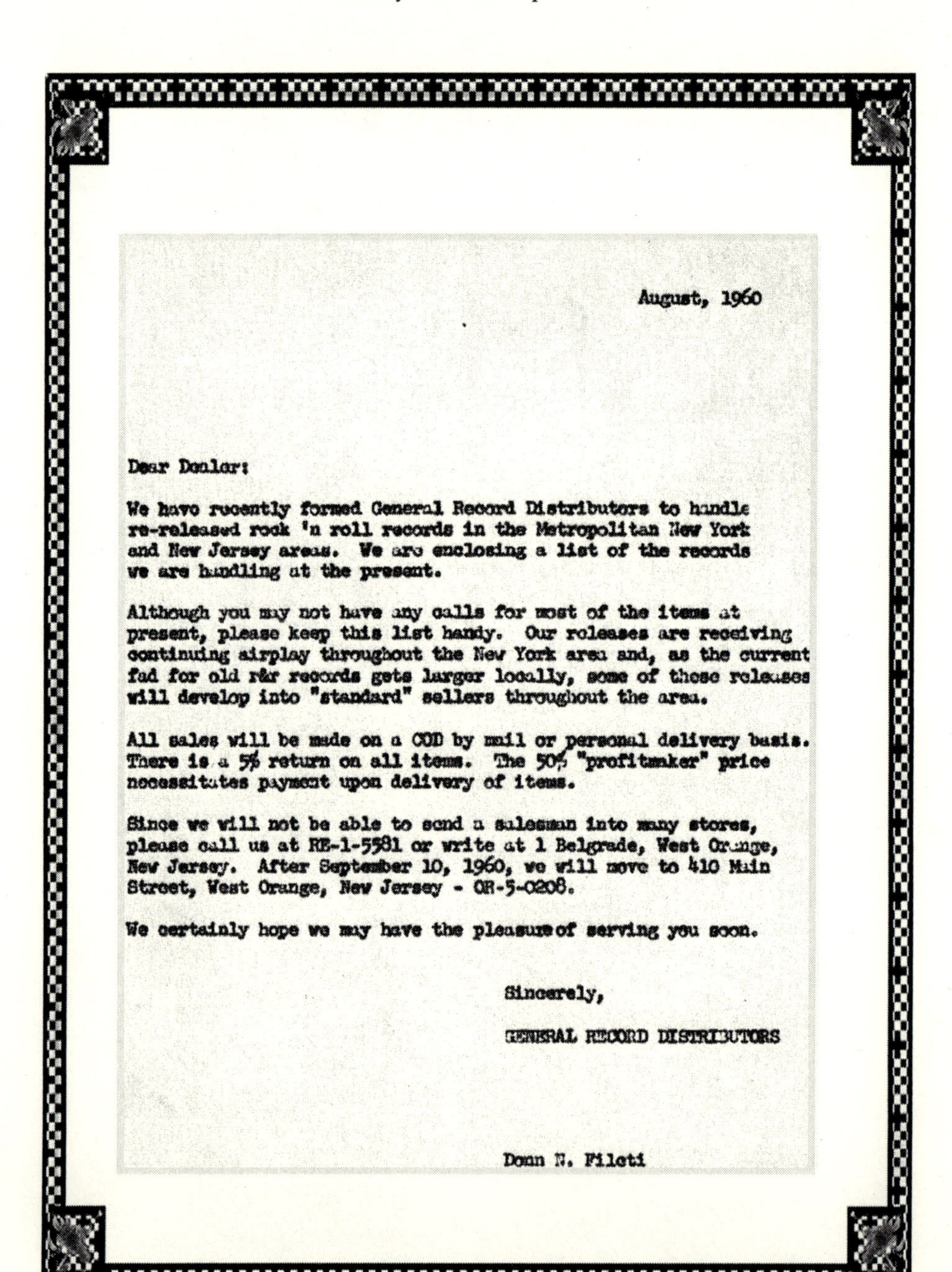

August, 1960

Dear Dealer:

We have recently formed General Record Distributors to handle re-released rock 'n roll records in the Metropolitan New York and New Jersey areas. We are enclosing a list of the records we are handling at the present.

Although you may not have any calls for most of the items at present, please keep this list handy. Our releases are receiving continuing airplay throughout the New York area and, as the current fad for old r&r records gets larger locally, some of these releases will develop into "standard" sellers throughout the area.

All sales will be made on a COD by mail or personal delivery basis. There is a 5% return on all items. The 50% "profitmaker" price necessitates payment upon delivery of items.

Since we will not be able to send a salesman into many stores, please call us at RE-1-5581 or write at 1 Belgrade, West Orange, New Jersey. After September 10, 1960, we will move to 410 Main Street, West Orange, New Jersey - OR-5-0208.

We certainly hope we may have the pleasure of serving you soon.

Sincerely,

GENERAL RECORD DISTRIBUTORS

Donn N. Fileti

Introductory Letter

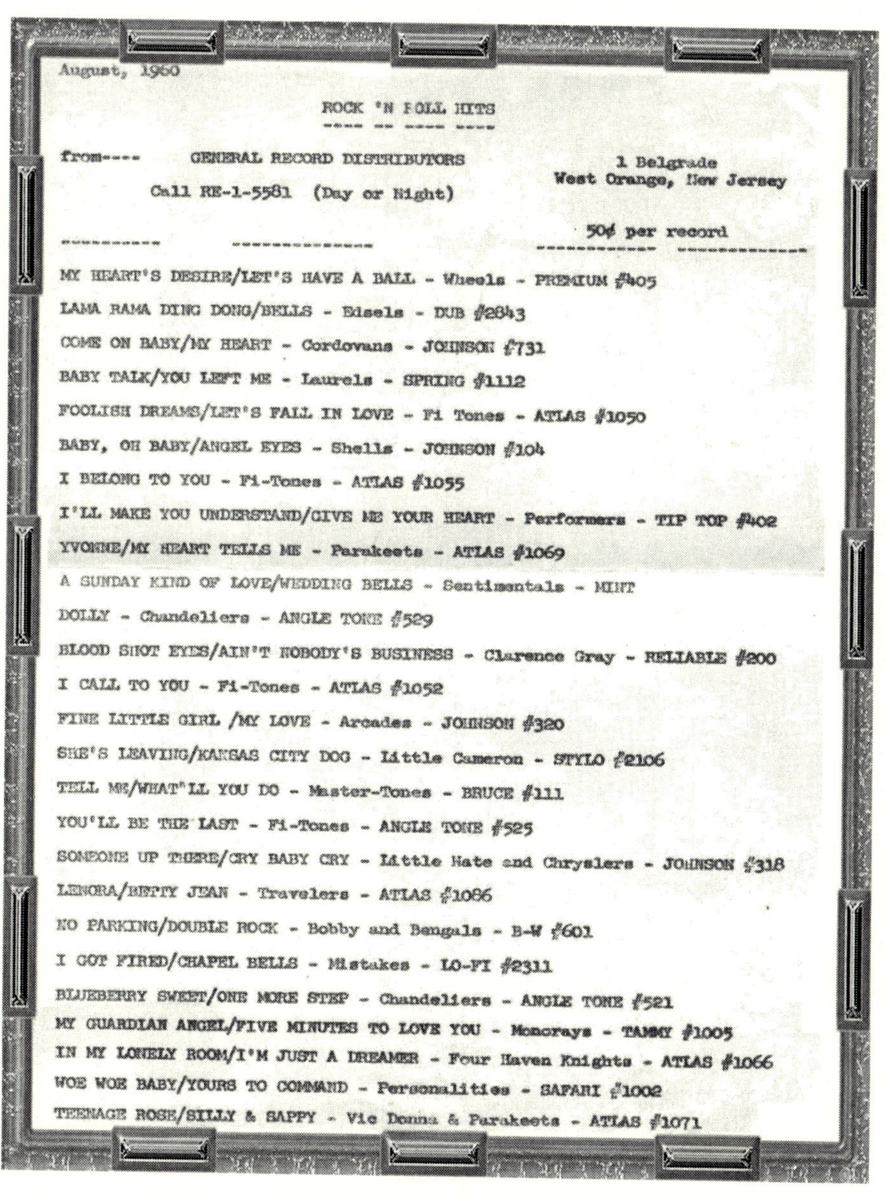
August, 1960

ROCK 'N ROLL HITS

from---- GENERAL RECORD DISTRIBUTORS
Call RE-1-5581 (Day or Night)

1 Belgrade
West Orange, New Jersey

50¢ per record

MY HEART'S DESIRE/LET'S HAVE A BALL - Wheels - PREMIUM #405
LAMA RAMA DING DONG/BELLS - Edsels - DUB #2843
COME ON BABY/MY HEART - Cordovans - JOHNSON #731
BABY TALK/YOU LEFT ME - Laurels - SPRING #1112
FOOLISH DREAMS/LET'S FALL IN LOVE - Fi Tones - ATLAS #1050
BABY, OH BABY/ANGEL EYES - Shells - JOHNSON #104
I BELONG TO YOU - Fi-Tones - ATLAS #1055
I'LL MAKE YOU UNDERSTAND/GIVE ME YOUR HEART - Performers - TIP TOP #402
YVONNE/MY HEART TELLS ME - Parakeets - ATLAS #1069
A SUNDAY KIND OF LOVE/WEDDING BELLS - Sentimentals - MINT
DOLLY - Chandeliers - ANGLE TONE #529
BLOOD SHOT EYES/AIN'T NOBODY'S BUSINESS - Clarence Gray - RELIABLE #200
I CALL TO YOU - Fi-Tones - ATLAS #1052
FINE LITTLE GIRL /MY LOVE - Arcades - JOHNSON #320
SHE'S LEAVING/KANSAS CITY DOG - Little Cameron - STYLO #2106
TELL ME/WHAT'LL YOU DO - Master-Tones - BRUCE #111
YOU'LL BE THE LAST - Fi-Tones - ANGLE TONE #525
SOMEONE UP THERE/CRY BABY CRY - Little Nate and Chryslers - JOHNSON #318
LENORA/BETTY JEAN - Travelers - ATLAS #1086
NO PARKING/DOUBLE ROCK - Bobby and Bengals - B-W #601
I GOT FIRED/CHAPEL BELLS - Mistakes - LO-FI #2311
BLUEBERRY SWEET/ONE MORE STEP - Chandeliers - ANGLE TONE #521
MY GUARDIAN ANGEL/FIVE MINUTES TO LOVE YOU - Moncrays - TAMMY #1005
IN MY LONELY ROOM/I'M JUST A DREAMER - Four Haven Knights - ATLAS #1066
WOE WOE BABY/YOURS TO COMMAND - Personalities - SAFARI #1002
TEENAGE ROSE/SILLY & SAPPY - Vic Donna & Parakeets - ATLAS #1071

General Records List...August, 1960

GENERAL RECORD PRODUCTS
410 Main Street
West Orange, N. J.

December, 1960 OR-5-0208

ELLS OF SAINT MARY/THE FAIREST	LEE ANDREWS	RAINBOW	[illegible]
Y HEART'S DESIRE/LET'S HAVE A BALL	THE WHEELS	PREMIUM	[illegible]
MPOSSIBLE/I'M LEAVING HOME	THE VELVATONES	NU KAT	[illegible]
OU CAME TO ME/OOW-WEE BABY	THE DUVALS	RAINBOW	[illegible]
AMA RAMA DING DONG/BELLS	THE EDSELS	DUB	2[illegible]
UNDAY KIND OF LOVE/WEDDING BELLS	THE SENTIMENTALS	MINT	[illegible]
TRANGE LOVE/CHERRLYN	THE NATIVE BOYS	COMBO	[illegible]
H LET ME DREAM/I'VE GOT THE FEELING	THE NATIVE BOYS	COMBO	[illegible]
Y GUARDIAN ANGEL/FIVE MINUTES TO LOVE	THE MONORAYS	TAMMY	1[illegible]
ENORA/BETTY JEAN	THE TRAVELERS	ATLAS	1[illegible]
O PARKING/DOUBLE ROCK	BOBBY AND THE BENGALS	B-U	[illegible]
OLLY/DANCIN IN THE CONGO	THE CHANDELIERS	ANGLE TONE	[illegible]
LUEBERRY SWEET/ONE MORE STEP	THE CHANDELIERS	ANGLE TONE	[illegible]
ABY TALK/YOU LEFT ME	THE LAURELS	SPRING	1[illegible]
Y LONELY FRIEND/KING OF ROCKING ROLL	THE CONTINENTALS	NU KAT	[illegible]
HE'S LEAVING/KANSAS CITY DOG	LITTLE CAMERON	STYLO	2[illegible]
AKE MY HEART/THUNDERBIRD BABY	THE PARAMOUNTS	COMBO	[illegible]
AUGHING LOVE	THE NATIVE BOYS	COMBO	
OMANCING IN THE SPRING/DON'T CRY DELLA	THE FIVE ROSES	NU KAT	[illegible]
HAPEL BELLS/I GOT FIRED	THE MISTAKES	LO FI	2[illegible]
'LL MAKE YOU UNDERSTAND/YOUR HEART	THE PERFORMERS	TIP TOP	4[illegible]
ELL ME/WHAT'LL YOU DO	THE MASTER-TONES	BRUCE	[illegible]

General Records List...December, 1960

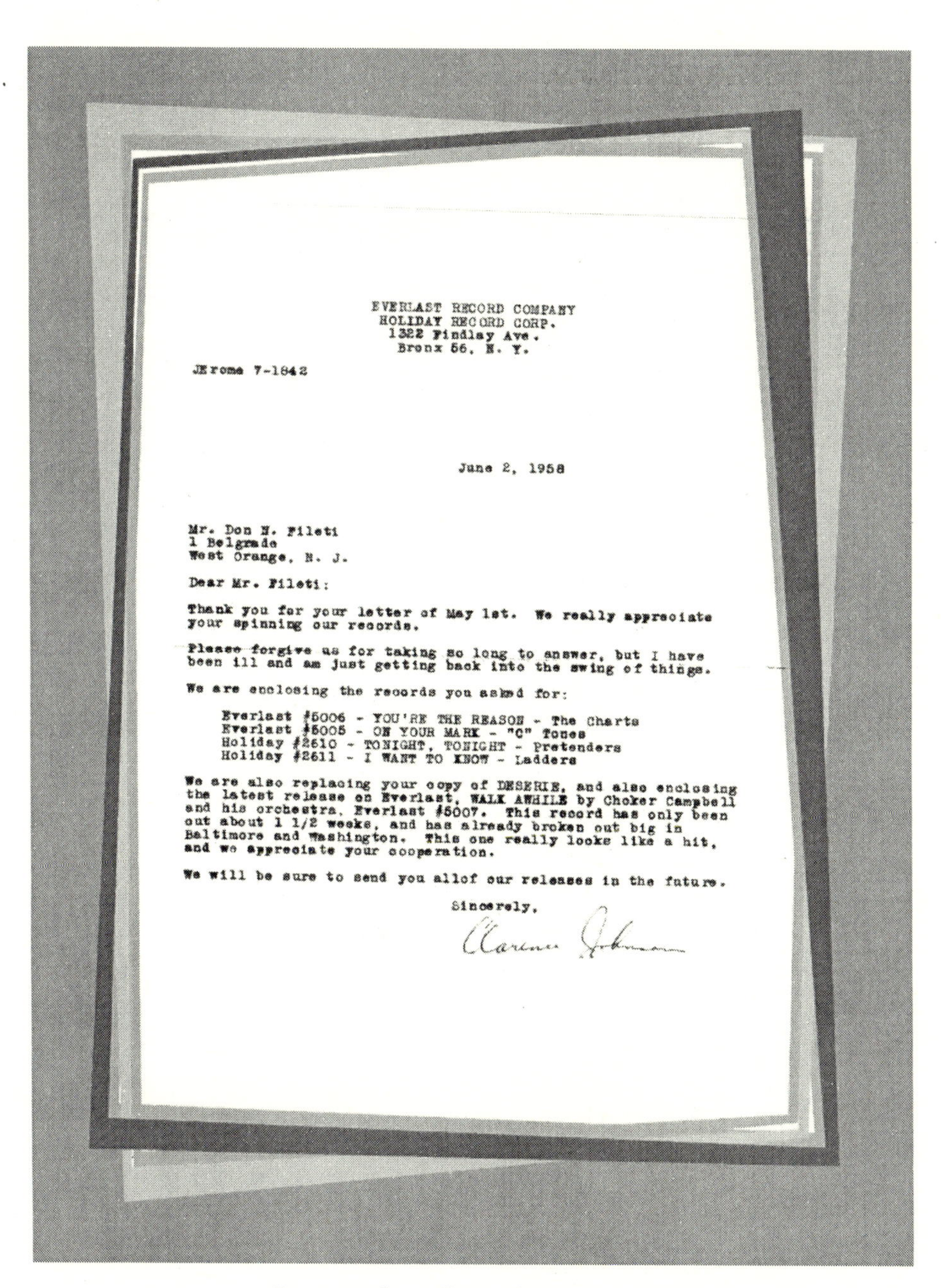

EVERLAST RECORD COMPANY
HOLIDAY RECORD CORP.
1322 Findlay Ave.
Bronx 56, N. Y.

JErome 7-1842

June 2, 1958

Mr. Don N. Fileti
1 Belgrade
West Orange, N. J.

Dear Mr. Fileti:

Thank you for your letter of May 1st. We really appreciate your spinning our records.

Please forgive us for taking so long to answer, but I have been ill and am just getting back into the swing of things.

We are enclosing the records you asked for:

Everlast #5006 - YOU'RE THE REASON - The Charts
Everlast #5005 - ON YOUR MARK - "C" Tones
Holiday #2610 - TONIGHT, TONIGHT - Pretenders
Holiday #2611 - I WANT TO KNOW - Ladders

We are also replacing your copy of DESERIE, and also enclosing the latest release on Everlast, WALK AWHILE by Choker Campbell and his orchestra, Everlast #5007. This record has only been out about 1 1/2 weeks, and has already broken out big in Baltimore and Washington. This one really looks like a hit, and we appreciate your cooperation.

We will be sure to send you allof our releases in the future.

Sincerely,

Clarence Johnson

Correspondence From Clarence Johnson

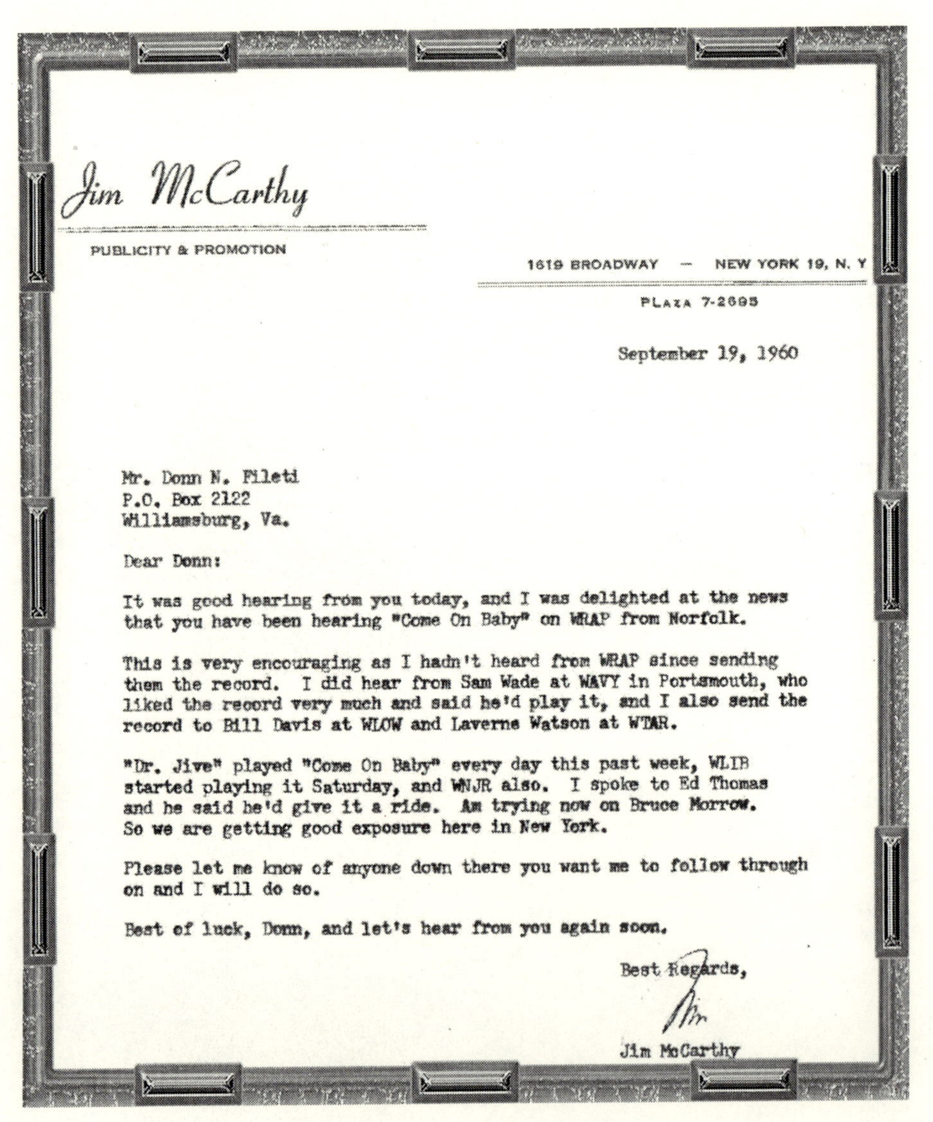

Jim McCarthy

PUBLICITY & PROMOTION

1619 BROADWAY — NEW YORK 19, N. Y

PLAZA 7-2695

September 19, 1960

Mr. Donn N. Fileti
P.O. Box 2122
Williamsburg, Va.

Dear Donn:

It was good hearing from you today, and I was delighted at the news that you have been hearing "Come On Baby" on WRAP from Norfolk.

This is very encouraging as I hadn't heard from WRAP since sending them the record. I did hear from Sam Wade at WAVY in Portsmouth, who liked the record very much and said he'd play it, and I also send the record to Bill Davis at WLOW and Laverne Watson at WTAR.

"Dr. Jive" played "Come On Baby" every day this past week, WLIB started playing it Saturday, and WNJR also. I spoke to Ed Thomas and he said he'd give it a ride. Am trying now on Bruce Morrow. So we are getting good exposure here in New York.

Please let me know of anyone down there you want me to follow through on and I will do so.

Best of luck, Donn, and let's hear from you again soon.

Best Regards,

Jim

Jim McCarthy

Correspondence Jim McCarthy

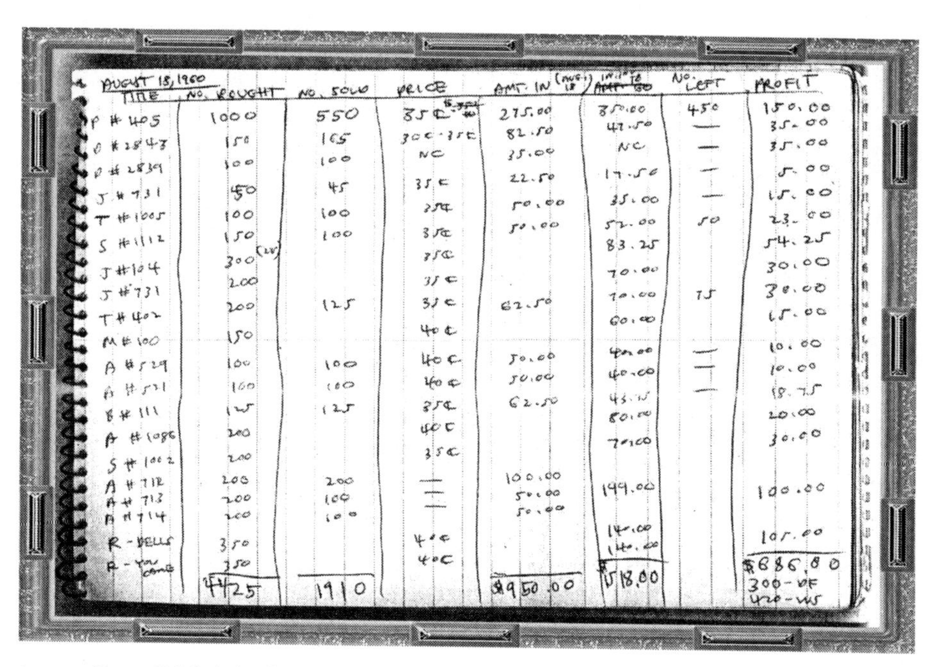

AUGUST 18, 1960

TITLE	NO. BOUGHT	NO. SOLD	PRICE	AMT. IN (AUG. 18)	[illegible]	NO. LEFT	PROFIT
P #405	1000	550	35¢ [illegible]	275.00	350.00	450	150.00
O #2843	150	165	30¢-35¢	82.50	47.50	—	35.00
O #2839	100	100	NC	35.00	NC	—	35.00
J #731	450	45	35¢	22.50	17.50	—	5.00
T #1005	100	100	35¢	50.00	35.00	—	15.00
S #1112	150	100	35¢	50.00	52.00	50	23.00
J #104	300 (25)		35¢		83.25		54.25
J #731	200		35¢		70.00		30.00
T #402	200	125	35¢	62.50	70.00	75	30.00
M #100	150		40¢		60.00		15.00
A #529	100	100	40¢	50.00	40.00	—	10.00
A #531	100	100	40¢	50.00	40.00	—	10.00
B #111	125	125	35¢	62.50	43.75	—	18.75
A #1086	200		40¢		80.00		20.00
S #1002	200		35¢		70.00		30.00
A #712	200	200	—	100.00	199.00		100.00
A #713	200	100	—	50.00			
A #714	200	100	—	50.00			
R - BELLS	350		40¢		14.00		105.00
R - YOU CAME	350		40¢		140.00		
	4425	1910		$950.00	$518.00		$686.80
							300 - VF
							420 - WS

Copy Of Original Notebook Entry Donn Fileti Used For General Record Distributors...List Of Transactions For The Week Of August 18, 1960

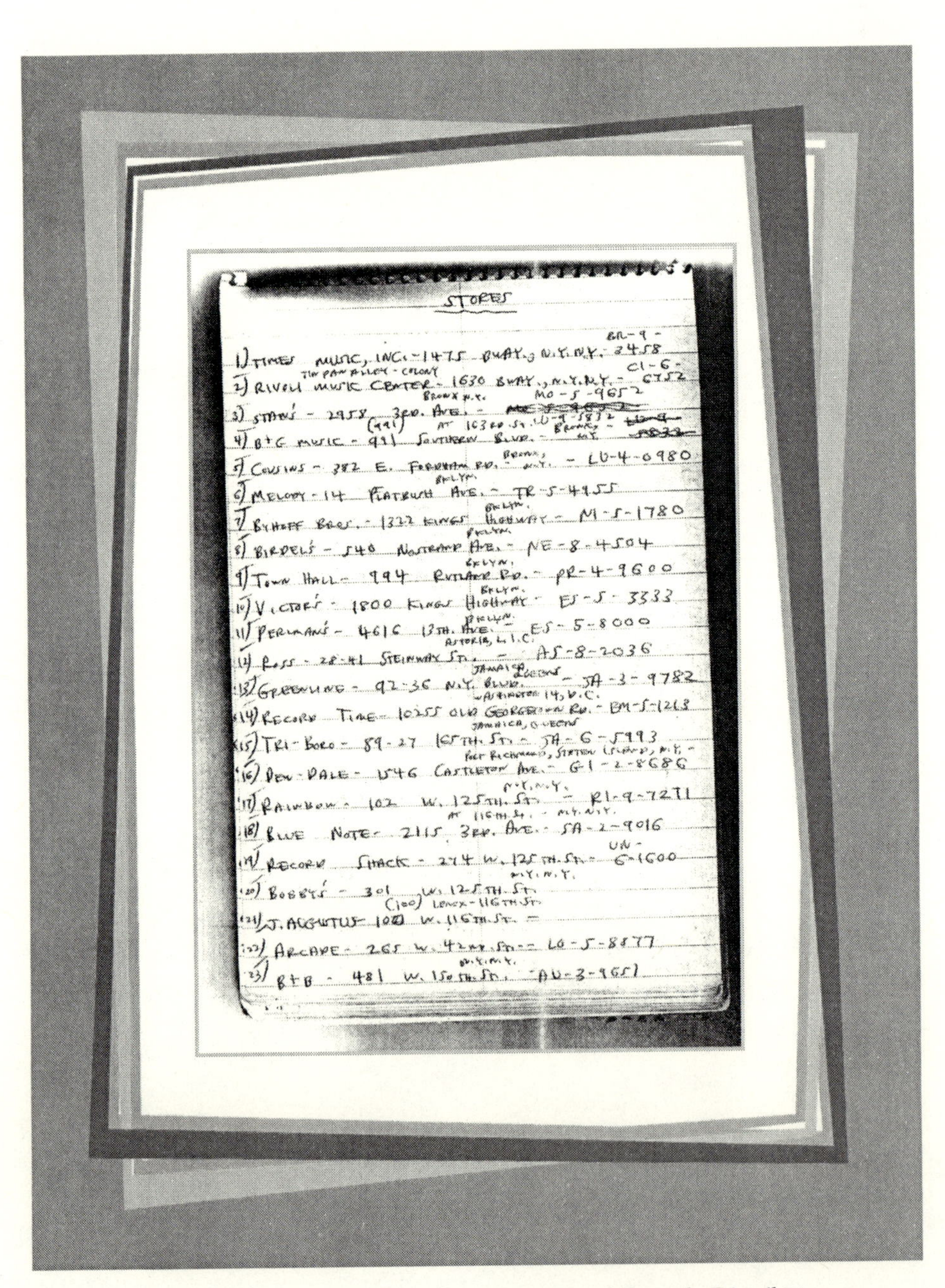

STORES

1) TIMES MUSIC, INC. - 1475 BWAY., N.Y. N.Y. - BR-9-2458
2) RIVOLI MUSIC CENTER - 1630 BWAY., N.Y. N.Y. - CI-6-6752
3) STAN'S - 2958 3RD. AVE. - BRONX N.Y. MO-5-9652
4) B+G MUSIC - 991 SOUTHERN BLVD. - (991) AT 163RD. ST. LU-9-5832 BRONX, N.Y.
5) COUSINS - 382 E. FORDHAM RD. - BRONX, N.Y. - LU-4-0980
6) MELODY - 14 FLATBUSH AVE. - BKLYN. TR-5-4955
7) BIHOFF BROS. - 1322 KINGS HIGHWAY - BKLYN. M-5-1780
8) BIRDEL'S - 540 NOSTRAND AVE. - BKLYN. NE-8-4504
9) TOWN HALL - 994 RUTLAND RD. - BKLYN. PR-4-9600
10) VICTOR'S - 1800 KINGS HIGHWAY - BKLYN. ES-5-3333
11) PERLMAN'S - 4616 13TH. AVE. - BKLYN. ES-5-8000
12) ROSS - 28-41 STEINWAY ST. - ASTORIA, L.I.C. AS-8-2036
13) GREENLINE - 92-36 N.Y. BLVD. - JAMAICA, QUEENS - JA-3-9782
14) RECORD TIME - 10255 OLD GEORGETOWN RD. - WASHINGTON 14, D.C. - EM-5-1213
15) TRI-BORO - 89-27 165TH. ST. - JAMAICA, QUEENS - JA-6-5993
16) DEW-DALE - 1546 CASTLETON AVE. - PORT RICHMOND, STATEN ISLAND, N.Y. - GI-2-8686
17) RAINBOW - 102 W. 125TH. ST. - N.Y. N.Y. - RI-9-7271
18) BLUE NOTE - 2115 3RD. AVE. - AT 116TH. ST. - N.Y. N.Y. - SA-2-9016
19) RECORD SHACK - 274 W. 125TH. ST. - UN-6-1600
20) BOBBY'S - 301 W. 125TH. ST. - N.Y. N.Y.
21) J. AUGUSTUS - 100 W. 116TH. ST. - (100) LENOX - 116TH ST.
22) ARCADE - 265 W. 42ND. ST. - LO-5-8877
23) B+B - 481 W. 150TH. ST. - N.Y. N.Y. - AU-3-9651

List Of Stores Kept By Donn Fileti For General Records Distributors

PHONE PL 5-9269

RES. PL 5-2773

TAMMY RECORDS CO.
334 Elm Street
STRUTHERS, OHIO

Aug 30, 1960.

Dear Donn:

All I can let you have for promotion records are as follows-. 10 for each release.

#1003- SHOWDOWN (Inclosed 10 Records)

#1004- RITA " " "

#1008- CRYING GUITAR " " "

NOTE! THE FOLLOWING TWO RECORDS ARE OUR LATEST RELEASES. LET ME KNOW WHAT YOU CAN DO FOR THEM

#1009 BY MICKEY FARRELL (BOTH SIDES ARE GOOD) 1 COPY INC.

1010 BY "THE EDSELS (BOTH SIDES GOOD) 1 COPY INCLOSED

LET ME HEAR FROM YOU SOON DONN.

Yours truly,

Tony March

Tony March

ALSO INCLOSED

10 - OF MY GUARDIAN-AN

Correspondence To Donn Fileti From Tony March At Tammy Records

West Orange Brdctg Co. Sept 18, 1959

WOMA

West Orange New Jersey

Dear Mr. Fileti,

Received your very nice letter. I am very sorry that you did not contact me sooner. As of now I am sponsoring time on the night train program saturday night, and it would be unfair to furnish other programs with records that are to be used on night train. Even so, I do not have any sort of a list of Records Available as I generally do not have over one or two copies of the real hard to get records, which in turn are sold as rapidly as they come in. However if you wish to purchase our

Correspondence Written By "Slim" To Donn Fileti Dated September 18, 1959...Note "Slim's" Signature...."Times Music"....

Records available at the time you
enter our store you are welcome
to do so. Or trade yours in
for ours which are on hand.

We have no set prices for
our records. the harder to get the more
they cost for instance if we have a
copy of W.P.L.J. right now it would
sell for $7.00 our trade in value on th
record is very high. Of course as an
example I have given you a top
priced record. Hundreds of hard to
get numbers run from one to three
dollars each. Its very hard to
understand our operation unless
you come in and see our price
list on offerings for old records
As we stated, you are more
than welcome to come in and

see for yourself. Sorry we can
not cooperate more fully with
you but at this time it can
not Be done, as we have an
obligation to Alan Fredricks and
the night train program

Respectfully
Times Music
1475 B'way
N.Y.C. N.Y.
Mrs Irving Rose

Wayne Stierle At Times...(Photo Taken By "Slim)"...With Donn Fileti Early 1990s...Cruising In His Car...Circa Early 1960s.....With Richard Blandon Of The Dubs....& The Original Underwood Typewriter Used For Business Transactions

Upper Left Photo....Lou Rallo, Robert Dickson & Wayne Stierle…Center Photo Wayne Stierle & Al Trommers...Bottom Photo George Grant of The Castelles, Wayne Stierle and Lou Rallo

Tony Williams & Wayne Stierle

George Grant (Castelles) Wayne Stierle & Lou Rallo "Over A Cup Of Coffee".......

Second Store Location Before The Move.....1963

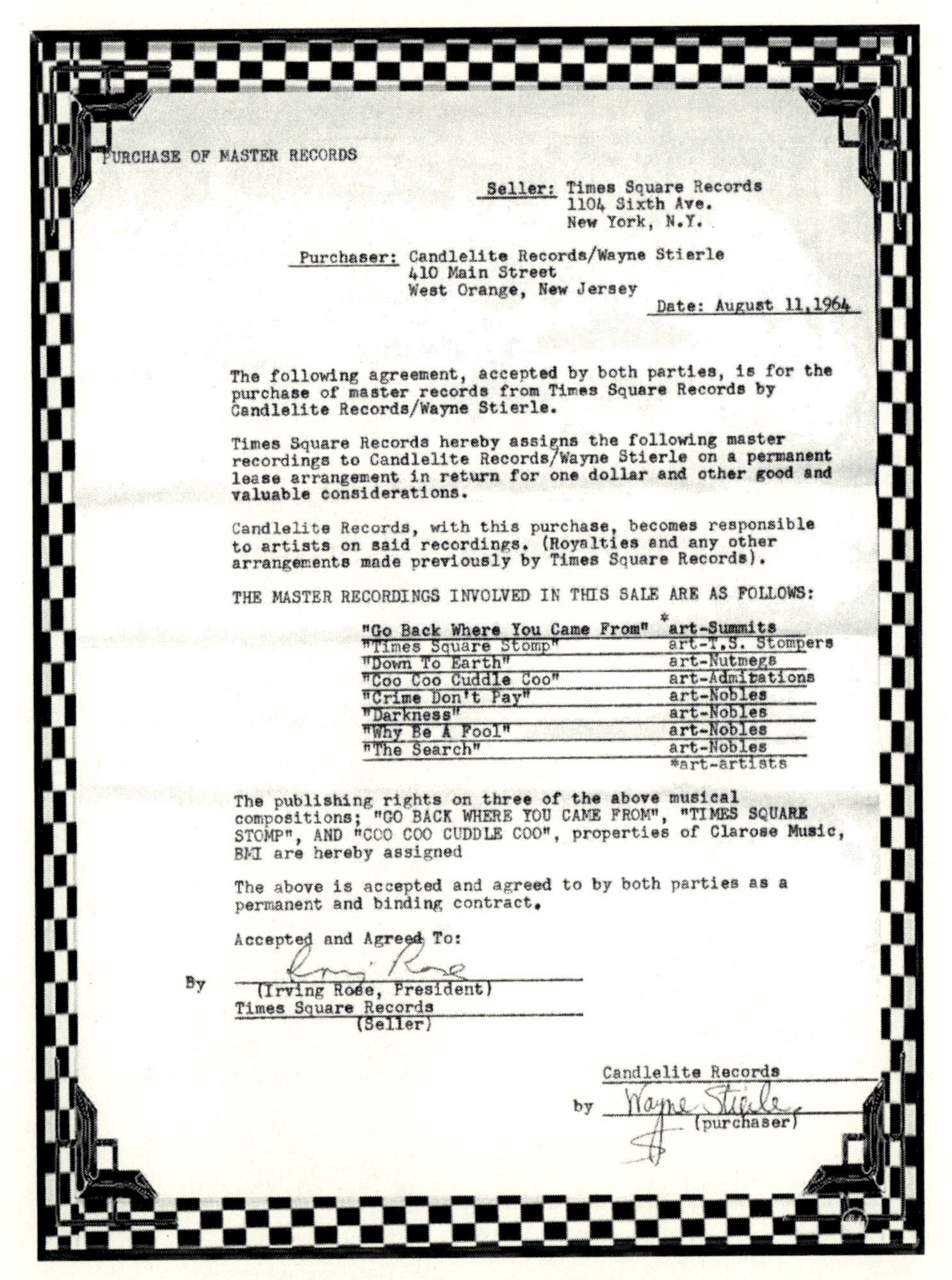

PURCHASE OF MASTER RECORDS

Seller: Times Square Records
1104 Sixth Ave.
New York, N.Y.

Purchaser: Candlelite Records/Wayne Stierle
410 Main Street
West Orange, New Jersey

Date: August 11,1964

The following agreement, accepted by both parties, is for the purchase of master records from Times Square Records by Candlelite Records/Wayne Stierle.

Times Square Records hereby assigns the following master recordings to Candlelite Records/Wayne Stierle on a permanent lease arrangement in return for one dollar and other good and valuable considerations.

Candlelite Records, with this purchase, becomes responsible to artists on said recordings. (Royalties and any other arrangements made previously by Times Square Records).

THE MASTER RECORDINGS INVOLVED IN THIS SALE ARE AS FOLLOWS:

"Go Back Where You Came From"	*art-Summits
"Times Square Stomp"	art-T.S. Stompers
"Down To Earth"	art-Nutmegs
"Coo Coo Cuddle Coo"	art-Admirations
"Crime Don't Pay"	art-Nobles
"Darkness"	art-Nobles
"Why Be A Fool"	art-Nobles
"The Search"	art-Nobles

*art-artists

The publishing rights on three of the above musical compositions; "GO BACK WHERE YOU CAME FROM", "TIMES SQUARE STOMP", AND "COO COO CUDDLE COO", properties of Clarose Music, BMI are hereby assigned

The above is accepted and agreed to by both parties as a permanent and binding contract.

Accepted and Agreed To:

By Irving Rose
(Irving Rose, President)
Times Square Records
(Seller)

Candlelite Records
by Wayne Stierle
(purchaser)

Contract Between "Slim" & Candlelite Records....

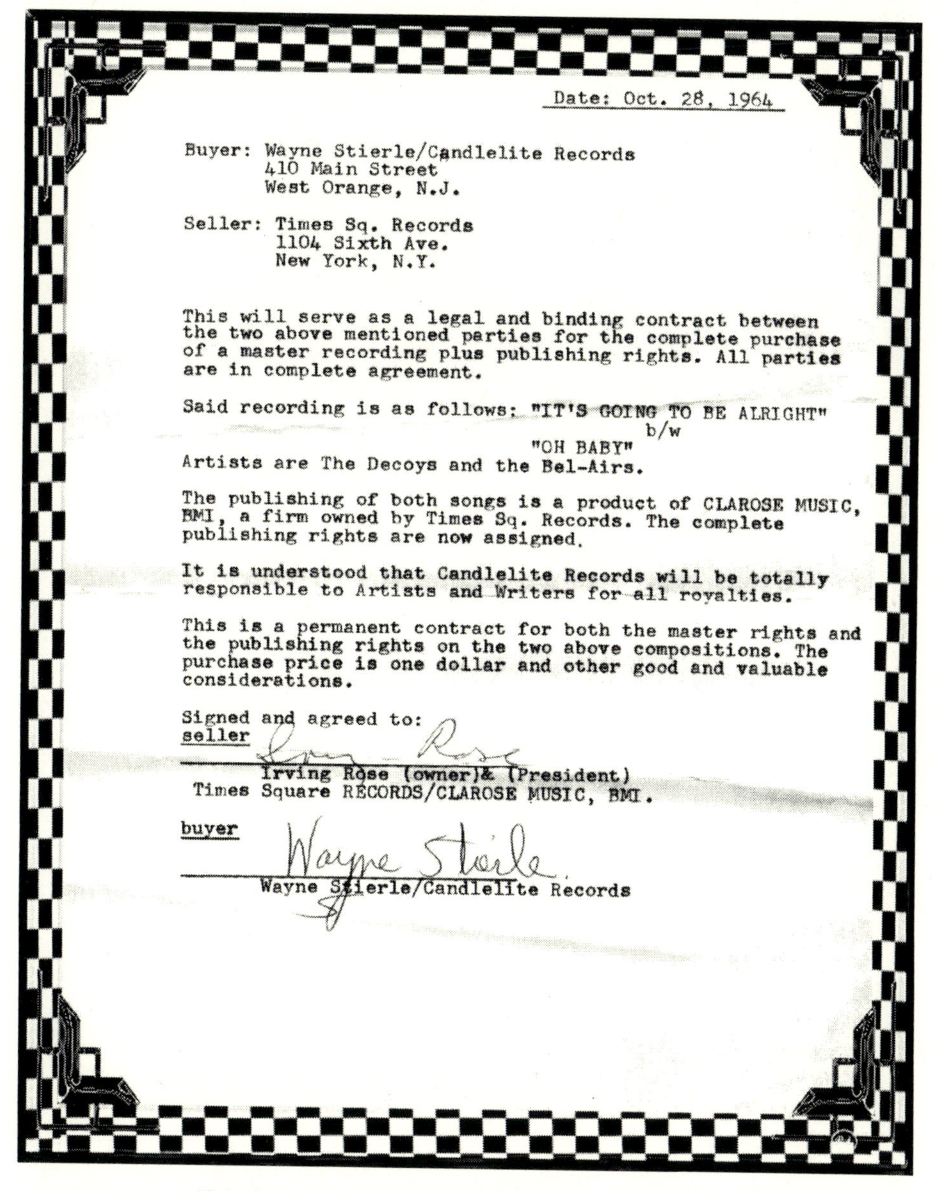

Date: Oct. 28, 1964

Buyer: Wayne Stierle/Candlelite Records
410 Main Street
West Orange, N.J.

Seller: Times Sq. Records
1104 Sixth Ave.
New York, N.Y.

This will serve as a legal and binding contract between the two above mentioned parties for the complete purchase of a master recording plus publishing rights. All parties are in complete agreement.

Said recording is as follows: "IT'S GOING TO BE ALRIGHT"
b/w
"OH BABY"
Artists are The Decoys and the Bel-Airs.

The publishing of both songs is a product of CLAROSE MUSIC, BMI, a firm owned by Times Sq. Records. The complete publishing rights are now assigned.

It is understood that Candlelite Records will be totally responsible to Artists and Writers for all royalties.

This is a permanent contract for both the master rights and the publishing rights on the two above compositions. The purchase price is one dollar and other good and valuable considerations.

Signed and agreed to:
seller

Irving Rose (owner)& (President)
Times Square RECORDS/CLAROSE MUSIC, BMI.

buyer

Wayne Stierle/Candlelite Records

"It's Going To Be Alright" / "Oh Baby" Contract....

September 21, 1963

THIS WILL SERVE AS A BINDING CONTRACT BETWEEN TIMES SQUARE RECORDS AND WAYNE STIERLE FOR THE PURCHASE OF A MASTER RECORDING BY WAYNE STIERLE FROM TIMES SQUARE RECORDS.............THE DATE IS September 20, 1963.
THE SALES DOES NOT INCLUDE PUBLISHING RIGHTS.

THE MASTER BEING PURCHASED IS "CAN I COME OVER"/"Gonna Get Together Again" By THE YOUNGTONES. THE AMMOUNT OF SALE IS ONE DOLLAR AND OTHER GOOD AND VALUABLE CONSIDERATIONS.

BOTH PARTIES ARE IN COMPLETE AGREEMENT ON THIS SALE.

SELLER:

TIMES SQUARE RECORDS

BY: Irving Rose

PURCHASER:

WAYNE STIERLE

BY: Wayne Stierle

"Can I Come Over" / "Gonna Get Together Again" Contract...

Date... April 16, 1963

This will serve as a binding contract between Times Square Records and Wayne Stierle for the purchase of this master: "Gonna Find My Pretty Baby"/"Lil' Lil' Lulu" by Norven Baskerville and The Admirations.

This a complete purchase, NOT including the publishing however.

This sale is on (date)..APRIL..16,.1963.....and is for one dollar and other good and valuable considerations.

Both parties are in total agreement.

Seller: TIMES SQUARE RECORDS

By Irving Rose

Purchaser: Wayne Stierle

By Wayne Stierle

"Gonna Find My Pretty Baby"/ "Lil" "Lil" LuLu" Contract.....

SEPTEMBER 20, 1963.

THIS WILL SERVE AS A BINDING CONTRACT BETWEEN TIMES SQUARE RECORDS AND WAYNE STIERLE. THE PURCHASE IS A MASTER RECORDING. THE SELLER IS TIMES SQUARE RECORDS, AND THE BUYER IS WAYNE STIERLE.

THE DATE IS: September 20, 1963

THE SALE DOES NOT INCLUDE ANY PUBLISHING RIGHTS.

J.W.S. IR THE MASTER BEING PURCHASED IS "Greatest Gift of All"/"Calypso Baby".

FIVE SOUNDS ← BY THE 5 SOUNDS .

THE SALE IS FOR ONE DOLLAR AND OTHER GOOD AND VALUABLE CONSIDERATIONS.

BOTH PARTIES ARE IN COMPLETE AGREEMENT.

SELLER:

TIMES SQUARE RECORDS.

BY:" Irving Rose .

PURCHASER:

WAYNE STIERLE

BY: Wayne Stierle.

"Greatest Gift Of All" Contract....

Date... December 28, 1962

This will serve as a binding contract between Times Square Records and Wayne Stierle for the purchase of a master: "She's Gone"/"The Voice" by Fred Parris & The Scarlets(formerely and now known as The 5 Satins).
This purchase is ~~is~~ complete, but does not include the publishing, which remains with its original owner.(Wall Music).
The sale is on (date) December 28, 1962, and is for one dollar and other good and valuable considerations.
Both parties are in total agreement.

Seller: TIMES SQUARE RECORDS

By Irving Rose, Pres.

Purchaser: Wayne Stierle

By Wayne Stierle

"She's Gone" / "The Voice" Contract......

Date... July 9, 1963

This will serve as a binding contract between Times Square Records and Wayne Stierle for the purchase of this master: "You I Adore"/"It's Over Now" by The Youngtones.

This is a complete purchase, but does NOT include the publishing of the songs........This sale is on July 9, 1963 and is for one dollar and other good and valuable ~~considerations~~ considerations.
Both parties are in total agreement.

Seller: TIMES SQUARE RECORDS
By Irving Rose, Pres.

Purchaser: Wayne Stierle
By Wayne Stierle

"You I Adore" / "It's Over Now" Contract.......

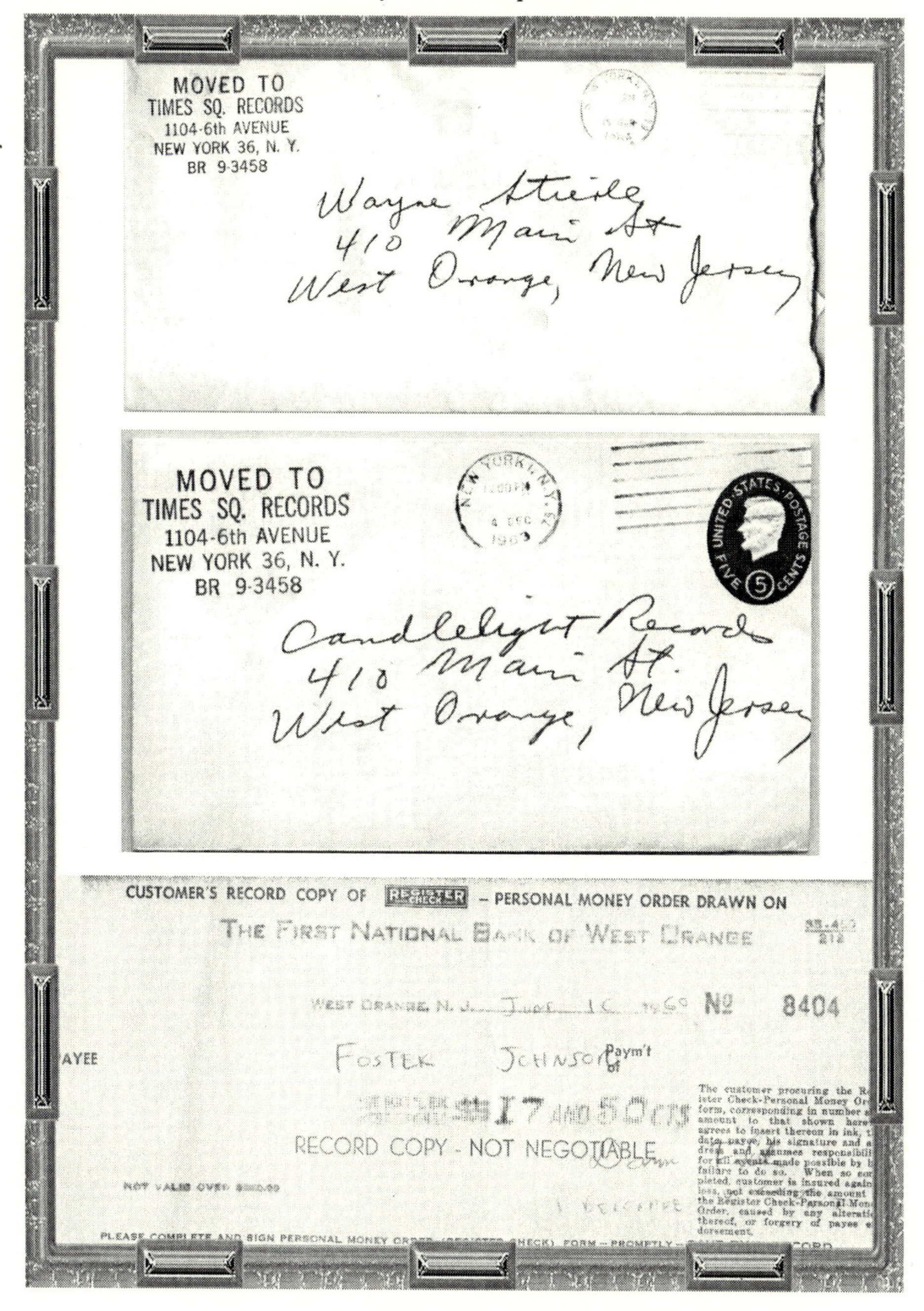
MOVED TO
TIMES SQ. RECORDS
1104-6th AVENUE
NEW YORK 36, N. Y.
BR 9-3458

Wayne Stierle
410 Main St
West Orange, New Jersey

MOVED TO
TIMES SQ. RECORDS
1104-6th AVENUE
NEW YORK 36, N. Y.
BR 9-3458

NEW YORK 1, N.Y.
4 DEC
1962

UNITED STATES POSTAGE
FIVE CENTS 5

Candlelight Records
410 Main St.
West Orange, New Jersey

CUSTOMER'S RECORD COPY OF REGISTER CHECK — PERSONAL MONEY ORDER DRAWN ON
THE FIRST NATIONAL BANK OF WEST ORANGE

WEST ORANGE, N. J. June 16 1960 № 8404

PAYEE Foster Johnson Paym't of

$17 AND 50 CTS

RECORD COPY - NOT NEGOTIABLE

NOT VALID OVER $100.00

PLEASE COMPLETE AND SIGN PERSONAL MONEY ORDER

Envelopes & Money Order Receipt

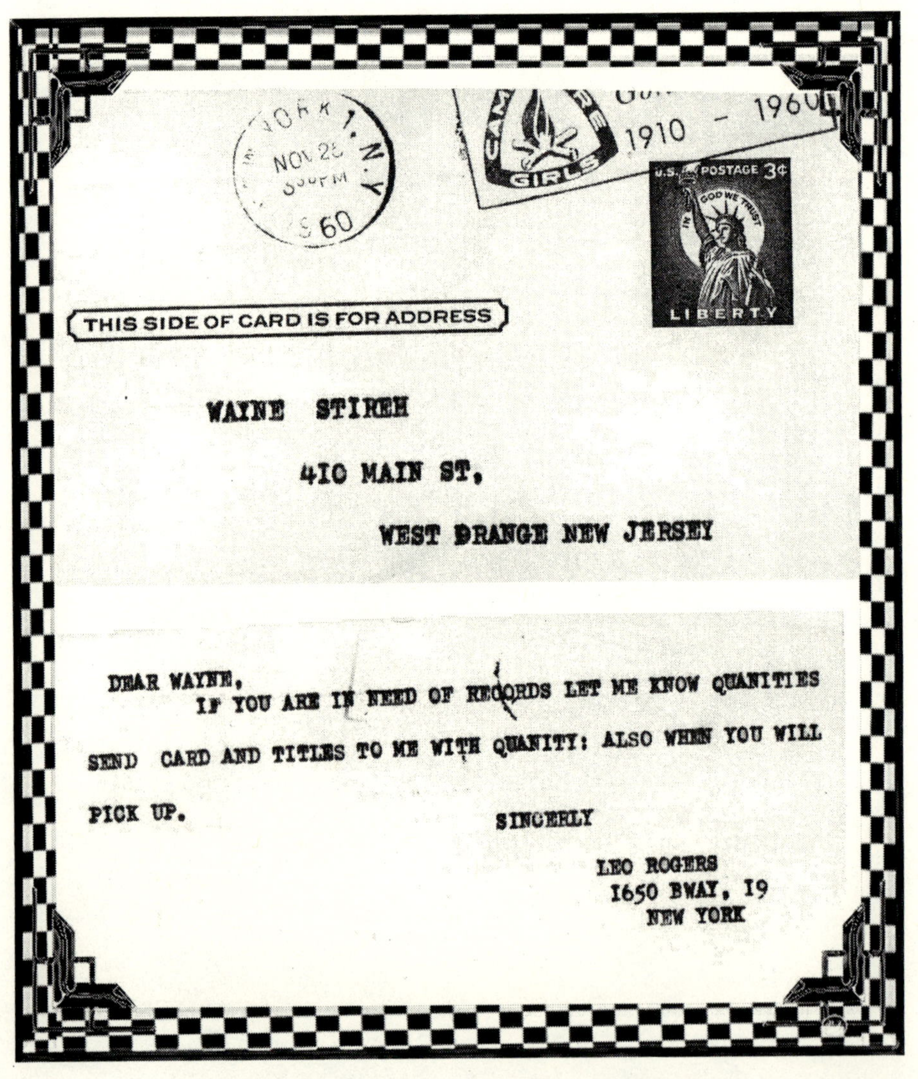

1910 - 1960

GIRLS

U.S. POSTAGE 3¢

IN GOD WE TRUST

LIBERTY

THIS SIDE OF CARD IS FOR ADDRESS

WAYNE STIREH

410 MAIN ST,

WEST BRANGE NEW JERSEY

DEAR WAYNE,
IF YOU ARE IN NEED OF RECORDS LET ME KNOW QUANITIES SEND CARD AND TITLES TO ME WITH QUANITY: ALSO WHEN YOU WILL PICK UP.

SINCERLY

LEO ROGERS
1650 BWAY, 19
NEW YORK

Post Card To Wayne Stierle From Leo Rogers

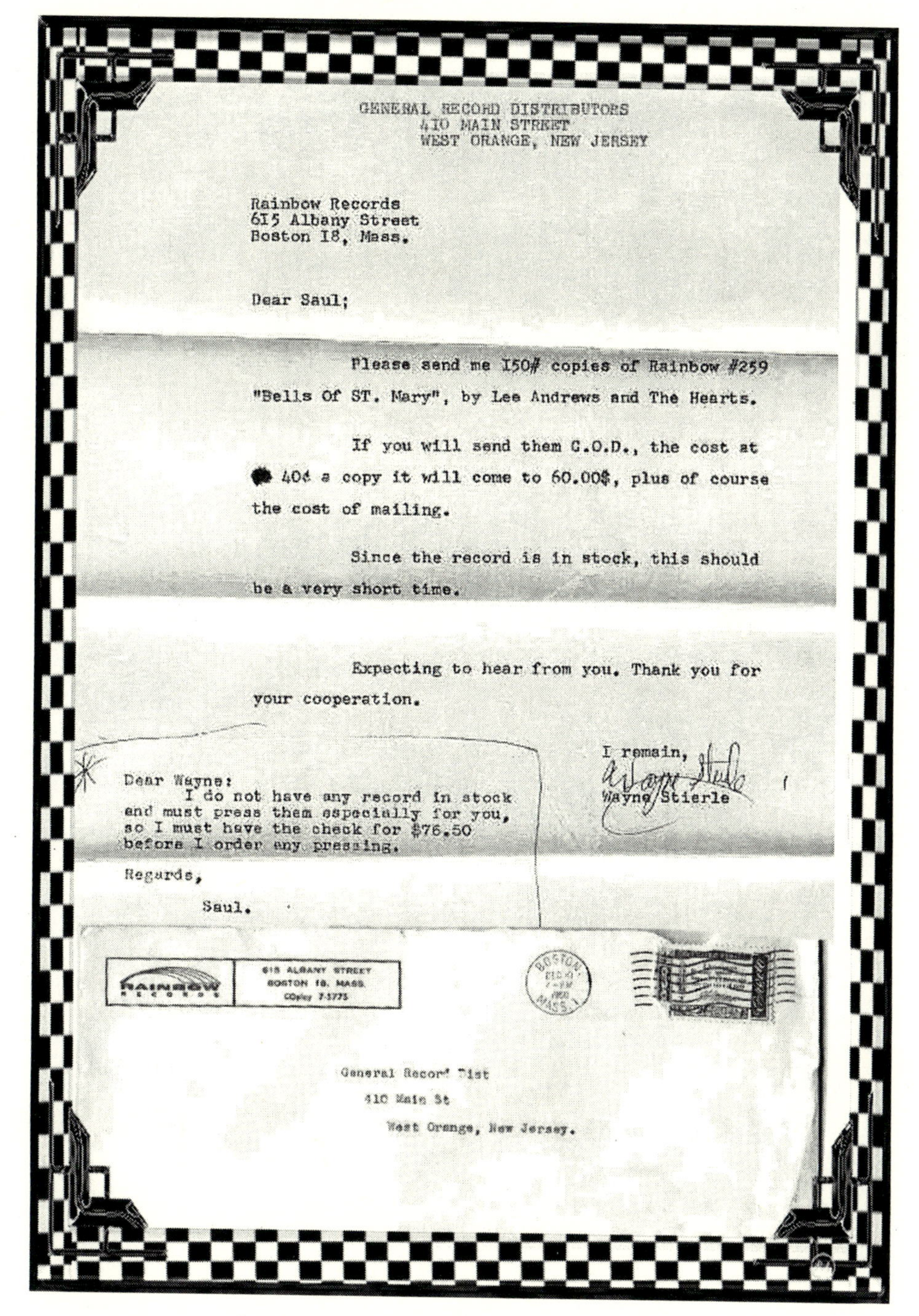

GENERAL RECORD DISTRIBUTORS
410 MAIN STREET
WEST ORANGE, NEW JERSEY

Rainbow Records
615 Albany Street
Boston 18, Mass.

Dear Saul;

Please send me 150# copies of Rainbow #259 "Bells Of ST. Mary", by Lee Andrews and The Hearts.

If you will send them C.O.D., the cost at 40¢ a copy it will come to 60.00$, plus of course the cost of mailing.

Since the record is in stock, this should be a very short time.

Expecting to hear from you. Thank you for your cooperation.

I remain,
Wayne Stierle

Dear Wayne:
I do not have any record in stock and must press them especially for you, so I must have the check for $76.50 before I order any pressing.

Regards,

Saul.

RAINBOW RECORDS
615 ALBANY STREET
BOSTON 18, MASS.
COpley 7-5775

BOSTON MASS.

General Record Dist
410 Main St
West Orange, New Jersey.

Correspondence To & From Rainbow Records

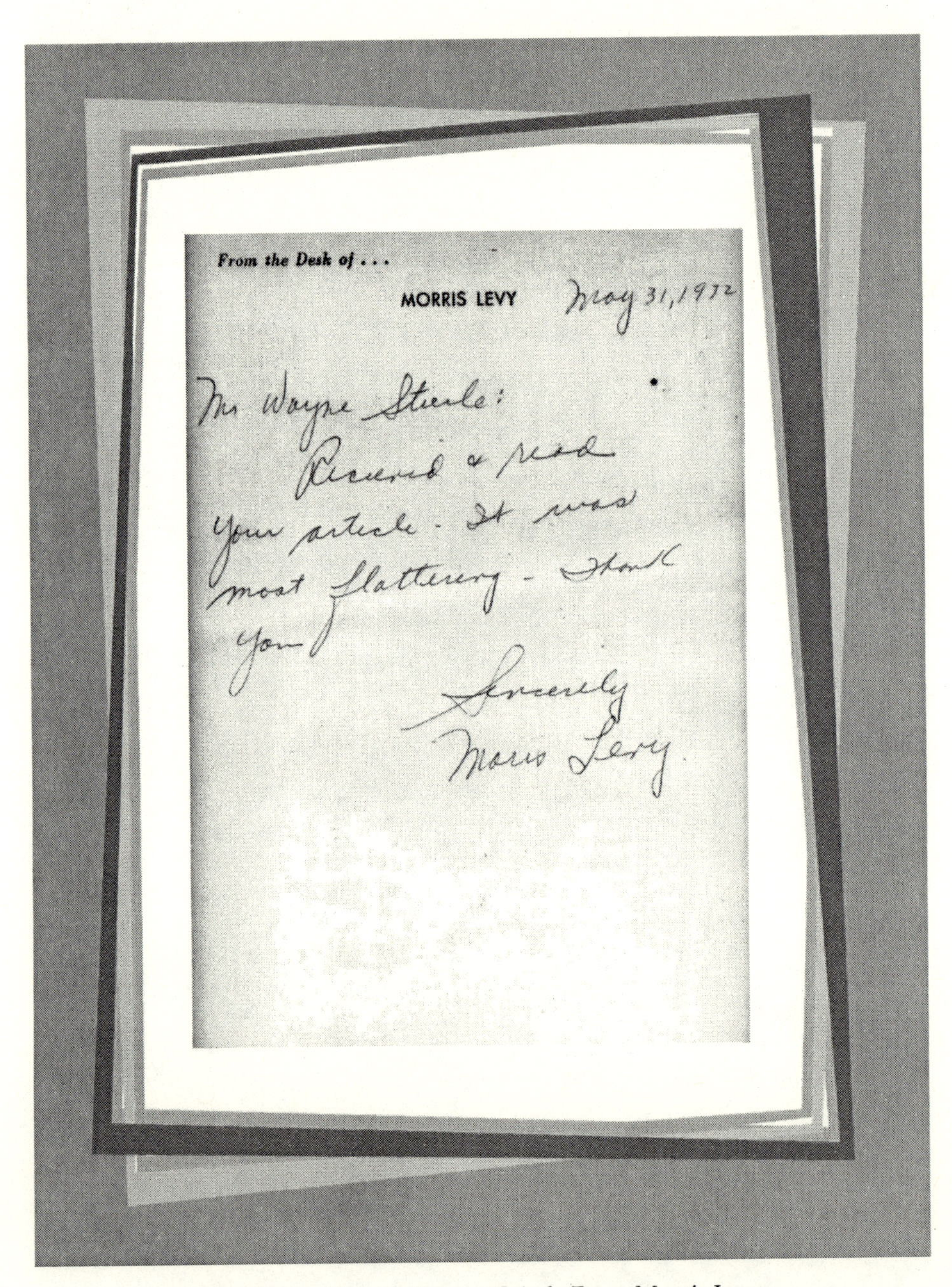

From the Desk of . . .

MORRIS LEVY May 31, 1972

Mr Wayne Stierle:

Received & read your article - It was most flattering - Thank you

Sincerely
Morris Levy

A Thank You Note To Wayne Stierle From Morris Levy...

SID TABACK RECORDS
We Buy and Sell All Types of Records
2540 West Pico Boulevard
Los Angeles 6, California

OUR NUMBER 7820
DATE
CUSTOMER'S ORDER
SALESMAN

Sold To General Record Dist.
410 Main St.
West Orange, N.J.
Shipped To
Address
Via Parcel Post

INVOICE

500 Dut 7843 [illegible] 75.00
Postage 2.50
77.50

Rediform 7H724

SID TABACK RECORDS
2540 WEST PICO BOULEVARD
LOS ANGELES 6, CALIF.

LOS ANGELES CALIF. 1960

BUILD YOUR FUTURE WISELY U.S. SAVINGS BONDS

General Record Dist.
410 Main St.
West Orange. N.J.

Purchase Invoice.....Sid Taback Records

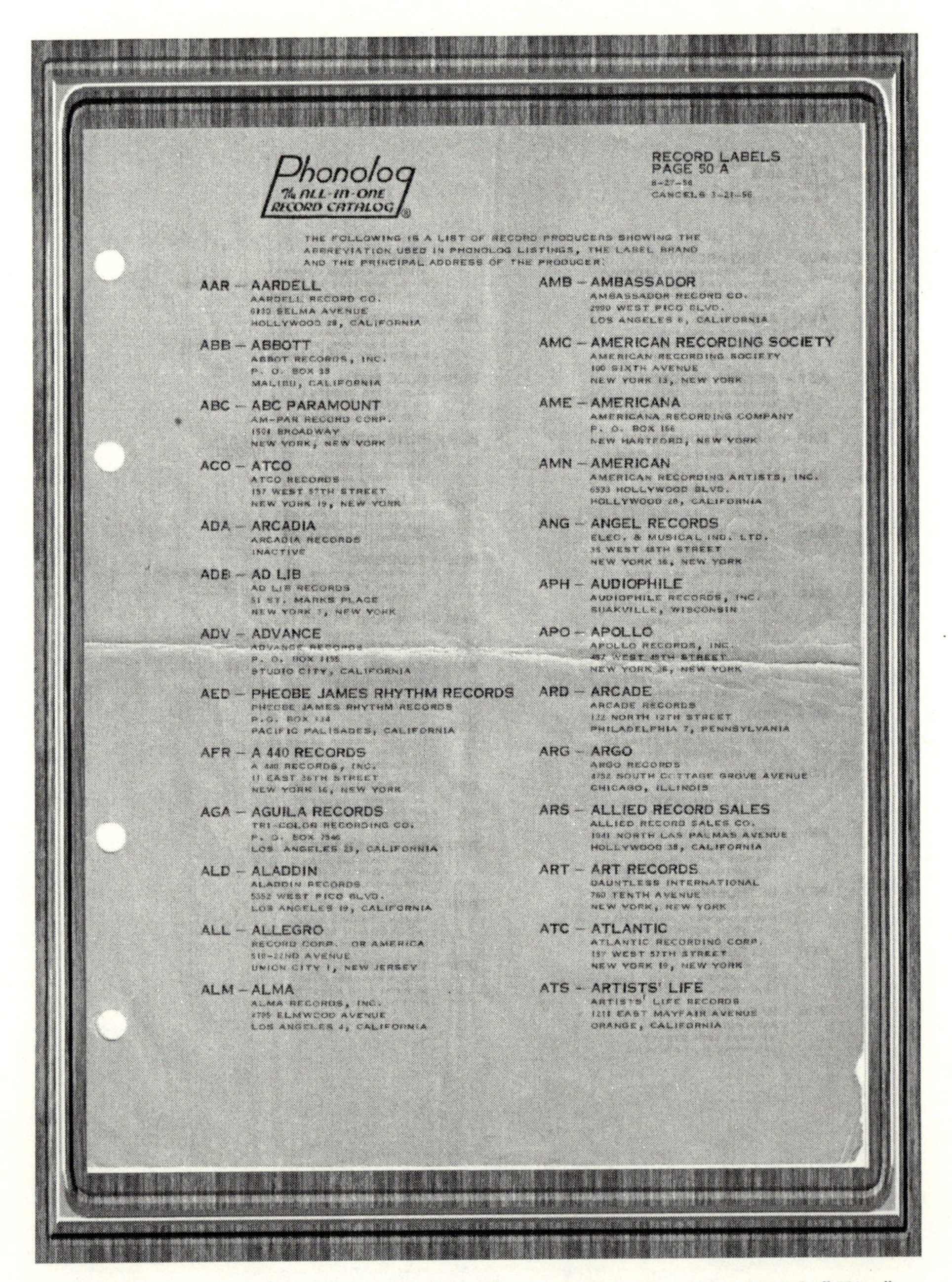

Phonolog
The ALL-IN-ONE RECORD CATALOG®

RECORD LABELS
PAGE 50 A
6-27-56
CANCELS 3-21-56

THE FOLLOWING IS A LIST OF RECORD PRODUCERS SHOWING THE ABBREVIATION USED IN PHONOLOG LISTINGS, THE LABEL BRAND AND THE PRINCIPAL ADDRESS OF THE PRODUCER:

AAR – AARDELL
AARDELL RECORD CO.
6930 SELMA AVENUE
HOLLYWOOD 28, CALIFORNIA

ABB – ABBOTT
ABBOT RECORDS, INC.
P. O. BOX 35
MALIBU, CALIFORNIA

ABC – ABC PARAMOUNT
AM-PAR RECORD CORP.
1501 BROADWAY
NEW YORK, NEW YORK

ACO – ATCO
ATCO RECORDS
157 WEST 57TH STREET
NEW YORK 19, NEW YORK

ADA – ARCADIA
ARCADIA RECORDS
INACTIVE

ADB – AD LIB
AD LIB RECORDS
51 ST. MARKS PLACE
NEW YORK 7, NEW YORK

ADV – ADVANCE
ADVANCE RECORDS
P. O. BOX 1155
STUDIO CITY, CALIFORNIA

AED – PHEOBE JAMES RHYTHM RECORDS
PHEOBE JAMES RHYTHM RECORDS
P.O. BOX 134
PACIFIC PALISADES, CALIFORNIA

AFR – A 440 RECORDS
A 440 RECORDS, INC.
11 EAST 36TH STREET
NEW YORK 16, NEW YORK

AGA – AGUILA RECORDS
TRI-COLOR RECORDING CO.
P. O. BOX 7546
LOS ANGELES 23, CALIFORNIA

ALD – ALADDIN
ALADDIN RECORDS
5352 WEST PICO BLVD.
LOS ANGELES 19, CALIFORNIA

ALL – ALLEGRO
RECORD CORP. OF AMERICA
510-22ND AVENUE
UNION CITY 1, NEW JERSEY

ALM – ALMA
ALMA RECORDS, INC.
4795 ELMWOOD AVENUE
LOS ANGELES 4, CALIFORNIA

AMB – AMBASSADOR
AMBASSADOR RECORD CO.
2990 WEST PICO BLVD.
LOS ANGELES 6, CALIFORNIA

AMC – AMERICAN RECORDING SOCIETY
AMERICAN RECORDING SOCIETY
100 SIXTH AVENUE
NEW YORK 13, NEW YORK

AME – AMERICANA
AMERICANA RECORDING COMPANY
P. O. BOX 156
NEW HARTFORD, NEW YORK

AMN – AMERICAN
AMERICAN RECORDING ARTISTS, INC.
6533 HOLLYWOOD BLVD.
HOLLYWOOD 28, CALIFORNIA

ANG – ANGEL RECORDS
ELEC. & MUSICAL IND. LTD.
35 WEST 48TH STREET
NEW YORK 36, NEW YORK

APH – AUDIOPHILE
AUDIOPHILE RECORDS, INC.
SUAKVILLE, WISCONSIN

APO – APOLLO
APOLLO RECORDS, INC.
457 WEST 45TH STREET
NEW YORK 36, NEW YORK

ARD – ARCADE
ARCADE RECORDS
122 NORTH 12TH STREET
PHILADELPHIA 7, PENNSYLVANIA

ARG – ARGO
ARGO RECORDS
4752 SOUTH COTTAGE GROVE AVENUE
CHICAGO, ILLINOIS

ARS – ALLIED RECORD SALES
ALLIED RECORD SALES CO.
1041 NORTH LAS PALMAS AVENUE
HOLLYWOOD 38, CALIFORNIA

ART – ART RECORDS
DAUNTLESS INTERNATIONAL
750 TENTH AVENUE
NEW YORK, NEW YORK

ATC – ATLANTIC
ATLANTIC RECORDING CORP.
157 WEST 57TH STREET
NEW YORK 19, NEW YORK

ATS – ARTISTS' LIFE
ARTISTS' LIFE RECORDS
1211 EAST MAYFAIR AVENUE
ORANGE, CALIFORNIA

The Phonolog Al Trommers Refers To In The First Chapter...Shared With "Slim".. It is dated June 27, 1956.

Phonolog
The ALL-IN-ONE RECORD CATALOG®

RECORD LABELS
PAGE 52 A
5-23-56
CANCELS 4-18-56

COOK LABORATORIES
SEE UNDER "SDS" IN RECORD LABEL SECTION

CAE – CAEDMON
CAEDMON PUBLISHERS
460 4TH AVENUE
NEW YORK 16, NEW YORK

CAM – CAMBRIDGE RECORD CO.
P. O. BOX 125
CAMBRIDGE 39, MASSACHUSETTS

CAP – CAPITOL
CAPITOL RECORDS, INC.
SUNSET & VINE
HOLLYWOOD 28, CALIFORNIA

CAR – CARIBBEAN
DAUNTLESS INTERNATIONAL
750 TENTH AVENUE
NEW YORK, NEW YORK

CAT – CAT
CAT RECORDING CORPORATION
234 WEST 56TH STREET
NEW YORK 19, NEW YORK

CAV – CAVALIER
CAVALIER RECORDS, INC.
298 – 9TH STREET
SAN FRANCISCO 3, CALIFORNIA

CBL – CYMBOL RECORDS
P. O. BOX 344
BURBANK, CALIFORNIA

CBO – COMBO
COMBO RECORDS
1107 EL CENTRO AVENUE
HOLLYWOOD 28, CALIFORNIA

CDA – CODA
SPANISH MUSIC CENTER
1291 SIXTH AVENUE
NEW YORK 19, NEW YORK

CDE – CADENCE
CADENCE RECORDS
40 EAST 49TH STREET
NEW YORK 17, NEW YORK

CDN – CAMDEN
CAMDEN RECORDS
155 EAST 24TH STREET
NEW YORK, NEW YORK

CDR – COMMODORE
COMMODORE RECORD CO., INC.
INACTIVE

CET – CETRA
CAPITOL RECORDS, INC.
1730 BROADWAY, DEPT. S
NEW YORK 19, NEW YORK

CFR – CHRISTIAN FAITH RECORDINGS
ALMA RECORDS, INC.
4705 ELMWOOD AVENUE
LOS ANGELES 4, CALIFORNIA

CHD – CHESTERFIELD
CHESTERFIELD RECORDS
BOX 3193
BEVERLY HILLS, CALIFORNIA

CHK – CHECKER
CHECKER RECORD COMPANY
4750 COTTAGE GROVE AVENUE
CHICAGO 15, ILLINOIS

CHS – CONCERT HALL SOCIETY
CONCERT HALL SOCIETY, INC.
45 COLUMBUS AVENUE
NEW YORK 23, NEW YORK

CHT – CHART
CHART RECORDS
1214 S. W. 8TH STREET
MIAMI, FLORIDA

CLA – CLAREMONT RECORDS
CLAREMONT RECORDS
224 YALE
CLAREMONT, CALIFORNIA

CLF – CLEF
CLEF RECORDS, INC.
451 NORTH CANON DRIVE
BEVERLY HILLS, CALIFORNIA

CLL – CARDILL
CARDILL RECORDS
88 WATER STREET
TORRINGTON, CONNECTICUT

CLS – CLASSIC EDITIONS
CLASSIC EDITIONS
719 TENTH AVENUE
NEW YORK 19, NEW YORK

CMP – COMMAND PERFORMANCE
COMMAND PERFORMANCE RECORDS, INC.
INACTIVE

CNT – C-NOTE
C-NOTE RECORDS
11739 BARRINGTON COURT
LOS ANGELES 49, CALIFORNIA

COA – COAST
COAST RECORD MFG., CO.
2534 WEST PICO BOULEVARD
LOS ANGELES 6, CALIFORNIA

COL – COLUMBIA
COLUMBIA RECORDS, INC.
1473 BARNUM AVENUE
BRIDGEPORT 8, CONNECTICUT

Phonolog Two

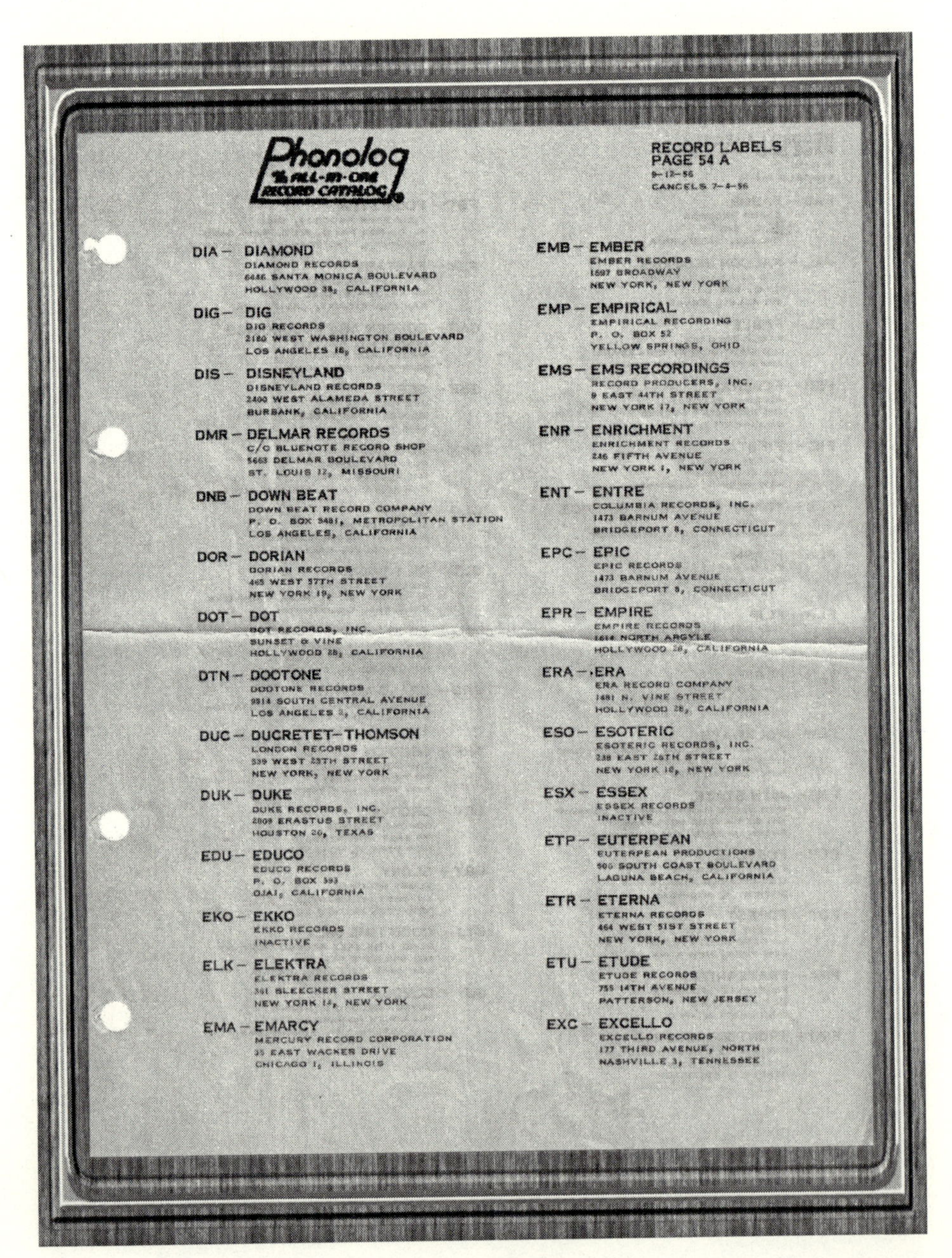

Phonolog
The All-In-One Record Catalog

RECORD LABELS
PAGE 54 A
9-12-56
CANCELS 7-4-56

DIA – DIAMOND
DIAMOND RECORDS
6686 SANTA MONICA BOULEVARD
HOLLYWOOD 38, CALIFORNIA

DIG – DIG
DIG RECORDS
2180 WEST WASHINGTON BOULEVARD
LOS ANGELES 18, CALIFORNIA

DIS – DISNEYLAND
DISNEYLAND RECORDS
2400 WEST ALAMEDA STREET
BURBANK, CALIFORNIA

DMR – DELMAR RECORDS
C/O BLUENOTE RECORD SHOP
5663 DELMAR BOULEVARD
ST. LOUIS 12, MISSOURI

DNB – DOWN BEAT
DOWN BEAT RECORD COMPANY
P. O. BOX 3481, METROPOLITAN STATION
LOS ANGELES, CALIFORNIA

DOR – DORIAN
DORIAN RECORDS
465 WEST 57TH STREET
NEW YORK 19, NEW YORK

DOT – DOT
DOT RECORDS, INC.
SUNSET & VINE
HOLLYWOOD 28, CALIFORNIA

DTN – DOOTONE
DOOTONE RECORDS
9514 SOUTH CENTRAL AVENUE
LOS ANGELES 2, CALIFORNIA

DUC – DUCRETET–THOMSON
LONDON RECORDS
539 WEST 25TH STREET
NEW YORK, NEW YORK

DUK – DUKE
DUKE RECORDS, INC.
2809 ERASTUS STREET
HOUSTON 26, TEXAS

EDU – EDUCO
EDUCO RECORDS
P. O. BOX 393
OJAI, CALIFORNIA

EKO – EKKO
EKKO RECORDS
INACTIVE

ELK – ELEKTRA
ELEKTRA RECORDS
361 BLEECKER STREET
NEW YORK 14, NEW YORK

EMA – EMARCY
MERCURY RECORD CORPORATION
35 EAST WACKER DRIVE
CHICAGO 1, ILLINOIS

EMB – EMBER
EMBER RECORDS
1697 BROADWAY
NEW YORK, NEW YORK

EMP – EMPIRICAL
EMPIRICAL RECORDING
P. O. BOX 52
YELLOW SPRINGS, OHIO

EMS – EMS RECORDINGS
RECORD PRODUCERS, INC.
9 EAST 44TH STREET
NEW YORK 17, NEW YORK

ENR – ENRICHMENT
ENRICHMENT RECORDS
246 FIFTH AVENUE
NEW YORK 1, NEW YORK

ENT – ENTRE
COLUMBIA RECORDS, INC.
1473 BARNUM AVENUE
BRIDGEPORT 8, CONNECTICUT

EPC – EPIC
EPIC RECORDS
1473 BARNUM AVENUE
BRIDGEPORT 8, CONNECTICUT

EPR – EMPIRE
EMPIRE RECORDS
1614 NORTH ARGYLE
HOLLYWOOD 28, CALIFORNIA

ERA – ERA
ERA RECORD COMPANY
1481 N. VINE STREET
HOLLYWOOD 28, CALIFORNIA

ESO – ESOTERIC
ESOTERIC RECORDS, INC.
238 EAST 26TH STREET
NEW YORK 10, NEW YORK

ESX – ESSEX
ESSEX RECORDS
INACTIVE

ETP – EUTERPEAN
EUTERPEAN PRODUCTIONS
905 SOUTH COAST BOULEVARD
LAGUNA BEACH, CALIFORNIA

ETR – ETERNA
ETERNA RECORDS
464 WEST 51ST STREET
NEW YORK, NEW YORK

ETU – ETUDE
ETUDE RECORDS
755 14TH AVENUE
PATTERSON, NEW JERSEY

EXC – EXCELLO
EXCELLO RECORDS
177 THIRD AVENUE, NORTH
NASHVILLE 3, TENNESSEE

Phonolog Three

Phonolog
The ALL-IN-ONE RECORD CATALOG®

RECORD LABELS
PAGE 56 A
8-1-56
CANCELS 3-4-56

HBR – HUMMING BIRD RECORDS
HUMMING BIRD RECORDS
INACTIVE

HER – HERALD
HERALD RECORDS
1697 BROADWAY
NEW YORK, NEW YORK

HIC – HICKORY
HICKORY RECORDS, INC.
2510 FRANKLIN ROAD
NASHVILLE 4, TENNESSEE

HIF – HI-FI RECORD
HIGH FIDELITY RECORDINGS, INC
6087 SUNSET BOULEVARD
HOLLYWOOD 28, CALIFORNIA

HIP – HIP
HIP RECORDS
6057 SUNSET BOULEVARD
HOLLYWOOD 23, CALIFORNIA

HMV – HIS MASTER'S VOICE
RCA VICTOR
155 EAST 24TH STREET
NEW YORK, NEW YORK

HNS – HANDEL SOCIETY
HANDEL SOCIETY, INC.
INACTIVE

HOL – HOLT
HENRY HOLT & CO.
383 MADISON AVENUE
NEW YORK 17, NEW YORK

HTG – HERITAGE
HERITAGE RECORDS
11 EAST 36TH STREET
NEW YORK 16, NEW YORK

HUL – HULL
HULL RECORD CO.
1595 BROADWAY
NEW YORK 19, NEW YORK

HWD – HOLLYWOOD
HOLLYWOOD RECORDS, INC.
1248 SOUTH BERENDO STREET
LOS ANGELES 6, CALIFORNIA

HYD – HAYDN SOCIETY
HAYDN SOCIETY, INC.
INACTIVE

IDL – IDEAL
RIO GRANDE MUSIC CO.
P. O. BOX 861
SAN BENITO, TEXAS

IMF – ISRAEL MUSIC FOUNDATION
DAUNTLESS INTERNATIONAL
750 TENTH AVENUE
NEW YORK, NEW YORK

IMP – IMPERIAL
IMPERIAL RECORDS
6425 HOLLYWOOD BOULEVARD
HOLLYWOOD 28, CALIFORNIA

INO – INTRO
INTRO RECORDS
5352 WEST PICO BOULEVARD
LOS ANGELES, CALIFORNIA

ISR – INTERNATIONAL SACRED
INTERNATIONAL SACRED RECORDINGS
6404 HOLLYWOOD BOULEVARD
HOLLYWOOD 28, CALIFORNIA

JOU – JOURNEY LANGUAGE
C/O GOLDSMITH'S MUSIC SHOP, INC.
401 WEST 42ND STREET
NEW YORK 36, NEW YORK

JOZ – JOSIE
JOSIE RECORD COMPANY
1650 BROADWAY
NEW YORK, NEW YORK

JUB – JUBILEE
JUBILEE RECORDS
1650 BROADWAY
NEW YORK, NEW YORK

JUM – JUMP
THE TURNTABLE
P. O. BOX 622, HOLLYWOOD STATION
HOLLYWOOD 28, CALIFORNIA

JZL – JAZZOLOGY
JAZZOLOGY RECORDS
131 SOUTH WOODLAND STREET
ENGLEWOOD, NEW JERSEY

JZM – JAZZ MAN
JAZZ MAN RECORD SHOP
P. O. BOX 2108
HOLLYWOOD, CALIFORNIA

JZW – JAZZ: WEST
JAZZ: WEST RECORDS
5352 WEST PICO
LOS ANGELES, CALIFORNIA

KAP – KAPP
KAPP RECORDS, INC.
119 WEST 57TH STREET
NEW YORK 19, NEW YORK

KEM – KEM
KEM RECORDS, INC.
1107 NORTH EL CENTRO
HOLLYWOOD 38, CALIFORNIA

KEY – KEY
KEY RECORDS
P. O. BOX 46128
HOLLYWOOD, CALIFORNIA

KGO – KING
KING RECORDS, INC.
1540 BREWSTER AVENUE
CINCINNATI 7, OHIO

KIS – KISMET
KISMET RECORD COMPANY
227 EAST 14TH STREET
NEW YORK 3, NEW YORK

Phonolog Four

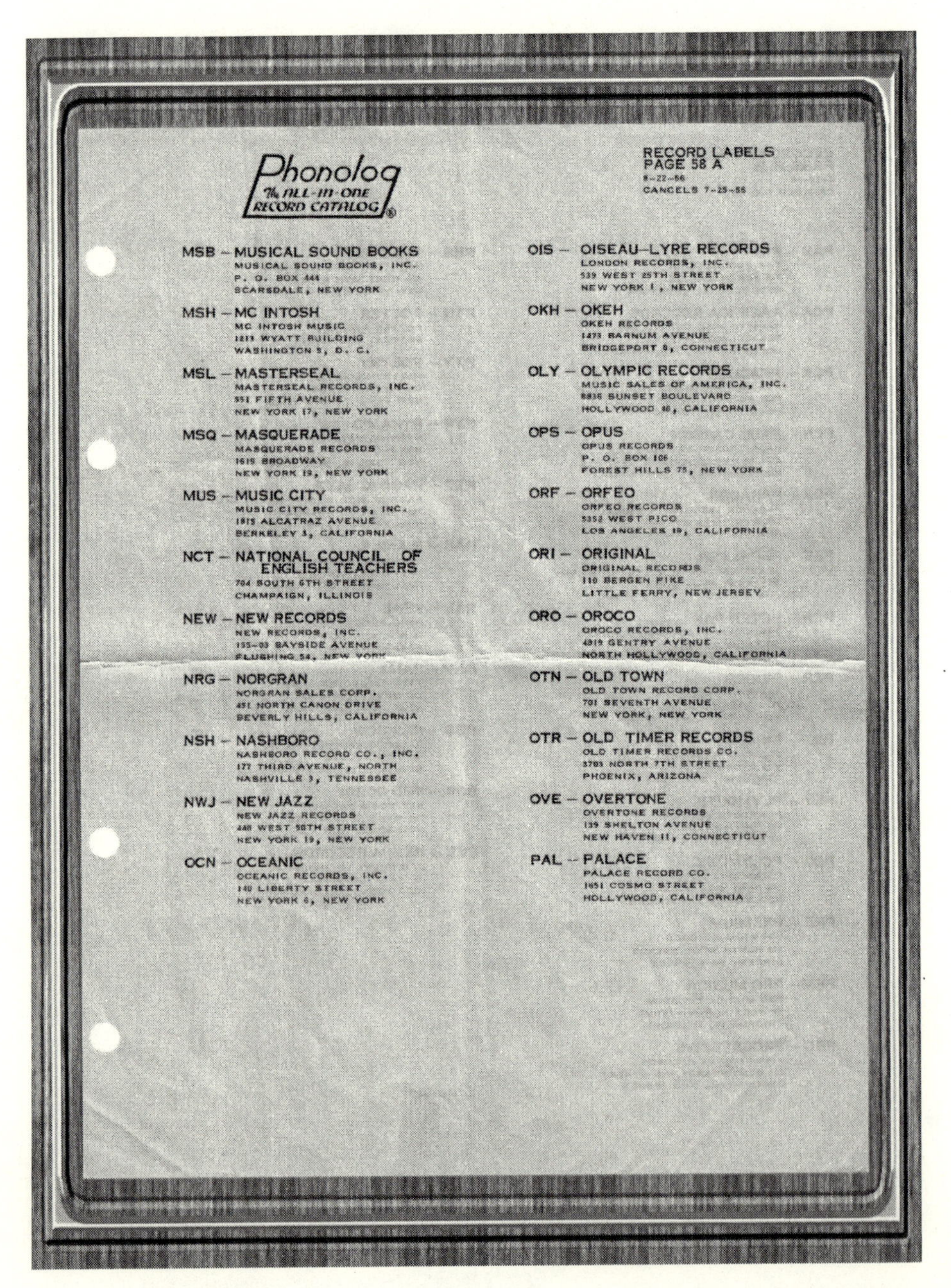

Phonolog
The ALL-IN-ONE RECORD CATALOG ®

RECORD LABELS
PAGE 58 A
8-22-56
CANCELS 7-25-55

MSB – MUSICAL SOUND BOOKS
MUSICAL SOUND BOOKS, INC.
P. O. BOX 444
SCARSDALE, NEW YORK

MSH – MC INTOSH
MC INTOSH MUSIC
1213 WYATT BUILDING
WASHINGTON 5, D. C.

MSL – MASTERSEAL
MASTERSEAL RECORDS, INC.
551 FIFTH AVENUE
NEW YORK 17, NEW YORK

MSQ – MASQUERADE
MASQUERADE RECORDS
1619 BROADWAY
NEW YORK 19, NEW YORK

MUS – MUSIC CITY
MUSIC CITY RECORDS, INC.
1815 ALCATRAZ AVENUE
BERKELEY 3, CALIFORNIA

NCT – NATIONAL COUNCIL OF ENGLISH TEACHERS
704 SOUTH 6TH STREET
CHAMPAIGN, ILLINOIS

NEW – NEW RECORDS
NEW RECORDS, INC.
155-03 BAYSIDE AVENUE
FLUSHING 54, NEW YORK

NRG – NORGRAN
NORGRAN SALES CORP.
451 NORTH CANON DRIVE
BEVERLY HILLS, CALIFORNIA

NSH – NASHBORO
NASHBORO RECORD CO., INC.
177 THIRD AVENUE, NORTH
NASHVILLE 3, TENNESSEE

NWJ – NEW JAZZ
NEW JAZZ RECORDS
446 WEST 50TH STREET
NEW YORK 19, NEW YORK

OCN – OCEANIC
OCEANIC RECORDS, INC.
140 LIBERTY STREET
NEW YORK 6, NEW YORK

OIS – OISEAU–LYRE RECORDS
LONDON RECORDS, INC.
539 WEST 25TH STREET
NEW YORK 1, NEW YORK

OKH – OKEH
OKEH RECORDS
1473 BARNUM AVENUE
BRIDGEPORT 8, CONNECTICUT

OLY – OLYMPIC RECORDS
MUSIC SALES OF AMERICA, INC.
8836 SUNSET BOULEVARD
HOLLYWOOD 46, CALIFORNIA

OPS – OPUS
OPUS RECORDS
P. O. BOX 106
FOREST HILLS 75, NEW YORK

ORF – ORFEO
ORFEO RECORDS
5352 WEST PICO
LOS ANGELES 19, CALIFORNIA

ORI – ORIGINAL
ORIGINAL RECORDS
110 BERGEN PIKE
LITTLE FERRY, NEW JERSEY

ORO – OROCO
OROCO RECORDS, INC.
4919 GENTRY AVENUE
NORTH HOLLYWOOD, CALIFORNIA

OTN – OLD TOWN
OLD TOWN RECORD CORP.
701 SEVENTH AVENUE
NEW YORK, NEW YORK

OTR – OLD TIMER RECORDS
OLD TIMER RECORDS CO.
3703 NORTH 7TH STREET
PHOENIX, ARIZONA

OVE – OVERTONE
OVERTONE RECORDS
139 SHELTON AVENUE
NEW HAVEN 11, CONNECTICUT

PAL – PALACE
PALACE RECORD CO.
1651 COSMO STREET
HOLLYWOOD, CALIFORNIA

Phonolog Six

Phonolog
The ALL-IN-ONE RECORD CATALOG®

RECORD LABELS
PAGE 62 A
7-25-56
CANCELS 4-4-56

STR – STARDAY
STARDAY RECORDS CO.
1248 SOUTH BERENDO STREET
LOS ANGELES 6, CALIFORNIA

STS – STATES
STATES RECORD CO.
5052 COTTAGE GROVE AVENUE
CHICAGO 15, ILLINOIS

STV – STRADIVARI
PERIOD MUSIC CO
884 TENTH AVENUE
NEW YORK 19, NEW YORK

SUN – SUN
SUN RECORDS
706 UNION AVENUE
MEMPHIS, TENNESSEE

SYC – SYCAMORE
SYCAMORE RECORDS
6768 SELMA AVENUE
HOLLYWOOD, CALIFORNIA

TAM – TAMPA
TAMPA RECORDS, INC.
2628 WEST PICO BLVD.
LOS ANGELES, CALIFORNIA

TEL – TELEFUNKEN
LONDON RECORDS, INC.
[illegible] WEST [illegible] STREET
NEW YORK 1, NEW YORK

TEM – TEMPO
TEMPO RECORD CO.
8540 SUNSET BLVD.
HOLLYWOOD 45, CALIFORNIA

THT – THOMAS TENNY RECORDS
MUSIC ON RECORDS
2983 COLLEGE AVENUE
BERKELEY 5, CALIFORNIA

TIC – TICO
TICO RECORDS
220 WEST 42ND STREET
NEW YORK, NEW YORK

TIF – TIFFANY
TIFFANY RECORDS
332 SOUTH MICHIGAN AVENUE
CHICAGO, ILLINOIS

TLY – TIMELY
TIMELY RECORDS
457 WEST 45TH STREET
NEW YORK 19, NEW YORK

TMW – THEATRE MASTERWORKS
THEATRE MASTERWORKS
30 ROCKEFELLER PLAZA, SUITE 1436
NEW YORK 20, NEW YORK

TNT – TNT
TANNER 'N' TEXAS
1422 WEST POPLAR
SAN ANTONIO 7, TEXAS

TRI – TRI-COLOR
TRI-COLOR RECORDING CO.
P. O. BOX 7546
LOS ANGELES 23, CALIFORNIA

TUR – TURQUOISE
TURQUOISE RECORDS
9683 OLYMPIC BLVD.
BEVERLY HILLS, CALIFORNIA

TWC – 20TH CENTURY
GOTHAM RECORD CORP.
1626-32 FEDERAL STREET
PHILADELPHIA 46, PENNSYLVANIA

UCN – UNICORN
UNICORN RECORDS
75 STATE STREET
BOSTON 9, MASSACHUSETTS

UNI – UNITED
UNITED RECORD CO.
5052 COTTAGE GROVE AVENUE
CHICAGO 15, ILLINOIS

UNQ – RKO UNIQUE
RKO-UNIQUE RECORDS
1697 BROADWAY
NEW YORK, NEW YORK

URA – URANIA
URANIA RECORDS, INC.
48 EAST 19TH STREET
NEW YORK 3, NEW YORK

UTC – UTC
UTC RECORDS
719 TENTH AVENUE
NEW YORK 19, NEW YORK

Phonolog Seven

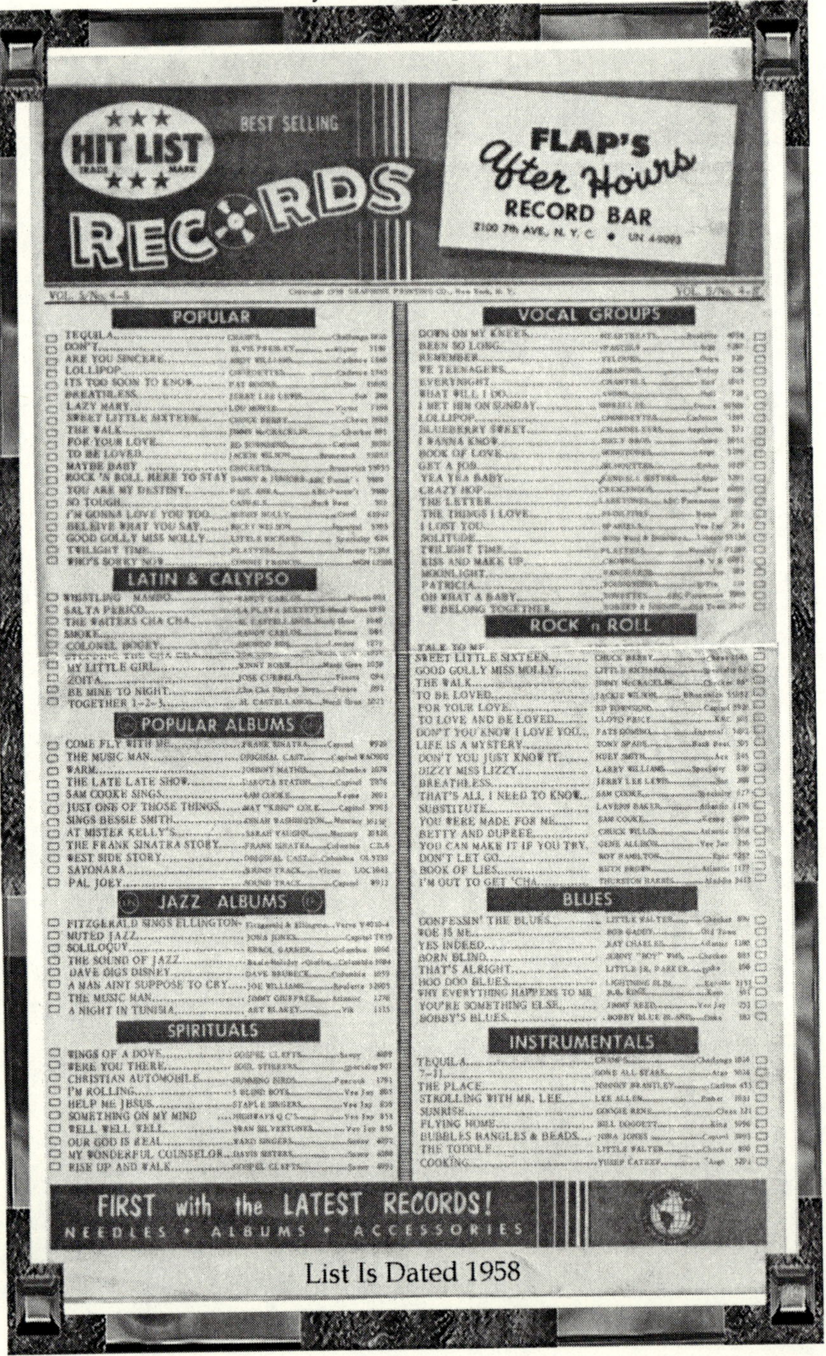

HIT LIST RECORDS — BEST SELLING

FLAP'S After Hours RECORD BAR

2100 7th AVE., N. Y. C.

POPULAR

Title	Artist	Label
TEQUILA	CHAMPS	Challenge
DON'T	ELVIS PRESLEY	Victor
ARE YOU SINCERE	ANDY WILLIAMS	Cadence
LOLLIPOP	CHORDETTES	Cadence
ITS TOO SOON TO KNOW	PAT BOONE	Dot
BREATHLESS	JERRY LEE LEWIS	Sun
LAZY MARY	LOU MONTE	Victor
SWEET LITTLE SIXTEEN	CHUCK BERRY	Chess
THE WALK	JIMMY McCRACKLIN	Checker
FOR YOUR LOVE	ED TOWNSEND	Capitol
TO BE LOVED	JACKIE WILSON	Brunswick
MAYBE BABY	CRICKETS	Brunswick
ROCK 'N ROLL HERE TO STAY	DANNY & JUNIORS	ABC Param't
YOU ARE MY DESTINY	PAUL ANKA	ABC-Param't
SO TOUGH	CASUALS	Back Beat
I'M GONNA LOVE YOU TOO	BUDDY HOLLY	Coral
BELIEVE WHAT YOU SAY	RICKY NELSON	Imperial
GOOD GOLLY MISS MOLLY	LITTLE RICHARD	Specialty
TWILIGHT TIME	PLATTERS	Mercury
WHO'S SORRY NOW	CONNIE FRANCIS	MGM

LATIN & CALYPSO

Title	Artist	Label
WHISTLING MAMBO		
SALTA PERICO	LA PLAYA SEXTETTE	
THE WAITERS CHA CHA		
SMOKE		
COLONEL BOGEY		London
STEPPING THE CHA CHA		
MY LITTLE GIRL		
ZOITA		
BE MINE TO NIGHT	Cha Cha Rhythm Boys	
TOGETHER 1-2-3		

POPULAR ALBUMS

Title	Artist	Label
COME FLY WITH ME	FRANK SINATRA	Capitol
THE MUSIC MAN	ORIGINAL CAST	Capitol
WARM	JOHNNY MATHIS	Columbia
THE LATE LATE SHOW	DAKOTA STATON	Capitol
SAM COOKE SINGS	SAM COOKE	Keen
JUST ONE OF THOSE THINGS	NAT "KING" COLE	Capitol
SINGS BESSIE SMITH	DINAH WASHINGTON	Mercury
AT MISTER KELLY'S	SARAH VAUGHN	Mercury
THE FRANK SINATRA STORY	FRANK SINATRA	Columbia
WEST SIDE STORY	ORIGINAL CAST	Columbia
SAYONARA	SOUND TRACK	Victor
PAL JOEY	SOUND TRACK	Capitol

JAZZ ALBUMS

Title	Artist	Label
FITZGERALD SINGS ELLINGTON	Fitzgerald & Ellington	Verve
MUTED JAZZ	JONA JONES	Capitol
SOLILOQUY	ERROL GARNER	Columbia
THE SOUND OF JAZZ		Columbia
DAVE DIGS DISNEY	DAVE BRUBECK	Columbia
A MAN AINT SUPPOSE TO CRY	JOE WILLIAMS	Roulette
THE MUSIC MAN	JIMMY GIUFFRE	Atlantic
A NIGHT IN TUNISIA	ART BLAKEY	Vik

SPIRITUALS

Title	Artist	Label
WINGS OF A DOVE	GOSPEL CLEFTS	Savoy
WERE YOU THERE	SOUL STIRRERS	
CHRISTIAN AUTOMOBILE	DIXIE HUMMING BIRDS	Peacock
I'M ROLLING	5 BLIND BOYS	Vee Jay
HELP ME JESUS	STAPLE SINGERS	Vee Jay
SOMETHING ON MY MIND	HIGHWAYS Q.C.'S	Vee Jay
WELL WELL WELL		Vee Jay
OUR GOD IS REAL	WARD SINGERS	Savoy
MY WONDERFUL COUNSELOR	DAVIS SISTERS	Savoy
RISE UP AND WALK	GOSPEL CLEFTS	Savoy

VOCAL GROUPS

Title	Artist	Label
DOWN ON MY KNEES	HEARTBEATS	
BEEN SO LONG		
REMEMBER		
WE TEENAGERS		
EVERYNIGHT	CHANTELS	
WHAT WILL I DO		
I MET HIM ON SUNDAY	SHIRELLES	Decca
LOLLIPOP	CHORDETTES	Cadence
BLUEBERRY SWEET		
I WANNA KNOW		
BOOK OF LOVE	MONOTONES	
GET A JOB	SILHOUETTES	
YEA YEA BABY		
CRAZY HOP		
THE LETTER		ABC Paramount
THE THINGS I LOVE		
I LOST YOU		
SOLITUDE		
TWILIGHT TIME	PLATTERS	
KISS AND MAKE UP	CROWNS	
MOONLIGHT		
PATRICIA		
OH WHAT A BABY		ABC Paramount
WE BELONG TOGETHER		

ROCK n ROLL

Title	Artist	Label
TALK TO ME		
SWEET LITTLE SIXTEEN	CHUCK BERRY	
GOOD GOLLY MISS MOLLY	LITTLE RICHARD	
THE WALK	JIMMY McCRACKLIN	Checker
TO BE LOVED	JACKIE WILSON	Brunswick
FOR YOUR LOVE	ED TOWNSEND	Capitol
TO LOVE AND BE LOVED	LLOYD PRICE	KRC
DON'T YOU KNOW I LOVE YOU	FATS DOMINO	Imperial
LIFE IS A MYSTERY	TONY SPADE	
DON'T YOU JUST KNOW IT	HUEY SMITH	Ace
DIZZY MISS LIZZY	LARRY WILLIAMS	Specialty
BREATHLESS	JERRY LEE LEWIS	Sun
THAT'S ALL I NEED TO KNOW	SAM COOKE	Specialty
SUBSTITUTE	LAVERN BAKER	Atlantic
YOU WERE MADE FOR ME	SAM COOKE	Keen
BETTY AND DUPREE	CHUCK WILLIS	Atlantic
YOU CAN MAKE IT IF YOU TRY	GENE ALLISON	Vee Jay
DON'T LET GO	ROY HAMILTON	Epic
BOOK OF LIES	RUTH BROWN	Atlantic
I'M OUT TO GET 'CHA	THURSTON HARRIS	

BLUES

Title	Artist	Label
CONFESSIN' THE BLUES	LITTLE WALTER	Checker
WOE IS ME		Old Town
YES INDEED	RAY CHARLES	Atlantic
BORN BLIND		Checker
THAT'S ALRIGHT	LITTLE JR. PARKER	
HOO DOO BLUES	LIGHTNING SLIM	
WHY EVERYTHING HAPPENS TO ME	B.B. KING	Kent
YOU'RE SOMETHING ELSE	JIMMY REED	Vee Jay
BOBBY'S BLUES	BOBBY BLUE BLAND	Duke

INSTRUMENTALS

Title	Artist	Label
TEQUILA	CHAMPS	Challenge
7-11	GONE ALL STARS	
THE PLACE		
STROLLING WITH MR. LEE	LEE ALLEN	Ember
SUNRISE		
FLYING HOME	BILL DOGGETT	King
BUBBLES BANGLES & BEADS	JONA JONES	Capitol
THE TODDLE	LITTLE WALTER	Checker
COOKING	YUSEF LATEEF	

FIRST with the LATEST RECORDS!

NEEDLES • ALBUMS • ACCESSORIES

List Is Dated 1958

Flap List

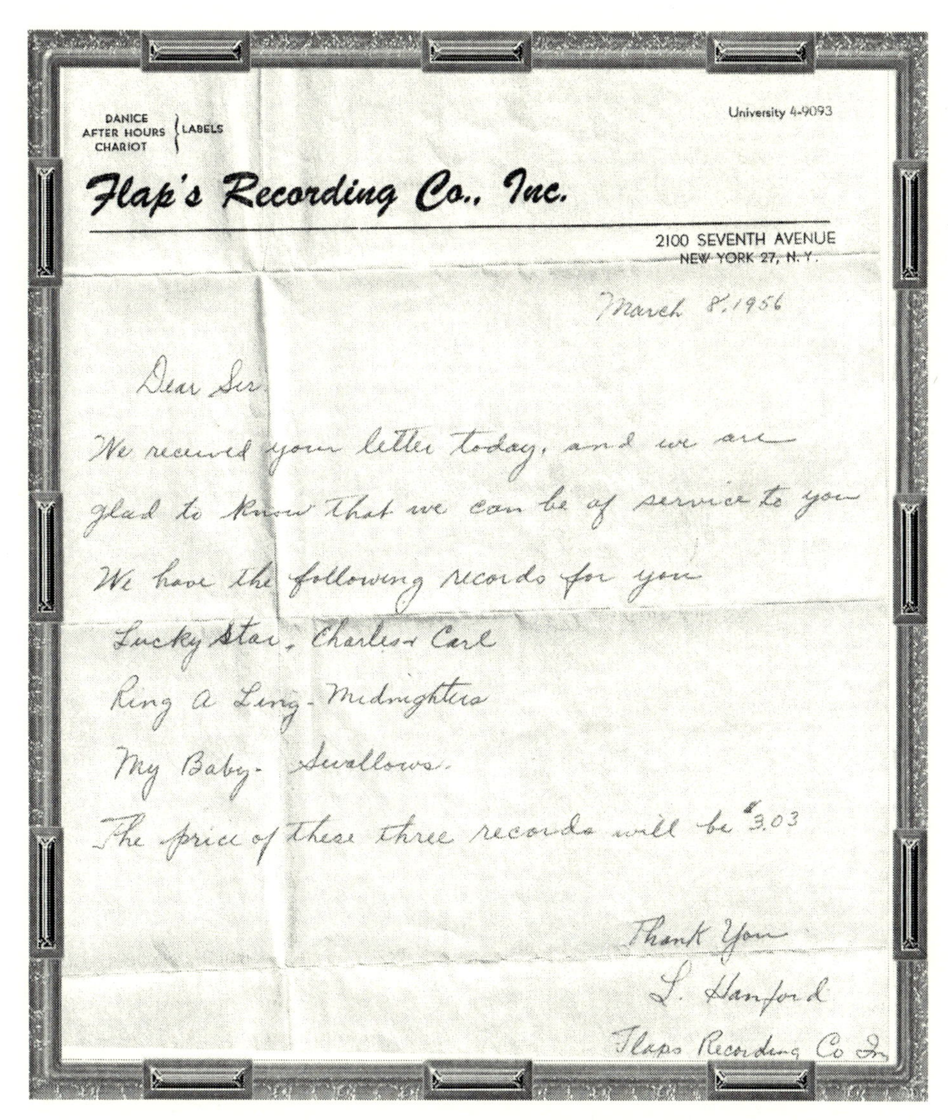

DANICE
AFTER HOURS
CHARIOT
LABELS

University 4-9093

Flap's Recording Co., Inc.

2100 SEVENTH AVENUE
NEW YORK 27, N. Y.

March 8, 1956

Dear Sir

We received your letter today, and we are glad to know that we can be of service to you

We have the following records for you

Lucky Star - Charles & Carl

Ring a Ling - Midnighters

My Baby - Swallows

The price of these three records will be $3.03

Thank You

L. Hanford

Flaps Recording Co In

Correspondence From Flap's Recording Company, Inc. To Al Trommers

GOTHAM RECORD CORP.

1626-32 FEDERAL ST. — PHILADELPHIA 46, PA. — DEwey 4-1115

Sept. 21, 1959

Al Trommers,
43 Bronx River Rd.,
Yonkers, N.Y.

Dear Mr. Trommers:

Thank you for your inquiry pertaining to Gotham 304.

We have this number in stock, and if you will send us a check for $15 we will send you the 25 that you want.

Hoping to hear from you, I remain,

Very truly yours,

Morris Ballen

Gotham
RECORD CORP.
1626-32 FEDERAL ST.
PHILADELPHIA 46, PA.

Mr. Al. Trommers
1165 Morris Avenue
Bronx 56, New York

Gotham Record Invoice To Al Trommers

GOTHAM RECORD CORP.
1526 FEDERAL STREET
PHILA: 46, PA.

CUST. ORDER NO. DATE 9-25-59

M Al Trommers c/o J. pless

ADDRESS 341 Madison Ave

NY NY

SOLD BY	CASH	C.O.D.	CHARGE	ON ACCT.	MDSE. RETD.	PAID OUT
	✓					

QUANTITY	DESCRIPTION	PRICE	AMOUNT
25	Goth # 304		15 00
	Paid In full		
	TAX		
	TOTAL		

ALL CLAIMS AND RETURNED GOODS MUST BE ACCOMPANIED BY THIS BILL.

No. 185 REC'D BY

IRVING TRUST COMPANY
New York

DATE Sept 24, 1959 No 4784
Fill in date here and on check

MEMORANDUM STUB
DETACH AND RETAIN

Remittance Sent TO Gotham Record Corp
Fill in name of payee here and on check

PAY 15 dol's 00 cts

FOR 25 records
Fill in purpose of remittance

BE SURE TO SIGN YOUR OWN NAME ON CHECK

Al Trommers Pays The Gotham Record Invoice

Standard Grand Record Company Contract

AGREEMENT made this day of 1953 by and between HERBERT SLOTKIN, trading as GRAND RECORD CO., hereinafter referred to as GRAND and

hereinafter referred to as ARTISTS.

WITNESSETH:

WHEREAS, GRAND is about to arrange and record certain musical compositions

and exert its best efforts to publicize, promote and distribute same.

WHEREAS such publicity, promotion and distribution will materially benefit any and all artists whose talent is used in said recordings, and

WHEREAS, ARTISTS desire that their talent be used in the recording of said musical compositions and,

WHEREAS, GRAND is willing to incorporate ARTISTS' talents in making said recordings, upon the following terms and conditions.

NOW, THEREFORE, for and in consideration of the following covenants, it is agreed as follows:

1. GRAND agrees to use and incorporate ARTISTS and their talents as leader, instrumentalists and vocalists for recording sessions of the said musical compositions,

2. ARTISTS agree to render their professional services and talents as leader, instrumentalists and vocalists in the said recording sessions, so that same may be incorporated in the recording of the said musical compositions.

3. ARTISTS agree that for and during the term of this Agreement GRAND shall receive as compensation or commission the following percentages of the gross weekly earnings received by ARTISTS as entertainers after the date of this Agreement:
10% where ARTISTS' gross weekly earnings are from $300.00 to $400.00.
15% where ARTISTS' gross weekly earnings are from $400.00 to $500.00.
20% where ARTISTS' gross weekly earnings are from $500.00 to $1000.00.
25% where ARTISTS' gross weekly earnings are over $1000.00.
provided, however, that GRAND is to receive no compensation or commission until thirty days after the first public release of the recording of the said musical composition and provided further that GRAND is to receive no percentage of ARTISTS' gross weekly earnings up to $200.00.

4. It is agreed and understood that compensation or commission due GRAND is separate and distinct from any commission or fee paid to a booking agent or booking agents and that said compensation due GRAND is to be paid from the gross earnings before the deduction of any such commission or fee paid to booking agent or booking agents. ARTISTS hereby agree to pay over to GRAND said compensation or commission due them under this Agreement within one week after the said weekly gross earnings have been received by ARTISTS, and each and every week ARTISTS are to render a true and correct statement to GRAND of the gross earnings earned by ARTISTS for the preceding week.

5. ARTISTS further agree that GRAND shall have the sole and exclusive right to all recordings and transcriptions made by ARTISTS for and during the term of this Agreement, whether made in the United States or elsewhere, and that ARTISTS will not for and during the said term record, transcribe or make any recordings or transcriptions for any other person, firm or corporation. In addition to the foregoing, it is further agreed that for and during the term of this Agreement GRAND shall be and ARTISTS hereby appoint GRAND as ARTISTS' personal manager with reference to all recordings and transcriptions made or to be made by ARTISTS, including among other things, the right to represent ARTISTS, negotiate and enter into contracts on ARTISTS' behalf with reference thereto. ARTISTS hereby acknowledge that their professional services are unique and extraordinary.

6. ARTISTS represent and agree that they are free from any obligation to any other person, firm or corporation with reference to other professional services to record or transcribe or make recordings or transcriptions of musical compositions, and that any recordings or transcriptions of musical compositions, and that any recording or transcription made for GRAND and reproductions therefrom are free and clear of any claim whatsoever by ARTISTS.

7. GRAND agrees that ARTISTS are to receive the following royalties for each record incorporating ARTISTS' professional services, whether same be manufactured and sold by GRAND or not:

> On the first ten records recorded by ARTISTS, said ARTISTS as a group are to receive cent a side for each side that incorporates their services for such record sold over and above copies. Thereafter, on each record sold that incorporates their services, ARTISTS as a group are to receive cent a side for each side that incorporates their services, on each record sold.

It is understood, however, that ARTISTS shall not be entitled to any monies received by GRAND as a result of the sale or leasing of the metal Masters' recordings, and ARTISTS hereby waive same.

8. It is understood and agreed that an accounting for royalties is to be made and royalties are to be paid to ARTISTS every three months beginning with
and payments to be made to
for and on behalf of all ARTISTS involved herein.

9. ARTISTS agree that they will pay their dues and otherwise remain in good standing in any union or professional or artists' guild, of which they are presently members or may henceforth during the term of this Agreement, become members.

10. The term of this agreement shall be from the date hereof, but if neither party gives the other written notice of termination of said Agreement within ninety days prior to the end of said then and in that event, this Agreement is to continue for another term of and thereafter from year to year until either party shall give the other written notice of termination within ninety days of the then current term. In the event that said notice of termination either of the original term or any extension thereof, is given in writing to GRAND by ARTISTS within the time aforesaid, it is agreed and understood nevertheless that such termination can only be elected by ARTISTS if they contemplate making recordings or transcriptions for some other person, firm or corporation, and in that event ARTISTS shall have the duty of forthwith presenting to GRAND a bona fide contract or the terms thereof which ARTISTS intend to sign or enter into and GRAND shall have the first right to make and enter into a similar contract with ARTISTS and if GRAND does so elect and desires to make and enter into such a contract, then ARTISTS shall be obliged and hereby agree to continue their association with GRAND upon the terms and conditions similar to the said bona fide contract.

11. NOTWITHSTANDING, anything said above, it is agreed and understood that if all the compositions referred to above prove unsuccessful to GRAND after allowing a reasonable time for publicity and exploitation, then and in that event, both parties hereto may by writing mutually terminate this Agreement prior to the terms set forth above.

12. It is agreed that this Agreement sets forth the entire understanding by and between the parties and that there are no other understandings, terms or conditions.

IN WITNESS WHEREOF, the parties hereto have hereunto set their hands and seals the day and year first above written.

WITNESS: (SEAL)

FOR GRAND RECORD CO.

Original Copy Of Grand Records Contract

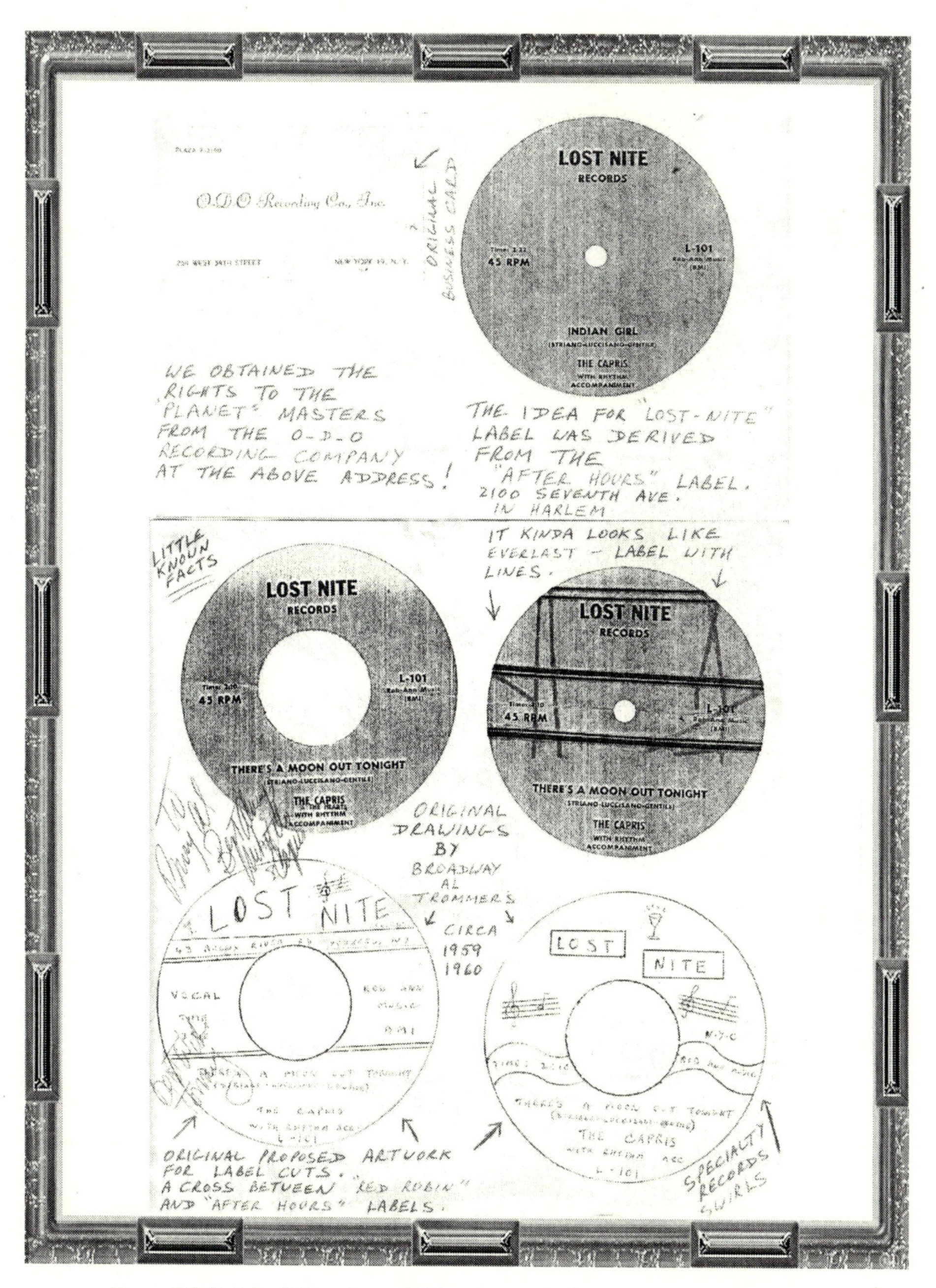

Copy Of Original Sketches Al Trommers Did For The Lost Nite Label

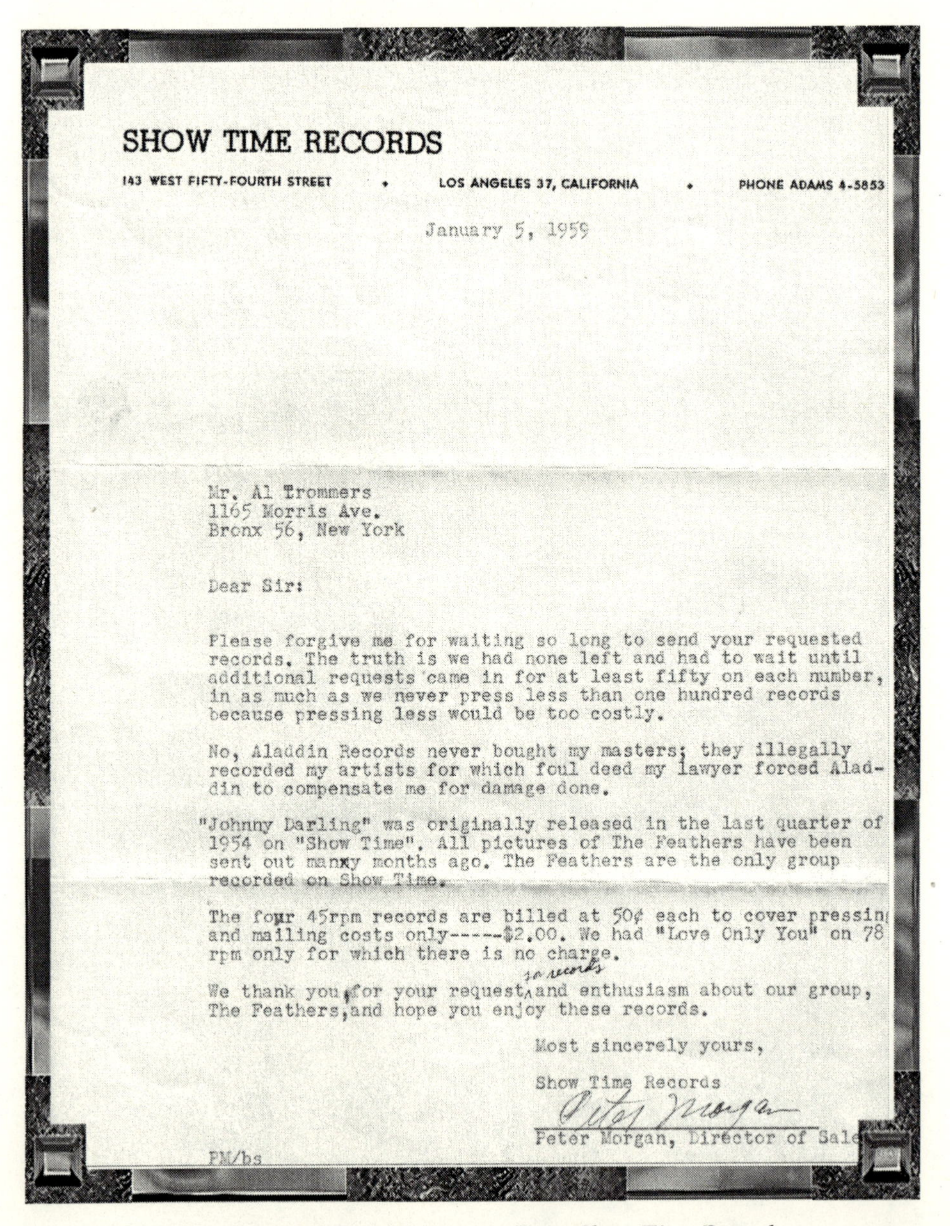

SHOW TIME RECORDS

143 WEST FIFTY-FOURTH STREET • LOS ANGELES 37, CALIFORNIA • PHONE ADAMS 4-5853

January 5, 1959

Mr. Al Trommers
1165 Morris Ave.
Bronx 56, New York

Dear Sir:

Please forgive me for waiting so long to send your requested records. The truth is we had none left and had to wait until additional requests came in for at least fifty on each number, in as much as we never press less than one hundred records because pressing less would be too costly.

No, Aladdin Records never bought my masters; they illegally recorded my artists for which foul deed my lawyer forced Aladdin to compensate me for damage done.

"Johnny Darling" was originally released in the last quarter of 1954 on "Show Time". All pictures of The Feathers have been sent out manxy months ago. The Feathers are the only group recorded on Show Time.

The four 45rpm records are billed at 50¢ each to cover pressing and mailing costs only-----$2.00. We had "Love Only You" on 78 rpm only for which there is no charge.

We thank you for your request for records and enthusiasm about our group, The Feathers, and hope you enjoy these records.

Most sincerely yours,

Show Time Records

Peter Morgan

Peter Morgan, Director of Sales

PM/bs

Correspondence To Al Trommers From Show Time Records

Al Trommers With Wife Upper Left & Upper Right Corner....Left Photo On His Wedding Day....Right Photo Village Oldies Records Owned By Al Trommers...His Car Parked In Front Of Building

Al Trommers Upper Left & Right Corners....Johnny Esposito & Jared Weinstein…Circa Late 1950's…Early 1960's

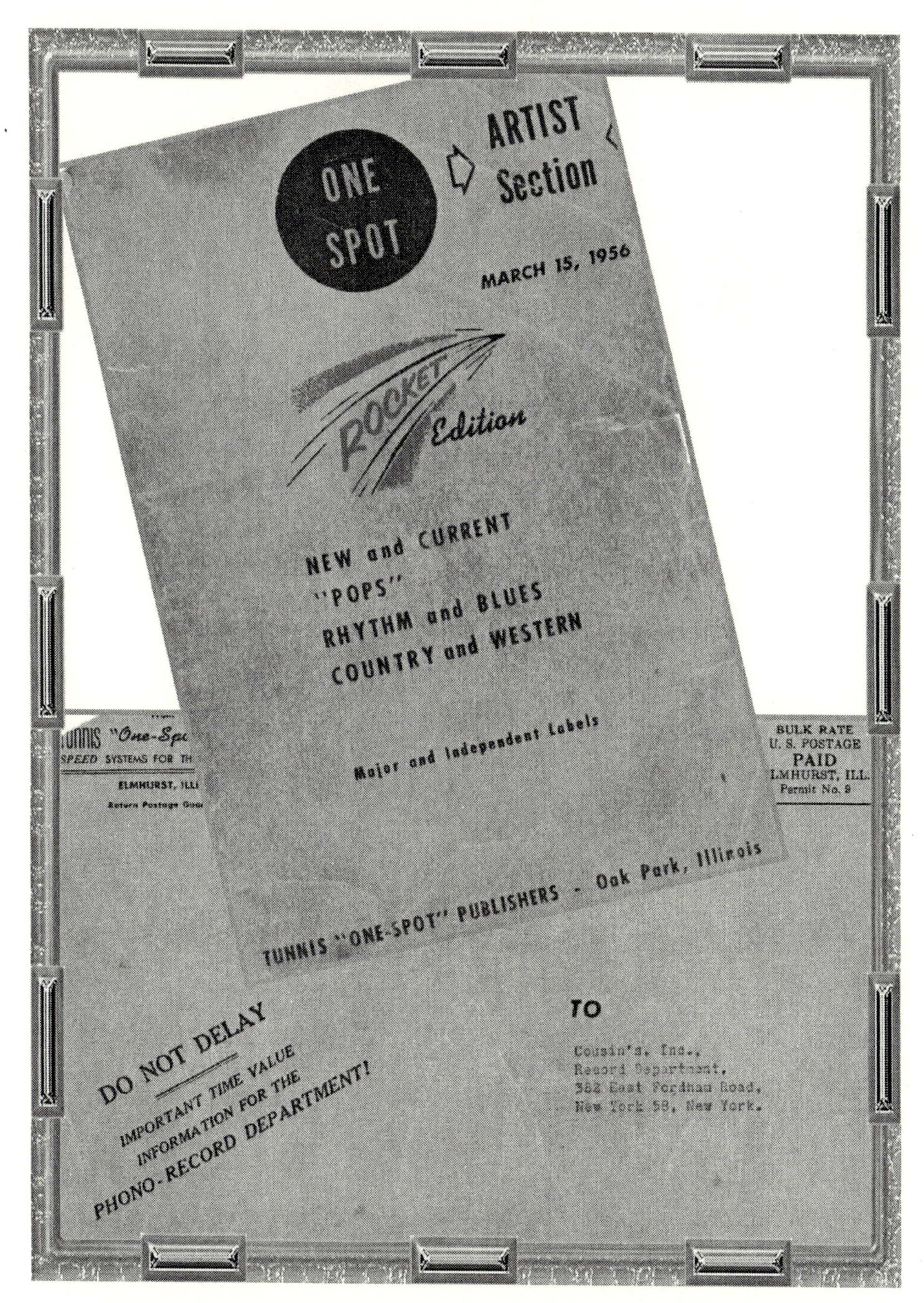

One Spot Sent To Cousins' Records Where Al Trommers Worked

Various Business Cards Al Trommers Maintained For His Records

NUMBER 4 | SHARES 19

INCORPORATED UNDER THE LAWS OF THE STATE OF NEW YORK

TIMES SQUARE MUSIC INC.

100 SHARES WITHOUT PAR VALUE

NOTICE is hereby given pursuant to Sections 616 and 709 of the Business Corporation Law that the Certificate of Incorporation contains provisions authorized by Sections 616 and 709 of said Law prescribing special provisions for quorum, vote or consent of shareholders and directors and the holder of this certificate is charged with knowledge thereof and holds the same subject to said provisions.

This Certifies that EDWARD J. GRIES is the registered holder of —(19) nineteen Shares

TIMES SQUARE MUSIC INC. Fully Paid and Non-Assessable

transferable only on the books of the Corporation by the holder hereof in person or by Attorney upon surrender of this Certificate properly endorsed.

In Witness Whereof, the said Corporation has caused this Certificate to be signed by its duly authorized officers and its Corporate Seal to be hereunto affixed this 15TH day of MARCH A.D. 1965

Edward J. Gries — SECRETARY-TREASURER

Harold M. Ginsburg — PRESIDENT

For Value Received ______ hereby sell, assign and transfer unto ______ Shares of the Capital Stock represented by the within Certificate, and do hereby irrevocably constitute and appoint ______ Attorney to transfer the said Stock on the books of the within named Corporation with full power of substitution in the premises.

Dated ______ 19__

CERTIFICATE FOR SHARES OF THE

ISSUED TO

DATED

Stock Certificate For Times Square Music, Inc

$ 100.00 March 15 1965

August 30, 1965 after date, for value received, we promise to pay to the order of TIMES SQUARE RECORDS, INC.

- - - One Hundred and no/100 - - - - - - - - - - - - - - - - - - Dollars

at Manufacturers Hanover Trust Co., 510 Fifth Ave. Br., New York City

with ~~interest at per cent.~~ no interest.

This note is one of a series of 45 notes of even date herewith, aggregating $ 4,500.00

It is understood and agreed that in the event of the non-payment of any one of said series and such default continue for a period of five days, then at the option of the holder of any of the said notes, all of any part of the remaining unpaid notes shall forthwith become due and payable. The failure to assert this right shall not be deemed a waiver thereof.

No. 24 Due Aug. 30, 1965

TIMES SQUARE MUSIC, INC.

No. 1000N Serial Note—Julius Blumberg, Inc., 80 Exchange Place, New York

FOR VALUE RECEIVED THE UNDERSIGNED AND EACH OF THEM HEREBY FOREVER WAIVES PRESENTMENT, DEMAND, PROTEST, NOTICE OF PROTEST AND NOTICE OF DISHONOR OF THE WITHIN NOTE AND THE UNDERSIGNED AND EACH OF THEM GUARANTEES THE PAYMENT OF SAID NOTE AT MATURITY AND CONSENTS WITHOUT NOTICE TO ANY AND ALL EXTENSIONS OF TIME OR TERMS OF PAYMENT MADE BY HOLDER OF SAID NOTE.

DOMESTIC COLLECTION M. O. AUG 27 1965 TELEPHONE 770-1331

Bank Note Signed By All Parties

Donn Fileti, Lillian Leach & Eddie Gries.... Eddie Gries & The Late Billy Pensabene...

Eddie Gries with "Slim" at UGHA in 1977. It would be the last public appearance for "Slim". Eddie Gries with Donn Fileti in the 1970's

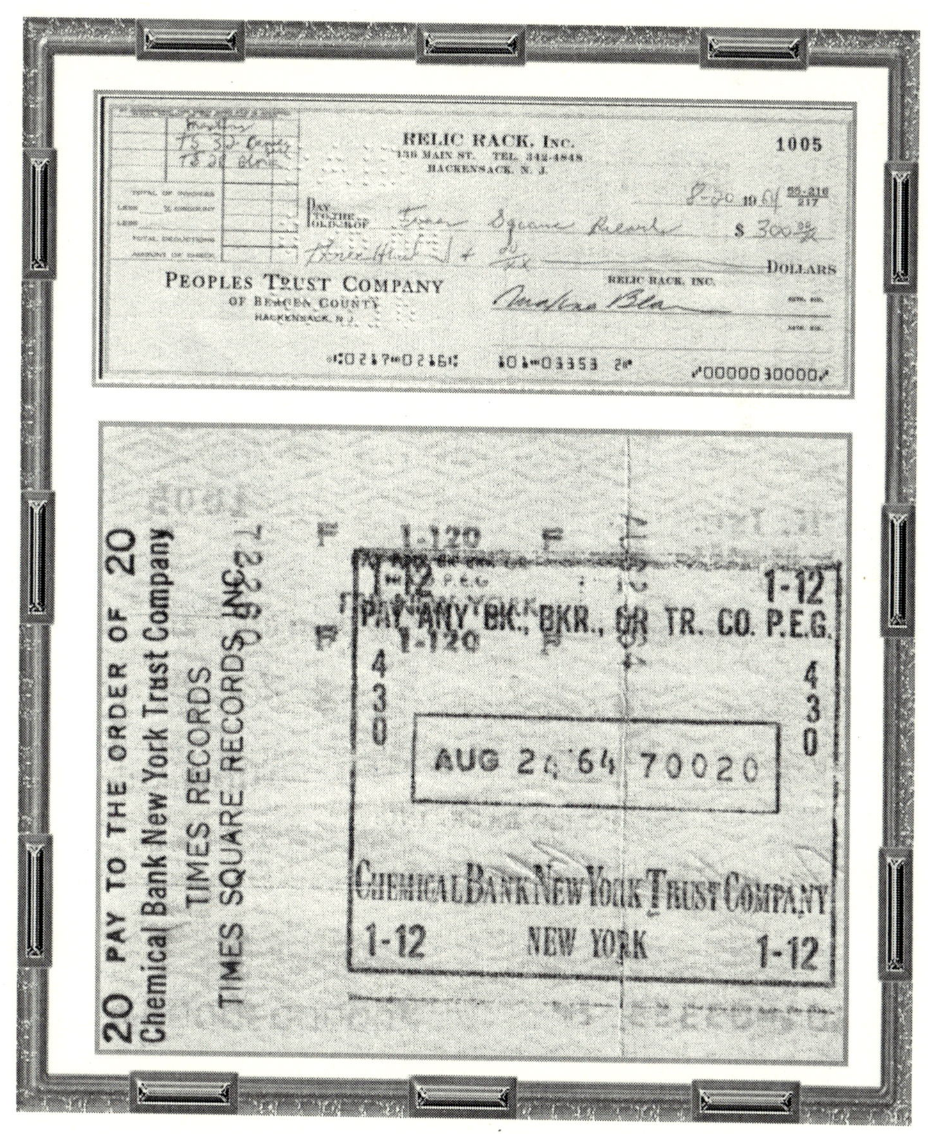
RELIC RACK, Inc.
138 MAIN ST. TEL. 342-4848
HACKENSACK, N. J.

1005

8-20 1964 55-216/217

PAY TO THE ORDER OF Times Square Records $ 300 00/xx

DOLLARS

PEOPLES TRUST COMPANY
OF BERGEN COUNTY
HACKENSACK, N. J.

RELIC RACK, INC.

⑆0217⑆0216⑆ 101⑈03353 2⑈ ⑈0000030000⑈

20 PAY TO THE ORDER OF 20
Chemical Bank New York Trust Company
TIMES RECORDS
TIMES SQUARE RECORDS, INC.

1-12 PAY ANY BK., BKR., OR TR. CO. P.E.G. 1-12
430 430
AUG 24 '64 70020
CHEMICAL BANK NEW YORK TRUST COMPANY
1-12 NEW YORK 1-12

"Slim's Competitor...The Relic Rack....Copy Of Check

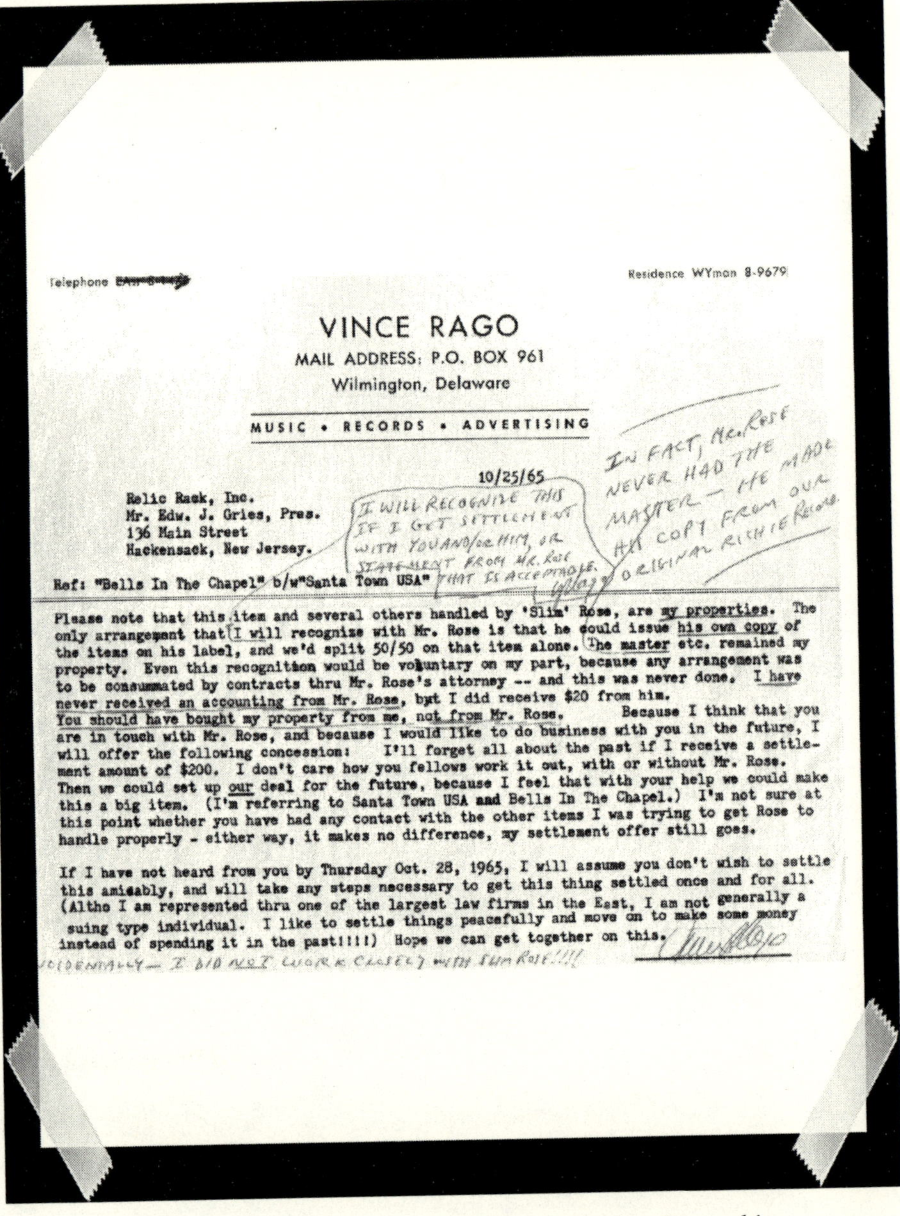

Telephone [illegible]

Residence WYman 8-9679

VINCE RAGO
MAIL ADDRESS: P.O. BOX 961
Wilmington, Delaware

MUSIC • RECORDS • ADVERTISING

10/25/65

Relic Rack, Inc.
Mr. Edw. J. Gries, Pres.
136 Main Street
Hackensack, New Jersey.

I WILL RECOGNIZE THIS IF I GET SETTLEMENT WITH YOU AND/OR HIM, OR STATEMENT FROM MR. ROSE THAT IS ACCEPTABLE.

IN FACT, MR. ROSE NEVER HAD THE MASTER — HE MADE HIS COPY FROM OUR ORIGINAL RICHIE RECORD.

Ref: "Bells In The Chapel" b/w "Santa Town USA"

Please note that this item and several others handled by 'Slim' Rose, are my properties. The only arrangement that I will recognize with Mr. Rose is that he could issue his own copy of the items on his label, and we'd split 50/50 on that item alone. The master etc. remained my property. Even this recognition would be voluntary on my part, because any arrangement was to be consummated by contracts thru Mr. Rose's attorney -- and this was never done. I have never received an accounting from Mr. Rose, but I did receive $20 from him. You should have bought my property from me, not from Mr. Rose. Because I think that you are in touch with Mr. Rose, and because I would like to do business with you in the future, I will offer the following concession: I'll forget all about the past if I receive a settlement amount of $200. I don't care how you fellows work it out, with or without Mr. Rose. Then we could set up our deal for the future, because I feel that with your help we could make this a big item. (I'm referring to Santa Town USA and Bells In The Chapel.) I'm not sure at this point whether you have had any contact with the other items I was trying to get Rose to handle properly - either way, it makes no difference, my settlement offer still goes.

If I have not heard from you by Thursday Oct. 28, 1965, I will assume you don't wish to settle this amicably, and will take any steps necessary to get this thing settled once and for all. (Altho I am represented thru one of the largest law firms in the East, I am not generally a suing type individual. I like to settle things peacefully and move on to make some money instead of spending it in the past!!!!) Hope we can get together on this.

[signature]

INCIDENTALLY — I DID NOT WORK CLOSELY WITH SLIM ROSE!!!!

Letter From Vince Rago To Relic Rack Disputing Ownership

WAGE AND TAX STATEMENT 1965

FORM W-2 — U.S. Treasury Department, Internal Revenue Service

Copy D – For employer

INCOME TAX INFORMATION			SOCIAL SECURITY INFORMATION		State or City Income Tax Withheld
Federal income tax withheld	Wages[1] paid subject to withholding in 1965	Other compensation[2] paid in 1965	F.I.C.A. employee tax withheld	Total F.I.C.A. wages paid in 1965	
197.10	1620.00	-0-	58.72	1620.00	32.40

Type or print EMPLOYEE'S social security no., name and address below: DENNIS ARAKELIAN

S—If Single M—If Married | No. of Dependents

Type or print EMPLOYER'S identification number name and address: TIMES SQ MUSIC INC 13-2529715

[1]Before payroll deductions or "sick pay" exclusions.
EMPLOYER: This copy is provided for your convenience in keeping your withholding records.

WAGE AND TAX STATEMENT 1965

FORM W-2 — U.S. Treasury Department, Internal Revenue Service

Copy D – For employer

INCOME TAX INFORMATION			SOCIAL SECURITY INFORMATION		State or City Income Tax Withheld
Federal income tax withheld	Wages[1] paid subject to withholding in 1965	Other compensation[2] paid in 1965	F.I.C.A. employee tax withheld	Total F.I.C.A. wages paid in 1965	
164.25	1350.00	-0-	48.94	1350.00	27.00

Type or print EMPLOYEE'S social security no., name and address below: EDWARD GRIES

S—If Single M—If Married | No. of Dependents

Type or print EMPLOYER'S identification number name and address: TIMES SQUARE MUSIC INC 13-2529715

[1]Before payroll deductions or "sick pay" exclusions.
EMPLOYER: This copy is provided for your convenience in keeping your withholding records.

WAGE AND TAX STATEMENT 1965

FORM W-2 — U.S. Treasury Department, Internal Revenue Service

Copy D – For employer

INCOME TAX INFORMATION			SOCIAL SECURITY INFORMATION		State or City Income Tax Withheld
Federal income tax withheld	Wages[1] paid subject to withholding in 1965	Other compensation[2] paid in 1965	F.I.C.A. employee tax withheld	Total F.I.C.A. wages paid in 1965	
31.90	309.40	-0-	11.22	309.40	-0-

Type or print EMPLOYEE'S social security no., name and address below: LEO JARVIS

S—If Single M—If Married | No. of Dependents

Type or print EMPLOYER'S identification number name and address: TIMES SQUARE MUSIC INC 13-2529715

[1]Before payroll deductions or "sick pay" exclusions.
EMPLOYER: This copy is provided for your convenience in keeping your withholding records.

W-2 Forms....Times Square Music, Inc...Tax Year 1965

Night Train Fan Club Card

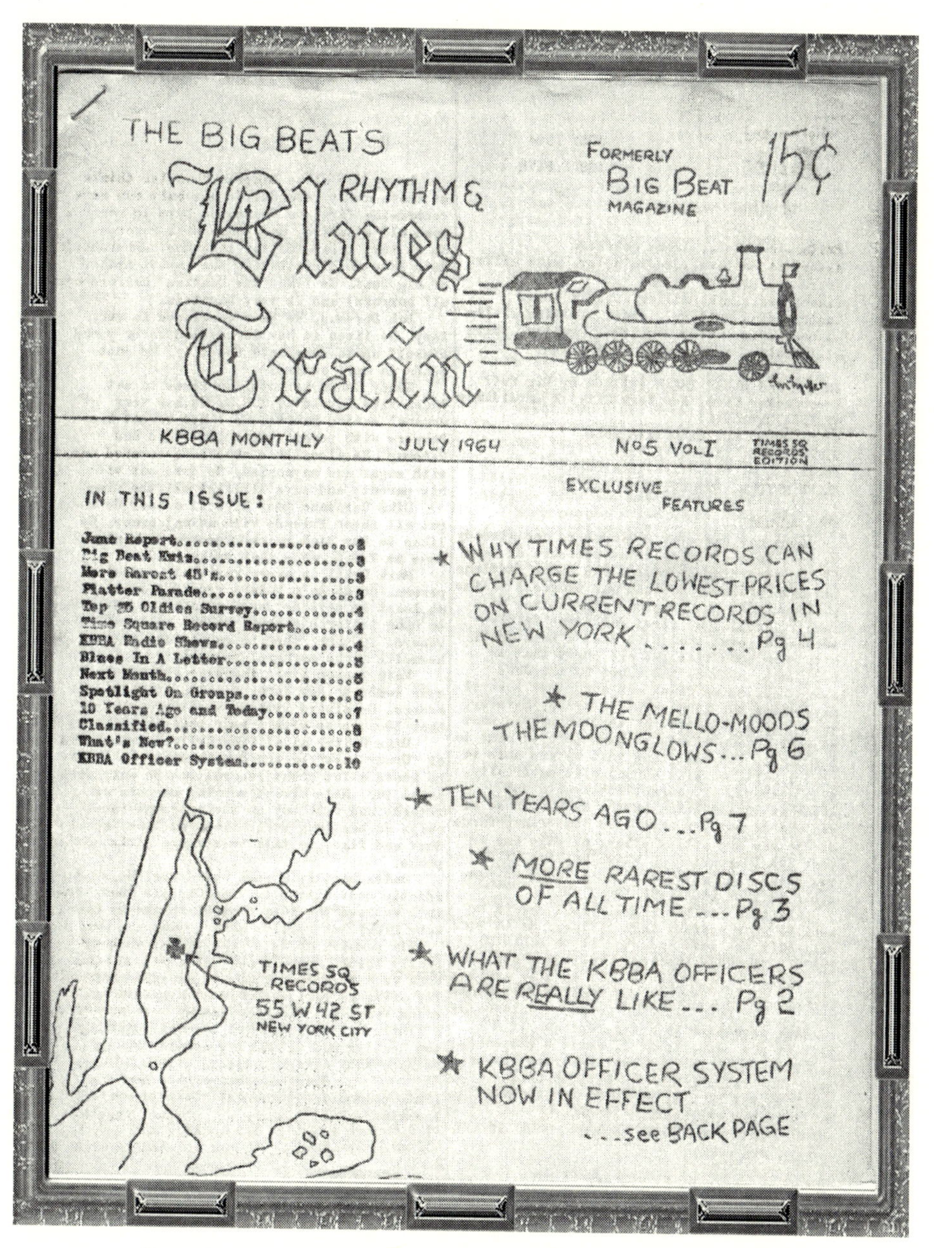

THE BIG BEATS
RHYTHM &
Blues
Train

FORMERLY
BIG BEAT
MAGAZINE

15¢

KBBA MONTHLY — JULY 1964 — No5 Vol I — TIMES SQ RECORDS EDITION

IN THIS ISSUE:

EXCLUSIVE FEATURES

★ WHY TIMES RECORDS CAN CHARGE THE LOWEST PRICES ON CURRENT RECORDS IN NEW YORK .... Pg 4

★ THE MELLO-MOODS THE MOONGLOWS ... Pg 6

★ TEN YEARS AGO ... Pg 7

★ MORE RAREST DISCS OF ALL TIME ... Pg 3

★ WHAT THE KBBA OFFICERS ARE REALLY LIKE ... Pg 2

★ KBBA OFFICER SYSTEM NOW IN EFFECT ... see BACK PAGE

TIMES SQ RECORDS
55 W 42 ST
NEW YORK CITY

"Slim" Advertising In An Issue Of "Rhythm & Blues Train"

About The Author

Nadine DuBois was born in Norristown, Pennsylvania in the early 1950's.

After graduating high school, she moved to Kingston, New York.
She attended college at the State University of New York at New Paltz.
She graduated with a degree in criminal justice.

While in New York, her career led her through a political maze. Starting out as a meter maid for the City of Kingston, New York she made her way through the City Court and County Court systems.

The year 1987 would bring many changes for the author. She left her "seasoned cushioned job" to give both her daughters a better life in rural New England.

In 1989, Ms. DuBois formed her own investigative company, which continues on to this day. She is now semi-retired.

Ms. DuBois has two grown married daughters. She has four grandchildren. Her oldest daughter has pursued a career with Bank of America while her youngest daughter is in her third year of law school following in the foot steps of her mother.

Ms. DuBois continues to reside in a small rural town in New Hampshire.

If you wish to contact Ms. DuBois her email address is timessquarerecords@yahoo.com

Her website is http://www.timessquarerecords.org

NOW! A RARE, COLLECTORS LIMITED EDITION COMPACT DISC! A CD THAT WILL BRING YOU BACK TO THOSE DAYS OF TIMES SQUARE RECORDS, EACH TIME YOU PLAY IT!

After reading the book, you might ask yourself... "Could "Slim" really sound and talk the way people describe him". The answer is a very strong "yes"! In addition to an amazing collection of rare records on this limited collectors edition cd, you will be getting a previously unreleased version of "Slim From Times", which includes some "Slim" items that have never been made available to the public before! "Slim From Times" is a hypnotic half hour, and that's without counting the rare records and exciting bonus tracks!

Included in the amazingly rare, full half hour of "Slim", you get highlights from the wild and often insane radio programs that starred "Slim" on shows he often called "The Times Square Records Supper Hour For Teens From 8 to 96". (The title of the show usually changed each week!). You will be drawn into the strange world of Times Square Records "live" as you hear excerpts of shows, conversations, and some of the wackiest mistakes ever made on radio! You will be treated to a heavy dose of what "Slim" sounded like and how he viewed the world! You will hear "Slim", Genni, Harold, Shandy, Wayne, and other characters that inhabited the almost neon world of Times Square Records! On top of that, you get rare records that were popular at Times, to the tune of over $250.00 worth of music, all on this unique limited edition compact disc!

The magic of "Times Square Records" was that it was the first and only home for the vocal group sound of the 1950's! The records that dominated Times became instant collector's items, as well as the wild vocal group recordings that were special favorites of "Slim" himself. In fact, "Slim" would try to make his own personal choices become the big hits of the store, and many times, he succeeded in doing just that! The music was "crazy" in a wonderful way, and the store itself was sometimes even crazier than the music! This was the first record store to become totally associated with this style of music! You will be transported back in time, just listening to this cd! It's a wild ride!

This is not just an ordinary cd, it is a "time machine" on a disc, and it includes the recording "Slim From Times", which when originally produced in a shorter form, carried with it the full blessings and gratitude of "Slim" himself. This cd is a personal listening experience between you, Times Square Records, and "Slim".

Here are many favorites that "Slim" played on his radio shows, and which were featured on the famous "wall" at Times Records, in addition to being played in the store all the time! These timeless classics include records from The Times Square Records label, as well as records originally re-released just for Times, and some in-store favorites as well. (Including a few tracks from the only label "Slim" ever distributed, Candlelite Records).

Directly from The Times Square Records label, comes "Go Back Where You Came From" by The Summits, one of the wildest cuts ever recorded especially for "Slim", and his personal favorite release. You will hear "It's Going To Be Alright" by The Decoys, one of the only Times Square Records to receive heavy airplay on regular am radio. Other Times Square Records include "Oh Baby" by The Bel-Airs, "Times Square Stomp", and some of the big Candlelite favorites including "My Lonely Friend" by The Continentals, "Impossible" by The Velvatones, and the almost unbelievable, “Jeannie” by The Thrashers. ("Slim" ran a contest for people to come up with the lyrics to "Jeannie", and no one won! By Times Records standards, “that’s” a record setter in itself!)

In addition to these wonderful recordings, are more gems that were favorites at Times or were recorded by some of the most sought after vocal groups to ever appear on the Times “wall”, or at a Times Records "live" show!

You'll thrill to such groups as the Shells, the Youngtones, the Admirations, the Sonics, the Youngsters, the Cameos, and more! As an added bonus, “Do You Remember Times” will take you back on your own personal journey to a place in time like no other. You will find yourself right there in Times!

Amazing original vocal group recordings, plus additional bonus tracks that include "Slim From Times", the astounding half hour retrospect of "Slim" himself, and even more bonus tracks! Almost an hour and a half of amazing, heartfelt memories, that you can re-live with each treasured play of this beautiful cd! Seventeen tracks in all!

The price for your own collector's edition cd is $15.98 plus $5.00 shipping for a total of $19.98.

You can obtain a copy of this cd, together with a copy of the fabulous book, "The History Of Times Square Records" upon visiting us at our website. (You can save money by buying book and cd together, or you can order them separately).

Visit us on the internet at http://www.timessquarerecords.org to order your copy now!!

In the heart of New York City lies the crossroads of the world, Times Square, where the ball drops on New Years Eve. It is a place known throughout the world, and a part of the folk lore of the greatest country on earth, the United States of America. Maybe you recall Guy Lombardo and New Years Eve, or maybe you don't remember Guy Lombardo, but you watched the ball drop with Dick Clark, or Ryan Seacrest. Directly below where the ball drops, and below street level, was Times Square Records! That gives you an idea of how amazing this story is.

There was a time that 42nd Street near Times Square was the sleaziest place in New York. Today it seems to be all multi-national corporations combined with "Disney", and associated with billions of dollars of advertising and sales. Come back with us before the area was too cleaned up, and 42nd Street was a dangerous place, and in the midst of this famous but often creepy place, was a record store, underground, that defied logic or reason. Come into the world of Times Square Records, down in the subway and near Huberts Flea Circus, that featured sideshow freaks once an hour. Step right in, with this recording and the great book that are your tickets to a world that did not exist at street level. A time when music mattered, and when dreams seemed possible, and nothing was odd about a raccoon sleeping on the counter. This is your chance to visit a place that you may never have seen, but wish you had, or re-visit a place that you actually did visit lo' those many years and decades ago. Times Square Records is alive and open again, and only in this unique cd and totally amazing book!